Internet Security and Firewalls

Internet
Security
and
Firewalls

V. V. Preetham

WITH

NIIT

Premier Press

Riverhead Free Library
330 Court Street
Riverhead, New York 11901

Important: Premier Press cannot provide software support. Please contact the appropriate software manufacturer's technical support line or Web site for assistance.

Premier Press and the author have attempted throughout this book to distinguish proprietary trademarks from descriptive terms by following the capitalization style used by the manufacturer.

Information contained in this book has been obtained by Premier Press from sources believed to be reliable. However, because of the possibility of human or mechanical error by our sources, Premier Press, or others, the Publisher does not guarantee the accuracy, adequacy, or completeness of any information and is not responsible for any errors or omissions or the results obtained from use of such information. Readers should be particularly aware of the fact that the Internet is an ever-changing entity. Some facts may have changed since this book went to press.

ISBN: 1-931841-97-7

Library of Congress Catalog Card Number: 2002111220

Printed in the United States of America

02 03 04 05 BH 10 9 8 7 6 5 4 3 2 1

Premier Press, a division of Course Technology
2645 Erie Avenue, Suite 41
Cincinnati, Ohio 45208

Publisher:
Stacy L. Hiquet

Marketing Manager:
Heather Buzzingham

Managing Editor:
Heather Talbot

Project Editor and Copy Editor:
Cathleen Snyder

Interior Layout:
LJ Graphics

Cover Design:
Phil Velikan

Indexer:
Sharon Shock

Acknowledgements

I would like to thank Vineet Whig and his development team at NIIT Ltd. for their excellent support, coordination, and guidance during the project. It has been a pleasure to work with Anita Sastry, Kuljit Kaur, and Nitin Pandey at NIIT on this project.

Special thanks go out to Stacy Hiquet for making this book happen. I would also like to thank the Project Editor, Cathleen Snyder, without whose help the book would not have been half as good as it is right now! Finally, thanks to Priyanka for creating the book's graphics.

About NIT

NIIT is a Global IT Solutions Corporation with a presence in 38 countries. With its unique business model and technology creation capabilities, NIIT delivers software and learning solutions to more than 1,000 clients around the world.

The success of NIIT's training solutions lies in its unique approach to education. NIIT's Knowledge Solutions Business conceives, researches, and develops all course materials. A rigorous instructional design methodology is followed to create engaging and compelling course content. NIIT has one of the largest learning material development facilities in the world, with more than 5,000 person-years of experience.

NIIT trains more than 200,000 people each year in Information Technology areas, using stand-up training, video-aided instruction, computer-based training (CBT), and Internet-based training (IBT). NIIT has been featured in the Guinness Book of World Records for the largest number of people trained in one year!

NIIT has developed more than 10,000 hours of instructor-led training (ILT) and more than 3,000 hours of Internet-based and computer-based training. IDC ranked NIIT among the Top 15 IT training providers globally for the year 2000. Through their innovative use of training methods and commitment to research and development, NIIT has been in the forefront of computer education and training for the past 20 years.

Quality has been the prime focus at NIIT. Most of the processes are ISO-9001 certified. NIIT was the twelfth company in the world to be assessed at Level 5 of SEI-CMM. NIIT's Content (Learning Material) Development facility is the first in the world to be assessed at this highest maturity level. NIIT has strategic partnerships with companies such as Computer Associates, IBM, Microsoft, Oracle, and Sun Microsystems.

About the Author

V. V. Preetham is the Chief Architect of ConceptUniv in Atlanta, Georgia. He is a Sun Certified Architect, a Sun Certified Java Programmer, a BEA WebLogic Enterprise Developer, a CIW Enterprise Developer, and a Microsoft Certified Product Specialist. He is also an IBM certified specialist on WebSphere 3.5, Visual Age, XML, and UML. He authored *Java Web Services Programming*. In his present job, he is involved in consulting, research, and development. V.V. has extensive knowledge of C, C++, C#, and Java. He has also done extensive work on Internet protocols, networking protocols, and OMG protocols for J2EE.

Contents at a Glance

	Introduction . . . . **xxiii**
1	Internet Overview. 1
2	Network Security Overview 25
3	Firewalls for Network Security 65
4	Firewall Technologies 81
5	Firewall Architectures 119
6	Firewall Design. 133
7	Bastion Hosts 159
8	Internet Services and Firewalls 197
9	Preventive Measures 219
10	Implementing Windows- and Linux-Based Firewalls . . . 225
11	Implementing Router-Based Firewalls. 259
A	Best Practices, Tips, and Tricks 293
B	Frequently Asked Questions 299
C	In the Wings. 311
	Index 313

Contents

Introduction xxiii

Chapter 1   Internet Overview **1**

What Is the Internet? 2
    The History of the Internet 3
    Basic Internet Primer 6
Understanding the OSI Model 10
Understanding TCP/IP 13
    TCP/IP Layered Architecture 13
    TCP/IP Protocols 15
    Internet Addressing 17
How the Internet Works 20
Summary 22
Check Your Understanding 22
    Multiple Choice Questions 22
    Short Questions 22
Answers 23
    Multiple Choice Answers 23
    Short Answers 23

Chapter 2   Network Security Overview **25**

Fundamental Elements of Security 26
    Drafting a Security Model 26
    Risk Analysis 29
    Ensuring the Success of a Security Model 30
    The Evolution of a Security Model 30
Basic Security Concepts 31
    Cryptography 31
    Authentication 33

Authorization. 33

Audits 33

Public Key Infrastructure 33

Digital Certificates. 34

Common Security Threats. 35

Footprinting. 35

Scanning 36

Enumeration 38

Social Engineering. 39

Application and Operating System Attacks 41

Network Attacks 48

Denial of Service Attacks. 51

Malicious Software. 52

Assessing Vulnerability 53

Evaluating the Threats 55

Analyzing Threats 55

Threat Modeling 56

Security Strategies. 57

Least Privilege 57

Defense In-Depth 58

Choke Point. 58

Weakest Link. 59

Fail-Safe Stance 59

Universal Participation 60

Diversity of Defense. 60

Simplicity. 60

Security through Obscurity 61

Summary 61

Check Your Understanding 62

Multiple Choice Questions. 62

Short Questions. 62

Answers 63

Multiple Choice Answers. 63
Short Answers 63

Chapter 3   Firewalls for Network Security. 65

The Origin and Need for Firewalls 66
The History of Firewalls 66
The Functions of Firewalls. 67
The Role of Firewalls in Network Security. 70
Types of Firewalls 72
Network-Layer Firewalls 72
Application-Layer Firewalls 74
Constraints and Future Trends of Firewalls 76
Limitations of Firewalls 76
Future Developments in Firewalls 77
Summary 77
Check Your Understanding 78
Multiple Choice Questions. 78
Short Questions 78
Answers 79
Multiple Choice Answers. 79
Short Answers 79

Chapter 4   Firewall Technologies 81

Introduction 82
TCP/IP Networking 84
Encapsulation 84
Demultiplexing 87
IP Routing. 87
Packet Filtering. 89
The Filtering Process 90
Advantages of Packet Filtering. 91
Disadvantages of Packet Filtering. 92

Proxy Servers. 92
    Features of a Proxy Server 93
    Requirements of a Proxy Service. 94
    SOCKS 95
    Advantages of Proxy Services 97
    Disadvantages of Proxy Services 97
User Authentication 98
    Kerberos 98
Network Address Translation. 100
    How NAT Works. 101
    Advantages of NAT 106
    Disadvantages of NAT 106
Virtual Private Networks 107
    VPN Requirements 109
    Tunneling. 110
    Point-to-Point Protocol 111
    Point-to-Point Tunneling Protocol 112
    Layer 2 Tunneling Protocol 112
    Internet Protocol Security (IPSec) Tunnel Mode 113
    Advantages of Virtual Private Networks 114
    Disadvantages of Virtual Private Networks 114
Summary 115
Check Your Understanding 116
    Multiple Choice Questions. 116
    Short Questions 116
Answers 117
    Multiple Choice Answers. 117
    Short Answers 117

Chapter 5   **Firewall Architectures** **119**

Dial-Up Architecture 120
Single Router Architecture 121
Dual Router Architecture 121

Dual-Homed Host Architecture 122

Screened Host Architecture 122

Screened Subnet Architecture 124

Variations to the Screened Subnet Architecture 125

    Multiple Bastion Hosts 125

    One Router Acting as the Interior and Exterior Router 126

    A Bastion Host Acting as the Exterior Router 127

    Multiple Exterior Routers 128

    Multiple Perimeter Networks 129

Summary 129

Check Your Understanding 130

    Multiple Choice Questions 130

    Short Questions 130

Answers 131

    Multiple Choice Answers 131

    Short Answers 131

Chapter 6   Firewall Design 133

Firewall Design Overview 134

Firewall Security Policy 135

    Need for a Security Policy 135

    Guidelines for Designing a Policy 136

    Policy Design Checklist 136

    Finalizing a Security Policy 139

Firewall Products 140

    Router-Based Firewalls 140

    Workstation-Based Firewalls 141

Evaluating Firewalls 143

    Parameters for Evaluation 143

    Additional Criteria for Selecting Firewalls 144

Firewall Configuration 144

    Split-Screened Subnet Architecture 145

Configuring a Packet-Filtering Architecture 149

Service Configuration. 151

Packet-Filtering Rules 152

Summary 155

Check Your Understanding 155

Multiple Choice Questions. 155

Short Questions 156

Answers 156

Multiple Choice Answers 156

Short Answers 157

Chapter 7   Bastion Hosts **159**

Introduction to Bastion Hosts 160

System Requirements 162

Hardware. 163

Operating System. 165

Services 166

Location 167

Hardening. 169

Hardware Setup 170

Operating System Setup. 170

Configuring Services 171

Security Measures 172

Connecting and Running 173

Windows Bastion Host 173

Installing the Services. 174

Services to Enable 179

Services to Disable 180

UNIX Bastion Host 181

Installing the Services. 182

Services to Enable 189

Services to Disable 190

Bastion Host Design 191

Summary 193

Check Your Understanding 193

    Multiple Choice Questions. 193

    Short Questions 194

Answers 194

    Multiple Choice Answers. 194

    Short Answers 194

Chapter 8   **Internet Services and Firewalls 197**

World Wide Web 198

    Web Servers. 199

    Securing Web Clients. 204

    HTTP Filtering Rules 205

Electronic Mail 205

    Mail System Components 206

    E-Mail Attachments 207

    Securing E-Mail Messages. 210

    Filtering Rules for SMTP and POP 212

File Transfer Protocol 212

    Accessing FTP Servers. 213

    Securing an FTP Server 214

Summary 214

Check Your Understanding 215

    Multiple Choice Questions. 215

    Short Questions 216

Answers 216

    Multiple Choice Answers. 216

    Short Answers 216

Chapter 9   **Preventive Measures. 219**

Remedial Measures 220

Legal Measures 222

Summary 223
Check Your Understanding 223
    Short Questions 223
Answers 224
    Short Answers 224

Chapter 10 Implementing Windows- and Linux-Based
Firewalls 225

Implementing Firewalls Using Microsoft ISA Server 2000 226
    Features of ISA Server 226
    ISA Installation Considerations 233
    Configuring Security on ISA Server 238
Implementing Firewalls in Linux 249
    Types of Firewalls in Linux 251
    IPchains 252
    IPtables 254
Summary 255
Check Your Understanding 256
    Multiple Choice Questions 256
    Short Questions 256
Answers 257
    Multiple Choice Answers 257
    Short Answers 257

Chapter 11 Implementing Router-Based Firewalls 259

An Introduction to Routers 260
Using Routers as Firewalls 262
    Rejecting Protocols 265
    IP Filtering 266
    Using IP Packet Filtering to Prevent IP Spoofing 266
Using Cisco Routers as Firewalls 267
Context-Based Access Control 268

CBAC Functions 269

Advantages of CBAC. 272

Limitations of CBAC. 273

How CBAC Works 273

Configuring CBAC 274

Summary 290

Check Your Understanding 290

Multiple Choice Questions. 290

Short Questions 291

Answers 291

Multiple Choice Answers. 291

Short Answers 291

Appendix A Best Practices, Tips, and Tricks 293

Best Practices 294

Tips and Tricks 297

Appendix B Frequently Asked Questions 299

Appendix C In the Wings 311

Index 313

Introduction

With the increasing use of the Internet in all business operations, it has become mandatory for all organizations to secure their corporate networks. If the security of a corporate network is breached, it can lead to enormous loss of revenue and customers.

You can effectively secure corporate networks by using firewalls, which provide a layer of protection between an external and internal network. This book provides in-depth coverage of firewalls and their implementation.

◆ Chapter 1 begins with an introduction to the Internet, the OSI model, and TCP/IP.

◆ Chapter 2 describes basic security concepts, such as cryptography and digital certificates, as well as common security threats such as network scanning and network attacks.

◆ Chapter 3 introduces firewalls and their types, use, and limitations.

◆ Chapter 4 carries on with the discussion begun in Chapter 3, and also describes firewall technologies such as proxy servers and virtual private networks.

◆ Chapter 5 describes firewall architecture, including the various architectures that you can apply to suit your specific network requirements.

◆ Chapter 6 discusses the steps to create a security policy, the firewall products available on the market, and the criteria for evaluating firewalls.

◆ Chapter 7 builds on the information covered in Chapter 6 and goes on to describe the steps to install and configure bastion hosts.

◆ Chapter 8 explores the role of firewalls in securing services available on the Internet, which include the Web, FTP, and e-mail.

◆ Chapter 9 explains the legal implications of network intrusion.

Chapter 1

Internet Overview

The Internet is one of the most important advents in history. Over the years, it has revolutionized the way people communicate and do business. This chapter explains what the Internet is and how it works. It also provides an overview of the history and timeline of the Internet and explains TCP/IP (*Transmission Control Protocol/Internet Protocol*), the backbone protocol of the Internet. Further, the chapter explains the current trends in the Internet and how they might affect future growth.

What Is the Internet?

The Internet is a major influence that has allowed communication to reach a new high. Communication is the essence of any transaction. In an earlier era, people used to tie messages to the legs of pigeons and hope they would reach the appropriate person. This was not easy because the pigeon had to be trained for its task as a mail agent. As modes of communication evolved, two major technological breakthroughs were invented—the telegraph and the telephone. At that time, the telegraph and the telephone were the most applicable technologies for end-to-end communication.

There was also a latent demand for an efficient alternative to the newspaper. The newspaper is a broadcasting medium, rather than an end-to-end real-time communication medium like the telephone. The advent of radio and television revolutionized the broadcasting and publishing industries.

While the broadcasting and telecommunications media provided information and entertainment to people, the Internet slowly started to take over as an alternative method of communication. As more research was funded toward networking, people realized the potential of such networks in alternative mailing, end-to-end communication, and broadcasting agents. The Internet has now become the primary medium for all types of communication, whether one-to-one, one-to-many, or many-to-many.

The Internet, by definition, is a galactic network that spans the globe with interconnected computing systems. The systems are devices that can be defined as entities that possess the basic qualities of computing. They can range from cameras to supercomputers. It is almost accurate to suggest that the Internet also spans outer space, because it is made up of devices such as artificial satellites that scan and monitor different planets.

The spread of the Internet into such a vast network is credited to the combined efforts of governments, business industries, and academia. Without these three influences, the Internet probably would not have grown to a dimension that spans geological and political boundaries. Anybody from any corner of the world can share his or her opinion on the Internet. People across the globe can share each other's ideas. This, in turn, helps speed the process of innovation. The dissemination of information at the speed of the Internet is another reason for new technological breakthroughs.

The History of the Internet

As you know, the Internet is a living, breathing system of millions of various computing devices connected to each other for some purpose. Initially, the Internet was formulated for the exchange of military information across a few computers. Slowly, universities found out that the Internet is a faster means to share information about the research that is conducted in college laboratories, and it grew from a few computers to a few hundred computers. Then the business community became curious about information sharing over the network. The Internet became more applicable for every community in one way or another. Needless to say, the main theme for the growth of the Internet was "information sharing." Almost everyone benefits from the growth of such a network. Information dissemination at the speed of electronic media has become a basic need of almost every human being. The growth and widespread acceptance of the Internet across political and geographic boundaries are indicators that sharing data and information electronically has become a necessity rather than a mere utility.

The following sections present a timeline of the events that occurred in the history of the Internet to help you understand its birth and growth. The timeline summarizes the events that occurred during the decades and influenced the evolution of the Internet.

The 1950s

One of the main events to trigger the conception of the Internet was the launch of the first artificial earth satellite by the USSR. The satellite was called Sputnik, and the event led to the formation of the ARPA (*Advanced Research Projects Agency*) within the United States Department of Defense.

The 1960s

A lot of network-related research was conducted in the 1960s. ARPA commissioned research on networking among time-sharing computers. Many universities were conducting research on networking. During this era, many papers presented different theories about networking. Also, the telecommunication giants got involved in the research and development of computer networks over existing telecommunication lines. The plan for the first ARPA network, called the ARPANET (*Advanced Research Projects Agency Network*), was drafted. ARPANET was the world's first principal packet-switching network.

The 1970s

During the 1970s, ARPANET was expanded to involve many different networks that existed in the research labs and universities. The first e-mail program was conceived during the early part of the 1970s, along with text-chat applications. The RFCs (*Request for Comments*) for Telnet and FTP (*File Transfer Protocol*) were created. The concept of Ethernet as a networking protocol was formed, and the concept of TCP and IP as transport and communication protocols emerged.

 NOTE

Ethernet is the most widely used LAN technology. Typically, Ethernet uses coaxial cable wires; it is also used in wireless LANs. TCP and IP (jointly used as TCP/IP) are the protocols of the Internet. They can also be used in a private network.

The 1980s

Many networks were formed during the 1980s, including BITNET, MILNET, CSNET, NSFNET, UUNET, and USENET. TCP/IP was becoming the backbone protocol for communication over many of these networks. Many RFCs were filed during this era, which influenced the growth of interconnectivity among different sub-networks. Also, many newsgroups were formed online.

The term "Internet" became a de facto representation to suggest a network made up of multiple sub-networks. Many UNIX-based desktop computers were deployed at university sites and businesses. DNS (*Domain Name System*) was introduced to manage the naming of Internet hosts among networks and sub-networks. In the early 1980s, viruses were accidentally introduced into the network, due to bugs. Such accidents originally brought the entire Internet to a halt. However, the Internet was better stabilized in the later part of the '80s, which also saw the outbreak of Internet worms. By the end of this era, there were almost 100,000 hosts across several countries connected to the Internet.

The 1990s

The ARPANET was decommissioned in the 1990s. Connections increased among different sub-networks spanning multiple countries. The CERN (*European Organization for Nuclear Research*) introduced the World Wide Web. Some countries formed Internet-related laws. Several countries researched privacy techniques to secure the Internet. The infrastructure for connectivity advanced at an accelerated speed. Many networks were introduced on a larger bandwidth connection that ranged from 1.5 Mbps T1 lines to 45 Mbps T3 lines. The capacity (bandwidth) of the Internet on the whole also improved during this era.

Many significant changes in the use of the Internet took place. E-mail was used extensively for faster communication. PCs became affordable. Many desktop systems and PCs were connected to the Internet. InterNIC (*Internet Network Information Center*) was created to monitor the directory, registration, and information services on the Web. Many communities, including universities, colleges, libraries, newsgroups, bulletin boards, and the governments of several countries, started to establish their presence on the Web.

Many ISPs set up their businesses on the network, providing dial-up access to different communities. The use of PCs and phone lines grew exponentially due to ISPs (*Internet Service Providers*). The concept of browsing the Web came into being. Many scripting languages were introduced to express information on the Internet, and HTML became the de facto standard for presenting information on the Web.

Thousands of RFCs were filed by this time. Many organizations started conducting business over the network. E-commerce was introduced during the later part of the 1990s. Stock trading, finance, banking, manufacturing, supply chains, and many other diverse groups of industries started participating in online commerce.

Distributed computing (the sharing of computing resources) also became the focal point for research scientists to harness the collective power of the Internet. Hackers became prominent by exposing the security holes in networks and network-related resources. Internet security became a prime concern for almost everyone using the network. Many technologies and protocols were invented to secure the Internet. Devices as small as a wristwatch or a cell phone started sharing the Internet space. Mobile Internet computing was invented. Due to the Y2K bug, the later part of the 1990s also became a stressful period for every business using computers. Many Internet resources were upgraded to counter the Y2K problem. The use of the Internet grew exponentially. (The number of hosts was in the millions.) The Internet eventually evolved to be more stable and reliable.

The Current Era

The TCP/IP addressing system is almost used up. New protocols like IPv6 (with much more address space) tackle the problem. Network commerce is growing at an exponential rate. People's trust in conducting commerce and business over the Internet is gaining by the hour. The number of hosts connected to the Internet is increasing alarmingly. The infrastructure capacity is being consumed at an accelerated speed.

The dependency of businesses and people on the Internet is almost frightening. If the Internet ever comes to a halt, it will be equivalent to the end for many businesses and several advanced countries that base most of their services on the Internet. Hackers, viruses, worms, and privacy invasion are prime concerns of everyone using the Internet. Major funding is going toward better security techniques for the Internet.

Diverse media content, such as video streaming, telephony, and HDTV (*High Definition Television*), is used across the Web. Average users (with a PC and a telephone line) are asking for more bandwidth to access this content on the Internet. Dial-up bandwidths are improving. ISDN and DSL connections with speeds of up to 600 Kbps are becoming increasingly available for the average user.

The network as a whole is not only used as a communication backbone, but also as a file server, a computer server, and an application server. In other words, the sharing of files, computing resources, and distributed applications over the network is increasing exponentially. New interconnecting paradigms and distributed networking technologies are evolving. The spread of the network is so mind-boggling that it is almost impossible to think of a world without such an all-encompassing concept.

Basic Internet Primer

The term *Internet* is derived from two roots—"inter" and "network." The ability to interconnect two networks introduces the definition of the Internet. How different is the Internet from a network? Well, not much. A network is made up of multiple computing devices, as shown in Figure 1.1.

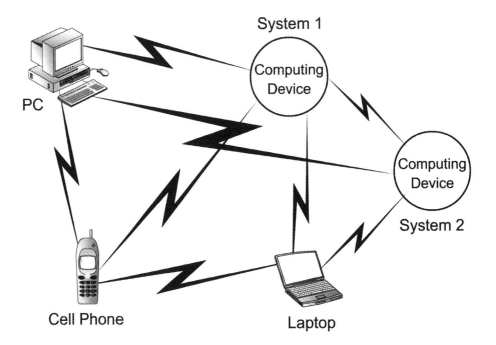

FIGURE 1.1 *A network with different computing devices*

A network can also be made up of multiple sub-networks, as shown in Figure 1.2.

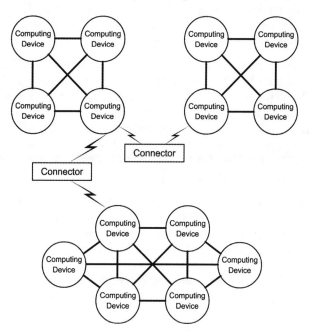

FIGURE 1.2 *A network with sub-networks*

The Internet is the mother of all networks. When you connect such huge networks and sub-networks to each other, you effectively derive the Internet, as shown in Figure 1.3.

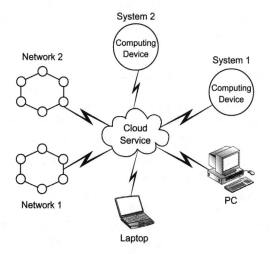

FIGURE 1.3 *Networks and sub-networks forming the Internet*

The preliminary stages of the Internet focused on one goal—developing strategic military-oriented communication among different computing devices. There was a basic need to share information across military bases in order to be current and effective in deploying military strategies.

When DARPA (*Defense Advanced Research Projects Agency*), the US military research agency, commissioned the ARPANET, the proposal was to come up with a foolproof network that was both rugged and reliable during warfare. This was the foremost principle behind the project, although there were a lot of other goals too. While designing the network, one goal was to ensure that there was no centralized command and control unit, so that there was no single point of attack where enemy missiles could bring down the entire network. It was, however, considered an almost impossible task to create an effective networking system without a centralized authority.

ARPANET worked on different designs before choosing packet-switched communication as its main protocol. The reason behind their choice was simple. The packet-switch network gave them the ruggedness and reliability that they needed. How? To begin with, a network is made up of multiple nodes. Each node has a node address and enough intelligence to manage its own status and efficiently communicate its status and availability to the other peer nodes. Every node is connected to every other node in the network directly or indirectly. Thus, there is more than one path to any given target node from a source node.

To explain further, whenever a source node is interested in communicating with a target node, it sends the information to the target node in the form of packets. A packet is a small package made up of information, which includes the source address, the destination address, and the information that must be transmitted from the source to the target. Usually the size of a packet does not vary. In other words, if the packet size for a given protocol is determined to be one byte, 100 one-byte packets are required to send 100 bytes of information. This is an example of how a large amount of information can be broken down into multiple packets to stream it from one node to another.

In the current scenario, if 100 bytes of information were sent from a source node to a target node, every packet would consist of the same source and destination addresses for the nodes from which they originated and to which they were destined, respectively. The source node would then release these packets on the network. Once this occurs, it is the responsibility of the network (collectively—a network is the sum of the nodes that are interconnected) to route the packets to the appropriate destination node.

How does the network achieve this? To begin with, whenever a packet leaves a source node, there is no predetermined path from the source to the destination. So how does the packet find its target? The first node that the packet comes across has some intelligence and suggests the next node to which the packet should be routed. The next node then routes the packet further, to the neighboring node that it determines is closer to the target. In this manner, the packet is routed across the network from one node to another to reach the target.

This is a very inefficient strategy because at any given point in time, the success or failure of a packet reaching the destination is not assured. However, the core idea behind such a networking protocol was to use this unreliability as an advantage.

You might wonder how this can be an advantage. Take the example of a network that spans cities named after the English alphabet. In other words, consider a network spanning City A to City Z. For the sake of the example, assume that every city is a unique node and that all cities are interconnected. Now assume that a hypothesized protocol is designed for communication across these cities. Imagine that this protocol requires a predetermined path for connection between the nodes. In other words, if City A needs to communicate with City N, it must travel via cities B, D, and G, as shown in Figure 1.4.

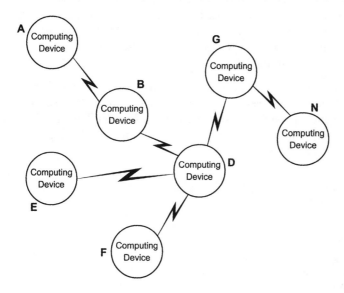

FIGURE 1.4 *A path connecting several "cities"*

In this scenario, if the node at City D shuts down for any reason, communication between City A and City N is totally halted. If the node at City D is also a vertex in the path among other cities, communication among several cities will be affected. This is a formula for disaster. Under the pretext of making the network efficient, you risk losing a lot more due to a single point of failure. The packet-switched network was designed so that there is no single point of failure. Even if one node in a packet-switched network ceases to operate, the packets can be routed through other nodes to their destinations. However, if the destination node ceases to operate, it is a different story! Although this protocol was not very efficient, it proved to be rugged.

The ARPANET was based on the design of a packet-switched network. This concept evolved due to the decentralization of control among different peers. The protocol that

ARPANET was using in the 1970s was called NCP (*Network Control Protocol*). As time passed and more funds were invested in research, TCP/IP was invented.

To understand the workings of the Internet, it is important to understand TCP/IP. However, to understand the TCP/IP suite of protocols, you must to understand the OSI (*Open Systems Interconnection*) model, derived by the ISO (*International Standards Organization*).

Understanding the OSI Model

The initial packet-switched networks were not as sophisticated as the current models. A limitation of the initial networks was that only nodes from the same vendor could talk to each other. (Here, *node* is used as a term used to encompass the manufactured hardware and proprietary software (operating system) that runs on a node.) While research was in progress, the ISO created a new model called the OSI model, which was meant to iron out the problems that existed in the initial network model.

The OSI model was designed to create a network from ground up, with heterogeneous computing devices from different vendors connected to each other. Whenever you study network architecture, it is a good idea to start with the OSI model. The model is made up of a layered architecture, in which every layer has its own responsibility. Figure 1.5 shows all of the layers within the OSI model.

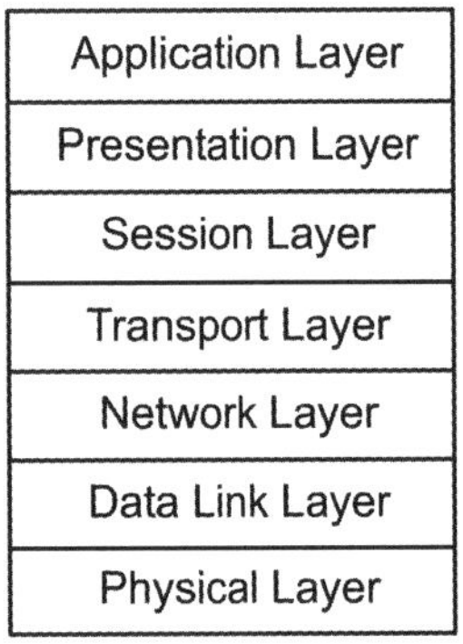

Application Layer
Presentation Layer
Session Layer
Transport Layer
Network Layer
Data Link Layer
Physical Layer

FIGURE 1.5 *The layers in the OSI model*

The OSI model is a hierarchical architecture. The basic idea behind such layering is to distribute a complex process among multiple layers in such a way that every layer claims responsibility for a particular task within the process. Also, such a layered architecture is considered to be *modular* because the responsibility of one layer is separated from the responsibilities of another. A modular architecture is more efficient and loosely coupled so that any layer within the model can be smoothly replaced without affecting the entire architecture.

Typically, OSI is a set of guidelines that you can follow to design any other network model. Therefore, the OSI model is also a reference model for other networking architectures. As shown in Figure 1.5, the OSI model has seven layers. A brief description of each layer follows.

◆ **Application layer**. This layer's responsibility is to interface the user application with the rest of the layers in the model. The Application layer is also responsible for providing an API (*Application Programming Interface*) to the user applications so the programmers who write code for the user interface don't have to worry about the implementation details of the interface. This means that the Application layer takes the responsibility of the networking details away from the user application so the user application does not have to know anything about the underlying implementation of the network. Some examples of user applications are file transfer services, printing services, e-mail services, network management consoles, client-server processes, and so on.

◆ **Presentation layer**. This layer's responsibility is to provide encoding standards for the network. The Presentation layer is also responsible for negotiating between the Application layer and the rest of the protocol stack. It provides a standard encoding streamer for the Application layer so that communication between the Application layer and the rest of the protocol stack is standardized across different operating environments. In other words, the Presentation layer provides translation and conversion functions to successfully transfer data to the underlying protocol stack. As an example, if the Application layer of a PC sends information in ASCII format, the Presentation layer is responsible for formatting the information in the standard network type. This standard network type, which is generic for the underlying protocol stack across different operating environments, would be transferred without further conversion. At the receiving end, it is again the Presentation layer's responsibility to convert the generic network format to a format that the receiving application can understand. Data encryption and decryption can also take place at the Presentation layer.

◆ **Session layer**. This layer's responsibility is to provide a communication channel between hosts. It provides a definition for managing the individual network channels, also called *sessions*, between two hosts. The Session layer is responsible for establishing a session between the hosts, as well as maintaining and ending the session. Some examples of the Session layer protocol are RPC (*Remote Procedure Call*), AppleTalk, and NFS (*Network File System*).

◆ **Transport layer**. This layer's responsibility is to control the transmission of data on the network. In other words, it provides flow control mechanisms to ensure data integrity between the nodes. The flow control mechanism acknowledges the receipt of every segment from the sending host and the proper sequencing of the segments. If the sender does not receive an acknowledgement from the recipient, the flow control mechanism at the sender's end is responsible for resending the segment. On the whole, the Transport layer's responsibility is to segment the data received from the Session layer and forward it to the Network layer. In addition, the Transport layer receives segmented data from the Network layer to reassemble the segments to forward them to the Session layer. The Transport layer is also responsible for establishing a logical connection between the destination node and the source node. Some examples of the Transport layer are TCP and UDP (*User Datagram Protocol*).

◆ **Network layer**. This layer's responsibility is to ensure the addressing of the hosts. It also ensures the routing of information between hosts across networks. In other words, the Network layer handles all of the transmission and traffic management among hosts. It also provides address resolution for the segments forwarded by the Data Link layer.

◆ **Data Link layer**. This layer's responsibility is to define how data is accessed from a physical medium. It provides a mechanism to format the information presented from a physical medium so the information can be passed to the Network layer. The information presented from a physical medium can be in the form of bits. The Data Link layer collates this information and formats it into *frames*. A frame is a unit of information that contains the destination address, the source address, an error checksum, and the data itself. The Data Link layer is also responsible for converting the information obtained from the Network layer into bits to forward it to the Physical layer. In addition, the Data Link layer is responsible for ensuring that the messages traversing the network reach the appropriate physical devices. This is possible because the Data Link layer manages the unique identity of the physical device on the network. It uses the concept of hardware addressing (MAC address) to identify a physical device. Some examples of the Data Link layer protocol are ARP (*Address Resolution Protocol*) and RARP (*Reverse Address Resolution Protocol*).

◆ **Physical layer**. This layer's responsibility is to manage the hardware details of sending and receiving binary data over a physical channel. The physical channel is typically made up of wires such as twisted-pair and fiber optic cables. It can also be made up of wireless media such as infrared or radio waves. In general, the Physical layer provides a specification for interfacing with a physical channel based on the electrical and mechanical functions of the medium. The connectors at the Physical layer have different topologies defined for different network designs. Topologies are the structures in which you set up your network. Some examples are the star topology, the ring topology, and the bus topology. One example of the Physical layer is the Ethernet standard, which is the network protocol that defines how different devices on the network communicate with each other over the Physical layer.

Now that you understand the OSI model, you need to understand the TCP/IP model.

Understanding TCP/IP

The TCP/IP suite of protocols is based largely on the OSI model. TCP/IP is a protocol suite that allows many computers running on different hardware and operating systems to communicate with each other. The main concept of the TCP/IP suite is to allow communication among heterogeneous computing platforms. There are some basic requirements for any computer to participate in a network. These requirements include

◆ **Computing hardware**. This refers to the CPU, the monitor, and the other hardware components.

◆ **Network interface card**. This is a piece of hardware within the CPU that connects the computer to the network via a network cable.

◆ **Operating system**. This is the software that controls the hardware and executes user-specific applications.

◆ **TCP/IP protocol suite**. This is the software that enables networking support on the system.

TCP/IP Layered Architecture

TCP/IP is an open protocol suite in which the implementation of the protocol is available almost free of charge for the public. It is the backbone protocol of the Internet. TCP/IP is a layered protocol, like any other networking protocol. Generally, a layer is a subsystem within the suite of protocols that shares a specific responsibility within the suite. Typically, TCP/IP is considered a four-layer protocol, as opposed to the seven layers in the OSI model. Figure 1.6 displays the different layers in the TCP/IP suite of protocols.

Application Layer
Transport Layer
Network Layer
Link Layer

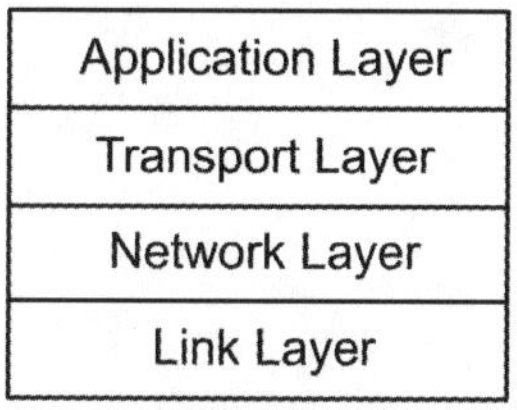

FIGURE 1.6 *The four layers of TCP/IP*

The following list explains these four layers.

◆ **Application layer**. This layer's responsibility is to provide a common interface for any user application to communicate with the underlying layers. In other words, the Application layer is responsible for providing an interface between the user application and the network.

♦ **Transport layer**. This layer's responsibility is to control the flow of data between two communicating hosts. The Transport layer is responsible for breaking down data into packets and sending and receiving them from the Network layer.

♦ **Network layer**. This layer's responsibility is to route packets across the network. It is also responsible for some message control and group management.

♦ **Link layer**. This layer's responsibility is to handle the hardware-related details of the system. In other words, the Link layer is responsible for interfacing the operating system to the network interface card within the computer.

Given a network of a number of nodes, each node must understand TCP/IP as the communication protocol to participate in the network. The communication between one node and another is simplified because every node talks TCP/IP (see Figure 1.7).

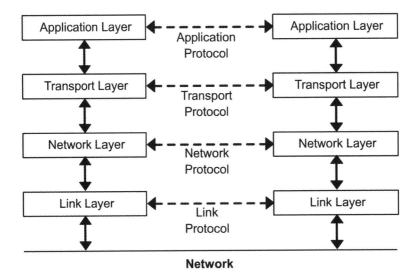

FIGURE 1.7 *The communication between TCP/IP-enabled nodes*

The communication between the Link layers of two nodes (or the Network layers of two nodes) is called *protocol communication*. It is important to understand that the Application layer is only involved in providing an interface between the user application and the network. The network is actually represented by the lower three layers of the TCP/IP suite. The lower three layers are responsible for handling network-oriented details without having to understand anything about the layout of the user application.

It is also important to note that the user application does not need to know anything about the way information is routed across the network by the lower three layers. Thus, the user application is completely separated from the networking details. The user applications at the two ends appear to be communicating directly with each other even though multiple layers of protocols are involved. You can say that TCP/IP is an example of a sophisticated, modularized, and layer-based communication protocol.

As I stated previously, the Internet is a galactic network that is made up of other networks. These networks are, in turn, made up of processing nodes, which are interconnected by direct network cables or through a *hub*. A hub is a piece of hardware that provides a junction for multiple nodes to connect to each other. If one network has to be connected to another network, you need a *router*, which is a piece of hardware that routes the packets that originated in one network to a destination in another network. Typically, the router uses the IP protocol to route the packet. Figure 1.8 shows two different networks connected to each other through a router.

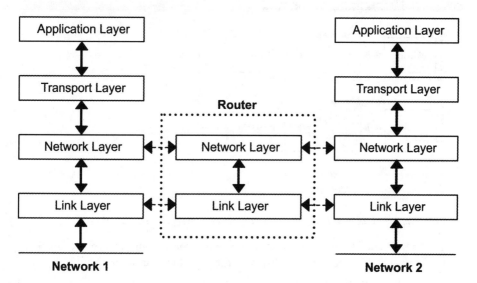

FIGURE 1.8 *Networks connected through a router*

A router uses the Network layer to connect two different networks. However, this can also be accomplished using a *bridge*. A bridge connects two different networks at the Link layer.

TCP/IP Protocols

TCP is considered a transport protocol; IP is considered a network protocol. IP provides a service to handle the movement of packets across the network. This service is unreliable because IP does not guarantee the delivery of a packet over the network. However, TCP guarantees the delivery. TCP is responsible for providing capabilities such as data flow control and transmission control between two hosts. It is also responsible for sending and receiving packets and acknowledging the receipt of a packet to the sending host.

The TCP/IP suite of protocols is actually made up of many other protocols that exist among the four main layers. Figure 1.9 shows the different protocols at the various layers of the TCP/IP protocol suite.

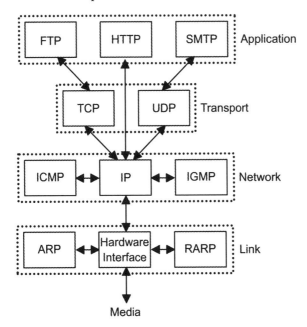

FIGURE 1.9 *Different protocols among the various layers of the TCP/IP suite*

TCP, UDP, and IP are the most important protocols among the protocol stack displayed in Figure 1.9. The following list explains these protocols in more detail.

◆ **TCP**. TCP is a reliable protocol that exists within the Transport layer and works on top of IP in the Network layer. Although IP is an unreliable protocol, TCP provides the transmission control mechanism that accounts for more reliable communication. TCP ensures that every packet it receives is acknowledged to the sender, so that the sender knows the packet has reached its destination. This way, the sender can rely on the network to send the necessary information.

◆ **UDP**. As I mentioned earlier, UDP stands for *User Datagram Protocol*. It is so named because the communication between two hosts happens by sending and receiving *datagrams*, which are units of information that carry predetermined sizes of data between hosts. UDP is considered an unreliable protocol compared to TCP. Like TCP, UDP also works within the Transport layer and uses the IP protocol that exists within the Network layer. Also like TCP, UDP is responsible for controlling the flow of data between two hosts. However, UDP does not ensure that all of the datagrams that are sent from the source reach their destinations. This is because UDP is a connectionless protocol—it has no mechanisms for connection establishment or termination. You can consider UDP unreliable for this purpose. Since UDP is much simpler than TCP, it is also much faster.

◆ **IP**. IP is a protocol within the Network layer. As shown in Figure 1.9, IP is used as a central point among many protocols such as TCP, UDP, ICMP, and IGMP. The IP protocol is responsible for routing the packets that are sent from the Transport layer across the network.

Internet Addressing

Now that you know how the TCP/IP layered architecture works, you can look into the details of Internet addressing. Every node on the Internet requires a unique address, called an *IP address*, to identify and distinguish it from other nodes.

An IP address is a 32-bit Internet addressing system. If a node needs to participate on the network, it must have its own IP address that is unique among the other addresses assigned to the different nodes on the Internet. An IP address is made up of a network portion and a host portion. The network portion represents the identity of the network to which the node belongs; the host portion represents the identity of the node itself within the network. This 32-bit address is written as four decimal numbers, with each decimal number separated by a dot. To better understand this concept, consider the following address.

140.252.133.33

This notation is also called a *dotted decimal notation* or a *dotted quad notation*. Since an IP address is made up of 32 bits, the number of bits assigned to each decimal is eight (in other words, one byte per decimal). Each byte is also referred to as an *octet*, which can have values ranging from 0 to 255.

An IP address can belong to one of the five different classes of the addressing scheme, represented as Class A, B, C, D, and E (see Figure 1.10).

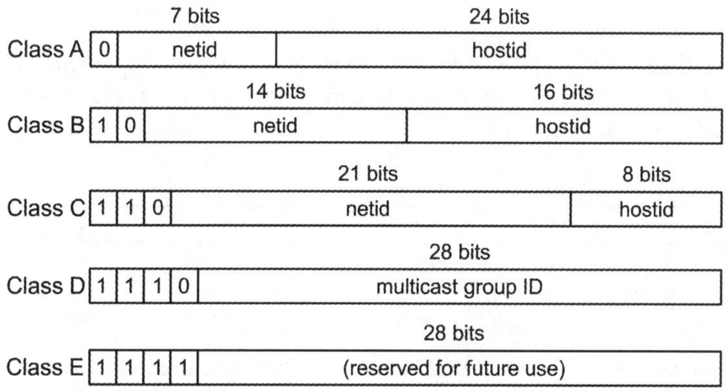

	7 bits	24 bits
Class A	0	netid	hostid

	14 bits	16 bits
Class B	1 0	netid	hostid

	21 bits	8 bits
Class C	1 1 0	netid	hostid

	28 bits	
Class D	1 1 1 0	multicast group ID

	28 bits	
Class E	1 1 1 1	(reserved for future use)

FIGURE 1.10 *The five classes of IP addresses*

Every class of IP addresses has a range of values assigned to it, which provides a distinguished boundary to identify the class of an IP address (see Figure 1.11).

Class	Range
A	**0**.0.0.0 to **127**.255.255.255
B	**128**.0.0.0 to **191**.255.255.255
C	**192**.0.0.0 to **223**.255.255.255
D	**224**.0.0.0 to **239**.255.255.255
E	**240**.0.0.0 to **255**.255.255.255

FIGURE 1.11 _The range of values for the different classes of IP addresses_

The following list describes the different classes of IP addresses.

◆ **Class A address**. The first octet of a Class A address represents the network portion of the address; the remaining three octets provide the host portion of the address (see Figure 1.12).

	7 bits	24 bits
Class A	0	netid	hostid

FIGURE 1.12 _The Class A address format_

Effectively, the Class A address has 24 bits to represent the host portion and only seven bits to represent the network portion. The most significant bit, or the left-most bit of the first octet, is set to 0 for a Class A address. Therefore, the range of values for the first octet of a Class A address lies between 1 and 127. Since there can be just 127 Class A networks, these have been assigned to government agencies and very large organizations, such as IBM.

◆ **Class B address**. The first two octets of a Class B address represent the network portion of the address; the remaining two octets represent the host portion of the address (see Figure 1.13).

	14 bits	16 bits
Class B	1 0	netid	hostid

FIGURE 1.13 _The Class B address format_

Compared to Class A addresses, Class B addresses can represent more networks. However, a Class A address can have more hosts than a Class B address.

As shown in Figure 1.13, the most significant bit of the first octet of a Class B address is set to 1, and the next bit is set to 0 for all Class B addresses. This means that the range of values for the first octet of the Class B address lies between 128 and 191. Class B addresses are assigned to large organizations.

◆ **Class C address**. The first three octets of a Class C address represent the network portion of the address; the last octet represents the host portion (see Figure 1.14).

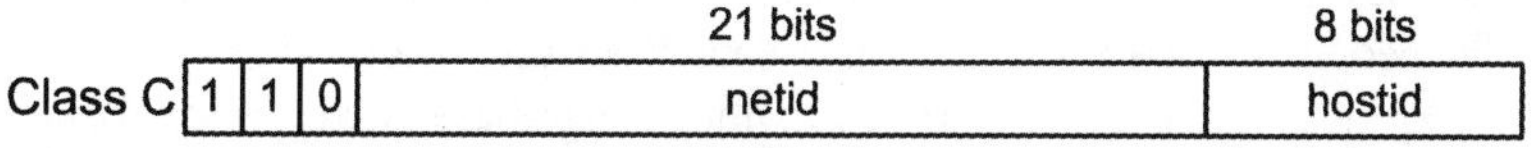

	21 bits	8 bits
Class C 1 1 0	netid	hostid

FIGURE 1.14 *The Class C address format*

A Class C address can represent more networks than either a Class A or a Class B address, while trading off the number of hosts that it can represent. In other words, for any network in the Class C address, there can be only be 1 to 254 hosts within the network because two values are reserved. The first three bits of the first octet of a Class C address are set to 1, 1, and 0, as shown in Figure 1.14. Therefore, the value of the first octet of a Class C address ranges from 192 to 223.

◆ **Class D address**. Class D is a special address class for the sake of representing a multicast group. A Class D address has the first four bits of the first octet set to 1, 1, 1, and 0, which typically means that the addresses range from 224 to 239. Note that a Class D address does not have a network portion or a host ID. In general, it is always considered a multicast group ID. Figure 1.15 represents the Class D address format.

	28 bits
Class D 1 1 1 0	multicast group ID

FIGURE 1.15 *The Class D address format*

◆ **Class E address**. Class E is also a special address class, and it is reserved for future use. The first four bits of the first octet of a Class E address are set to 1, 1, 1, 1. This means that the range of values in the first octet lies between 240 and 255. Figure 1.16 shows the Class E address format.

	28 bits
Class E 1 1 1 1	(reserved for future use)

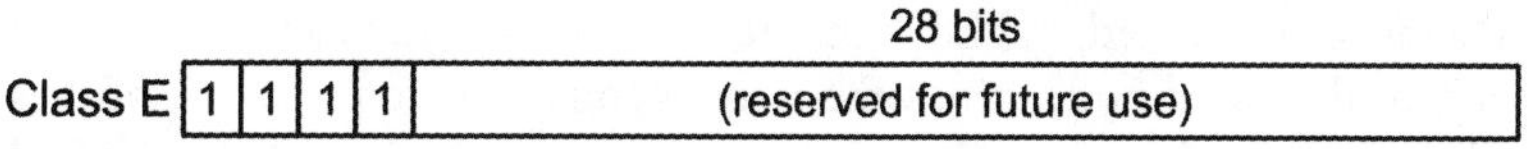

FIGURE 1.16 *The Class E address format*

Now that you know the different classes of IP addresses, you can understand how a unique address can be specified for a particular node. A controlling body provides a unique address that can be assigned to any node. InterNIC is the controlling authority for assigning IP addresses on the World Wide Web. InterNIC assigns only a network ID. The task of assigning the respective post ID is left to the administrator or the ISP to which the node is connected.

If two nodes need to communicate with each other, the source node needs to know the address of the destination node. Remembering the dotted quad format of the IP address is difficult for people, so DNS is an alternative naming system for the nodes on the Internet. DNS is an addressing schema that provides a database with a host name and its respective mapping to a unique IP address on the network. To be more precise, DNS is a distributed database system that provides the host name resolution protocol for any given host. In other words, if the name of a host is provided, DNS can resolve it to its respective IP address. DNS also works the other way around—if the IP address of the host is provided, the system can derive the respective host name mapped to the IP address.

You have now learned the basics of the OSI model and the TCP/IP architecture. The following section explains how the Internet works.

How the Internet Works

By now you know that the Internet is a collection of multiple computers and networks. The objective of the Internet is to provide a medium for communication among all of these interconnected systems. On a basic level, users have Web browsers to surf the Internet. A *browser* is a software utility that allows a user to view the information that is available on the Internet. You can think of a browser as a window to the world of the Internet. Consider a scenario in which a user opens a browser and starts to surf the Internet. First the user opens the browser on his or her computer and enters an appropriate Internet address in the Address field. The user presses Enter, and the browser reads the Internet address that has been entered.

The address is in a format similar to http://www.google.com/index.html. This format is called a URL (*Uniform Resource Locator*). The browser breaks up the URL into its protocol, a host name, and a file name. In the current example, the protocol is http, the host name is www.google.com, and the file name is index.html. After the browser has broken up the URL into these three parts, it immediately establishes communication with the host. To do so, the browser looks for a host with the name www.google.com.

A DNS server available on the Internet resolves the host name to its respective IP address. Once an IP address is obtained, the DNS server translates the host name into an IP address and returns it to the client node. Once the node is found, the browser establishes a connection with it. Usually there is a Web server running on the host system. The browser hooks up to the server on a specific port based on a given protocol. In the current example the protocol is http, so the browser hooks up to the default port (port 80) of the Web server.

The browser then submits a query to the Web server to obtain the file specified in the URL. In this example, the file is index.html and it resides on the root of the Web server. If the file is found, the same http connection that was established between the browser and the Web server is used to return the file. Once index.html is streamed back to the browser, an HTML parser that is available within the browser parses the HTML and displays the appropriate information within the context of the browser.

For all of these events to happen, the user's computer must support the basic hardware, software, and connection that are necessary to talk to the Internet. The basic required hardware can be something as simple as a PC with a *modem*. A modem is a modulator and demodulator that actually encodes and decodes the information sent back and forth between the user's computer and the Internet. If the user does not have a modem that accesses the Internet through a LAN (*Local Area Network*), he or she probably has a network interface card. The user might connect to the Internet via a proxy server in this situation. Regardless, once the prerequisites of the hardware are satisfied and there is some way to connect to the network, the user is ready to surf the Internet. The basic software that is required includes some kind of an operating system and a simple Internet browser. In most cases, Internet users have a home-based system with a modem and a telephone line. The user also needs a dial-up account with an ISP. Figure 1.17 shows a basic diagram of a user system connecting to the Internet through a modem and a telephone line.

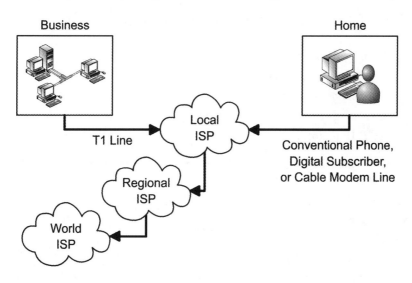

FIGURE 1.17 *A PC connected to the Internet through an ISP*

Summary

This chapter covered the basics of the Internet, including the history and a timeline of its evolution, and provided details on the OSI model. It also covered the TCP/IP architecture and provided an overview of the different layers of the TCP/IP model. The chapter went on to explain how the Internet works. The next chapter will introduce you to the concepts of network security.

Check Your Understanding

Multiple Choice Questions

1. Which layer of the OSI model provides a communication channel between hosts?

   a. Application layer

   b. Presentation layer

   c. Session layer

   d. Network layer

2. Which of the following is not a requirement for a computer to participate in a network?

   a. Computing hardware

   b. Network Interface Card

   c. Application software

   d. Operating system

   e. TCP/IP protocol suite

3. Which of the following classes of IP addresses are assigned to government agencies and very large organizations?

   a. Class A

   b. Class B

   c. Class C

   d. Class E

Short Questions

1. Why was DNS introduced?

2. What are the various classes of IP addresses?

Answers

Multiple Choice Answers

1. c. The Session layer provides a communication channel between hosts.
2. c. Application software is not a requirement for a computer to participate in a network.
3. a. Class A addresses are assigned to government agencies and very large organizations.

Short Answers

1. DNS was introduced as an alternative naming system for IP addresses because it is difficult for humans to remember the dotted quad format of the IP address.
2. The various classes of IP addresses are

    - **Class A address.** In this address, the first octet represents the network portion and the remaining three octets refer to the host portion.
    - **Class B address.** In this address, the first two octets represent the network portion and the remaining two octets refer to the host portion.
    - **Class C address.** In this address, the first three octets represent the network portion and the last octet refers to the host portion.
    - **Class D address.** In this address, the first four bits of the first octet are set to 1, 1, 1, 0 and the range of the first octet is between 224 and 239.
    - **Class E address.** In this address, the first four bits of the first octet are set to 1, 1, 1, 1 and the range of the first octet is between 240 and 255.

Chapter 2

The Internet is growing at an exponential rate. While it is a great boon for technological evolution, it is also an unsafe zone. Privacy on the Internet has become a prime concern of users. Hackers, viruses, worms, sniffing, phreaking, and many other buzzwords are used to define different security threats. This chapter discusses some fundamental elements of network security and provides an overview of the security threats. It also explains how to evaluate these threats and take appropriate measures. Finally, it covers various security strategies to counter the threats.

Fundamental Elements of Security

The term "security" is subjective. To begin with, no system is totally secure. Any system that is connected to the Internet is, in one way or another, subject to security threats. Only a system that is not connected to the network and is switched off is totally secure. Even then, it is subject to physical threats, like the theft of the hard disk. The degree of security varies depending on context. Generally, you discuss security in terms of levels, and there can be multiple levels of security.

You define security levels after you carefully assess the risks and threats involved. There might be very few levels of security in one security model and many levels of security in another. This determination of levels is subjective and relative to the user's perspective.

It is important to understand the fundamental elements of any given security model. The prime virtue of any security model is its ability to identify an estimated amount of threats for a given system. In fact, the success of a security model is based completely on identifying the threats. The higher the number of threats estimated, the better your chances of securing a system.

Usually when you speak of security, the discussion is specific to the system being used. If the system in use is a PC, you only have to strategize an appropriate security model for the PC. If the system is a network, evaluating and strategizing a security model for the specific network (without considering any other network) is more appropriate.

Drafting a Security Model

Whenever you draft a security model for a system, you must keep two entities in mind—the components that belong to the system and those that don't. The components that belong to the system are within the boundaries of the system, and can also be referred to as the *internal components* of the system. The components that don't belong to the system are those that are outside the boundaries of the system, and can also be referred to as *external components*. Figure 2.1 illustrates the components of a network system.

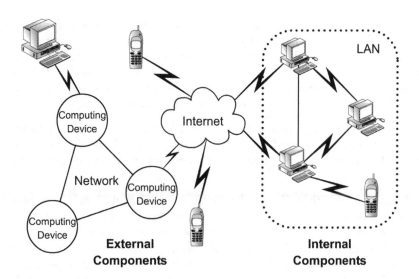

FIGURE 2.1 *A network with multiple components*

Before you draft a security model, you must identify all of the internal system components. This is essential because such identification provides a concise scope for the system in use. Once you know the scope, it is easy to relate to the context of use of the system. Also, you must identify the scope of the system to know which components need to be secured.

The external components do not need to be subject to any security context. This is an important concept so that you don't waste resources on those components that might not mean much for the system. Also, all of the components that cannot be categorized as internal should be considered external components. Those components that are not yet defined should always fall into the external category. In other words, it is always a good idea to start with a default external state for all of the components until they are identified as internal. Once you identify a component as internal, you can eliminate it from the list of external components.

Once you list all of the internal and external components of a system, it is easier to identify threats. Threats are events that will cause the system to fail, things that can go wrong with the system, and possible attacks on the system. Some examples of events that can be considered threats are fire, faulty wiring in the network, and attacks on the system by a hacker.

It is nearly impossible to identify all of the threats to a given system, yet it is advisable to list all of the conceivable threats. An initial list should not distinguish between threats of different flavors. You should document a homogenous listing of all threats. This list can include all of the trivial and severe threats to a system.

Another fundamental principle for defining any security model is to consider all of the external components of a system as threats. This should always be your default assumption unless you have proved otherwise. An external component of a system is almost always a threat, but this does not mean that the internal components of a system are not threats. For example, a hacker is a threat to the system, but a hacker can be either an external component (an outsider) or an internal component (an inside user) of the system. Therefore, by simply determining the internal and external components, you are not ensuring that there are no threats from the internal system components.

When you consider securing a system, you typically talk about protecting the valuable and confidential information possessed by the internal components. Generally, when you talk about network security, you can consider the following elements fundamental to the security model.

◆ **Identity**. This is the ability to identify a user and all of the internal components of the system. For example, if you consider the network a system, it is important to identify all of the users, devices, hosts, servers, services, and applications as internal components. Also, you should identify any kind of resources, such as routers, switches, bridges, hubs, or connectors. There are technologies that enable the identification of internal components. These technologies include network authentication protocols (such as Kerberos), one-time password tools, RADIUS, and TACACS+. There are also other methods of identification, such as smart cards, digital certificates, and biometric devices.

 NOTE

Biometrics is an authentication system that uses unique human-based identification such as fingerprints, iris scans, face scans, voice prints, and other such unique human traits.

◆ **Perimeter security**. This helps you control the critical system resources so that only the properly authenticated components can access the resources within the system. Generally, perimeter security enforces access control rules based on policy files. A policy file contains a list of users who are allowed to access the internal resources of the system. The users are mapped to a table that suggests the limited resources that they are allowed to access within the system. Firewalls are an implementation of perimeter security because they restrict unauthorized external users from accessing the internal system. Firewalls are covered further in Chapter 3, "Firewalls for Network Security."

◆ **Data privacy**. This is the ability to secure or protect the information in the system from unauthorized users or unauthorized modification. Data privacy uses strategies such as layer 2 tunneling protocols, digital encryption, VPNs, and cryptography.

◆ **Security monitoring**. This is the ability to monitor and scrutinize the system under consideration. It helps you check the status of the current security model that is being employed. Security monitoring also provides a proactive measure to identify the vulnerabilities within the system. Additionally, it can act as an intrusion detector to monitor any attacks that can occur on the system.

◆ **Policy management**. This is also one of the key elements of security. A network security policy defines an organization's expectations for proper network and computer use and lays down the procedures to prevent and respond to security incidents. A network security policy outlines what assets are worth protecting and what actions or inactions threaten the assets. It is very important to have centralized policy management in huge networks that have complex interaction between devices.

Risk Analysis

One of the fundamental goals of network security is to protect the internal components of the system from the external components. You must understand the risks involved in securing the internal components of a system from its external environment.

There are always risks involved in identifying a proper security model, so it is important to perform risk analysis on any given security model. Risk analysis strategy helps you mitigate the risks or totally avoid them. You can perform risk analysis on a given security model in many distinct ways. More generically, risk analysis is broken down into two approaches—quantitative and qualitative risk analysis.

Quantitative Risk Analysis

Quantitative risk analysis is made up of two fundamental elements.

◆ The probability of event occurrence

◆ The likely loss, if the event should occur

Quantitative risk analysis estimates a risk by multiplying the potential loss by the probability of the event occurrence. This risk analysis is somewhat unreliable if the probability of the event occurrence is not calculated with acceptable precision.

Qualitative Risk Analysis

Qualitative risk analysis does not use any probability data to formulate a risk estimate. Instead, it uses interrelated elements including

◆ **Threats**. As I mentioned earlier, things that can go wrong with the system are called threats. Examples of threats include fire or a hacker attack.

◆ **Vulnerabilities**. Vulnerabilities are the weaknesses within the system that can be exploited by an external component, for example a PC connected to the Internet without a firewall.

◆ **Controls**. Controls are measures to circumvent the system's vulnerabilities. There are basically four types of controls for a system.

- **Deterrent controls**. These help decrease the probability of an intentional attack.
- **Preventive controls**. These help decrease the impact of an attack. In other words, they protect the vulnerabilities of the system to make any attack futile.
- **Corrective controls**. These help decrease the effects of an attack on the system.
- **Detective controls**. These help detect or identify attacks and activate the preventive or corrective control measures.

Ensuring the Success of a Security Model

You should perform the following tasks to ensure the success of the security model you are drafting.

1. Identify the internal and external system components.
2. Distinguish a clear boundary between the internal and external components.
3. Identify all of the threats against the system.
4. Identify all of the system's vulnerabilities.
5. Perform a qualitative risk analysis on the security model.

The Evolution of a Security Model

Security models are always evolving and iterative in nature. The evolution of a security model can occur through the following incremental phases.

1. **Establishing a security policy**. In this phase, you must identify the goals of the security model.
2. **Implementing network security**. In this phase, you consider a holistic approach (one in which you consider security with respect to the complete enterprise) toward the security model, so that the system does not rely on only one type of technology to solve the security issues.
3. **Performing audits**. In this phase, you audit the system on a regular basis to ensure that the security policy and security goals are being enforced without any irregularities. The results of the audits provide a new set of data you can analyze to identify new system vulnerabilities. This helps a security policy evolve from the existing version to the next incremental version.

Now that you have an overview of the fundamental elements of security, I will discuss some basic security concepts.

Basic Security Concepts

This section will describe the basic concepts in any given security architecture. There are multitudes of security concepts available, however this section will provide only some general concepts that are used extensively by all security models.

Cryptography

Cryptography is the science of encryption and decryption of data. Usually data is in its raw form, which can be easily read by any person. Such data is not secure because hackers can break in and read it. If you can disguise the data in a format that does not make sense, you have successfully encrypted it. Figure 2.2 illustrates the encryption process.

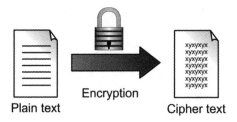

FIGURE 2.2 *Encryption*

Encrypting clear text data results in encrypted text, also called *cipher text*. Generally, the idea behind encryption is to hide the data from everybody except those people who should read it. People for whom the data is intended should be aware of the process to convert the encrypted text back to its original format, also called *decryption*. Figure 2.3 illustrates this process.

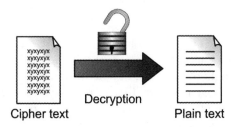

FIGURE 2.3 *Decryption*

Cryptography actually uses mathematics to encrypt and decrypt data. You can send such encrypted data across the Internet without worrying about the packets being sniffed because even if hackers can sniff the data, they won't know the correct mechanism to decrypt it.

NOTE

Sniffing is a process in which a hacker breaks into an easier component of a network to eavesdrop on the network traffic. For more details, refer to the "Sniffing" section later in this chapter.

To better understand the process of cryptography, you need to understand how a cryptographic algorithm, also called a *cipher*, works. A cipher is a mathematical algorithm that encrypts and decrypts the data. A cipher requires a key combination in which the key can be either a number or a string. The cipher uses the key to encrypt the clear text. Conventional cryptography uses the concept of *symmetric key encryption*, in which a single key is used for both encrypting clear text and decrypting cipher text (see Figure 2.4).

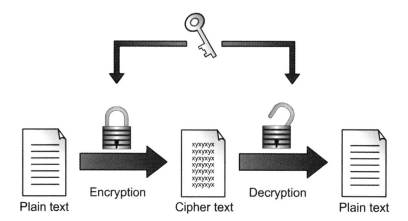

FIGURE 2.4 *Symmetric key encryption*

One example of conventional cryptography is Caesar's cipher, which uses the concept of "shift by three" encryption. Using Caesar's cipher, the letters in the English alphabet are replaced by the third letter down to the right of the letter. In other words, if you encrypt the word *password*, you get *sdvvzrug*, which is cipher text. To decrypt this, you have to use the same "shift by three" key in reverse. In other words, you shift three letters up to the left. This is a very simple example of symmetric key encryption. There are other encryption standards, such as DES (*Data Encryption Standard*), that use a much more complex encryption mechanism.

If you use symmetric encryption standards, you must share a key with the recipient. As long as the key is kept secret between the two parties, the communication between them is relatively secure. However, there is an inherent problem with this mechanism. If a hacker sniffs out the key value while you are sharing it with the recipient, the security of the cipher text is compromised.

Cryptography also uses another standard for encryption called *asymmetric encryption*, or *public key cryptography*. Public key cryptography uses a pair of keys to encrypt clear text. A public key and a private key comprise the pair. The public key is normally used to encrypt the data, while the private key is used to decrypt the data. The concept behind asymmetric encryption is that once you generate a pair of keys, you share your public key with the rest of the world and keep your private key a secret. Anyone who is interested in sending information to you must encrypt the data using your public key, and the cipher text can only be decrypted by using your private key. Therefore, even the person who intends to share information cannot decrypt the cipher text once it is encrypted using your public key. Public key cryptography eliminates the need to secretly share a single key between two parties (as in the case of symmetric encryption) because the public key can be freely distributed. It also eliminates another inherent problem of symmetric encryption— maintaining multiple keys for different people.

Authentication

Authentication is a process that uses an account name and a password to identify a user. There are different types of authentication, which range from a simple mechanism, such as an account name and a password, to complex authentication, such as biometrics.

Authorization

Authorization is a security measure that is employed by a security model after it authenticates a user's identity. This measure is also called *access control* in some security implementations. The goal of authorization is to provide limited or predefined access to a user. Predefined access is based on an access control list, which maps the user's identity to a list of resources that the user can access.

Audits

The goal of auditing within a security model is to set up an account quota for every user to limit the consumption of a resource. Auditing also ensures that most of the actions the user performs within the security model are logged so that they are traceable.

Public Key Infrastructure

PKI (*Public Key Infrastructure*) is a set of technologies and tools that provide secured communication for the system. It is responsible for verifying the confidentiality and authenticity of data between two communication end points. PKI uses the following three technologies based on cryptography to generate a security component.

- ◆ Symmetric key ciphers
- ◆ Asymmetric key ciphers
- ◆ One-way hash functions

Symmetric and asymmetric key ciphers were explained earlier, in the "Cryptography" section. One-way hash functions use a cryptographic algorithm, which encrypts clear text to cipher text; there is no decryption process. In other words, once the clear text is encrypted, it is relatively impossible to decrypt the cipher text. Such one-way hash functions can be used to store account passwords in a database so that even if there is a security breach of the passwords, it is impossible to decrypt them.

The PKI infrastructure uses one-way hash functions for authentication purposes. The first time an account is created within a system, a one-way hash function encrypts the password for the account and stores it within a system database. The next time the user tries to access the system, the PKI model asks him or her to enter the account name and password. Once the user does this, the password is encrypted using a one-way hash function, and the resulting cipher text is compared with the cipher text stored in the system database. If the cipher text matches, the user is permitted to access the system. One-way hash functions always generate the same cipher text for the given clear text, and the cipher text for two different pieces of clear text data is never equal. PKI uses these cryptographic technologies to ensure the privacy of data on a communication channel and security within the network.

Digital Certificates

The "Cryptography" section already explained the concept of public key ciphers. You'll recall that a public key cipher is an asymmetric encryption algorithm consisting of a pair of keys to secure data—a public key and a private key. As the holder of the private key, you are the only person who can decrypt data. There is an inherent problem with this mechanism. How can the sender of the data know that the public key really belongs to you? In reality, there is no way by which the sender can confirm this. The sender trusts that the key belongs to you and performs the relevant task. If a public key that is created by a hacker replaces your public key, the information sent will be compromised.

The concept of digital certificates was introduced to solve this problem. Digital certificates are based on the concept of a *digital signature*, which is a unique electronic fingerprint that can be assigned to a particular user. You can identify the authenticity of the user by verifying his or her digital signature. A certifying authority that vouches for the authenticity of the key can obtain these digital signatures. Usually, a certifying authority requires your public key and other relevant data such as your name, social security number, or any other unique identity that establishes your presence. Once you submit your public key and the relevant data, the certifying authority creates a digital certificate that contains your public key, a digital signature, an expiration date for the certificate, and the detailed information about the holder of the public key. This certificate can then be used as a verification tool to ensure that the public key really belongs to the person it represents. A hacker cannot tamper with such digital certificates. Verisign is one such third-party certifying authority that issues certificates conforming to International Telecommunications Union (ITU) Telecommunication Standardization (ITU-T) X.509 version 3.

Now that you have an overview of some basic security concepts, take a look at some common security threats.

Common Security Threats

As I mentioned earlier, threats are events that can occur on a system. They can also be called *attacks*. An attack on a system is performed for a purpose, such as:

◆ To vandalize the system

◆ For fun

◆ To gather intelligence

Vandalism is a process in which the purpose of the attacker is to destroy the target system. A vandal is not interested in gaining any information from the system for personal benefit. Usually, a vandal gets malicious satisfaction from creating such havoc on the Internet.

On the other hand, a person hacking for fun is being playful and trying to show off his or her prowess in hacking a system. People who hack for fun are only interested in breaching the secured boundary of the system; they are not interested in obtaining any information or destroying the resources within the system.

Intelligence gathering is a process in which a hacker tries to obtain information about the target system. The hacker is committed and focused on obtaining details about the configuration and operating environment of the system. There are three high-level processes that a hacker goes through to obtain information about the target system, which include

◆ Footprinting

◆ Scanning

◆ Enumeration

The following sections explain these categories in detail.

Footprinting

Footprinting is a process in which a hacker plans extensively to obtain information about the target system. The hacker systematically profiles the details of the target environment and creates profiles to devise an attack plan and a mode of attack for the target system. Footprinting is a process of reconnaissance, in which a methodical approach is applied to obtain information about the security model, the vulnerabilities of the system, and the control strategies used within the security model. The information gathered from footprinting a network can include

◆ The range of IP addresses used

◆ The types and addresses of the DNS servers used

◆ Information about the network's mail servers

◆ Contact details for administrative, technical, and billing tasks

◆ The mail addresses of the important resources that control the network

◆ Phone and fax numbers

◆ Details about hardware locations

◆ The mail addresses of system administrators

◆ The IP addresses of the Internet gateways

Footprinting is the initial and most important step in intelligence gathering. An intelligent hacker does not hack a system without profiling the system using extensive footprinting techniques. Usually, a hacker tries to determine the scope of operation for footprinting the system and than chooses an appropriate reconnaissance model.

Scanning

Scanning is another technique used by hackers to gain control of a system, whether it is a PC or a network. Scanning is the art of identifying a system's configuration in any given context. In this process, a hacker tries to detect the internal components that are reachable within the system. The internal components are the services, hosts, and applications that exist within a system. Network scanning is most often used as an attack method to infiltrate information storehouses. It usually consists of transmitting data over the network to elicit a response to determine the network's configuration. It is also a tool to identify the network's vulnerabilities.

Network vulnerability scanning is the process of identifying the vulnerability of a network. A hacker can use many techniques to scan a target network, some of which include

◆ Ping sweeps

◆ Port scans

◆ Operating system identification

The configuration information that the hacker can obtain by performing scans includes

◆ The type of UDP and TCP services that are running

◆ The type of operating system

◆ The system architecture

◆ The filtering systems between the hacker and the target system

◆ The IP addresses of the hosts

◆ The open ports

◆ An approximation of the network topologies

Scanning can be segregated into many categories. The major categories are sweeping, war dialing, war driving, and port scanning.

Sweeping

Sweeping is a process in which a hacker obtains a mapping of the network, which identifies all of the active internal system components. This helps the hacker determine the system status. In other words, it helps the hacker identify which components within the given network are alive.

A basic step in sweeping is to use an automated ping sweep to identify the range of IP addresses within the system. A ping sweep, also known as an ICMP (*Internet Control Message Protocol*) sweep, is a network scanning technique that is used to identify the range of IP addresses that map to live computers. Ping sweeping is one of the older and slower network scanning techniques. An automated ping sweep helps the hacker determine the active IP addresses that do not have any network block on them.

A ping is usually employed only on small networks. Employing the ping utility on a large network is not fruitful because it might take hours to determine the status of the network's resources. There are many tools that are available to execute ping sweeps, including `fping` and `nmap`.

War Dialing

War dialing is another technique to scan the network. This process employs a computer program called a *war dialer*, which dials a range of phone numbers to determine which numbers are connected to a modem. The war dialer then logs the phone numbers that return a successful modem handshake.

War dialing is used to find the entry points for unprotected systems on the Internet. Once a hacker obtains a log of numbers, he or she usually reviews the log and redials the numbers to obtain more information from the system. By war dialing, a hacker can obtain information about fax machines, modem access points, and PBX access points. War dialing software includes PhoneSweep, TeleSweep, and ToneLoc.

War Driving

War driving is a more recent technique hackers use to scan a network. It is derived from war dialing. In this process, a hacker drives around to search and scan unprotected 802.11 wireless networks. 802.11 is a wireless network protocol that enables wireless computing devices to network with each other. If a hacker can tap into this wireless network, it becomes fairly easy for him or her to eavesdrop on the network. The 802.11 access points use a security measure called WEP (*Wired Equivalent Protocol*) to prevent eavesdropping. However, many security loopholes have been recently identified within the WEP algorithm. Advanced hackers use these loopholes to gain access to wireless networks. Some of the tools used in war driving include GPS receivers, laptops, 802.11 PCMICA cards, and appropriate software.

Port Scanning

Port scanning is a process in which a hacker scans the availability of the listener ports at a given IP address. Hackers only use this process after they have identified the active IP addresses within a given system using other techniques, such as sweeping and war dialing. Many of the computers connected within a network listen on well-known and registered ports. The hacker's objective is to identify all of the active ports on a given system to determine the types of services running on the host. Once the hacker identifies these types of services, he or she can identify who owns the services and whether anonymous logins for the services are supported.

Port scanning is performed by sending a request message to every port for a given IP. Based on the type of response received, the hacker determines the status of a port, which can be either active or inactive. If the status of the port is active, the response might contain some information specific to the type of service that is listening on the port. This way, the hacker can explore different services on the system while he or she tries to exploit the system's vulnerabilities. There are many types of port scans, including

- ◆ **Vanilla**. In this type of port scan, the port scanner tries to connect to all of the 65,536 ports on a given system.
- ◆ **Strobe**. In this type of port scan, the port scanner tries to scan only the known services.
- ◆ **Fragmented packets**. In this type of port scan, the port scanner attempts to send undetectable packet fragments that can get through simple packet filters on the system. The fragments can contain control codes that might compromise the security of the system.
- ◆ **UDP**. In this type of port scan, the port scanner scans only for the UDP ports on the system.
- ◆ **Sweep**. In this type of port scan, the port scanner tries to scan only one pre-defined port on all of the systems.
- ◆ **FTP bounce**. In this type of port scan, the port scanner impersonates some other source to access an FTP server. Once in, the scanner can get the FTP server to send critical files to some other place. Such attacks are usually untraceable.

There are many tools to help a hacker to scan the ports within a network, some of which include Winscan, Netcat, Nmap, IpEye, Fscan, and Netscan.

Enumeration

Enumeration is a process that a hacker performs after he or she has footprinted and scanned a target system. In this process, the hacker identifies the valid user accounts and vulnerable resources within the target system. Enumeration is an information-gathering process that is considered more intrusive than footprinting or scanning.

During the process of enumeration, a hacker tries to use active connections to query the system for information. Enumeration uses many techniques to gather intelligence from the system, which can include

- User names
- Group names
- Network resources
- Network shares
- System banners
- Routing tables
- SNMP (*Simple Network Management Protocol*) information

The three phases of hacking (footprinting, scanning, and enumeration) employ many common techniques. The following section explains social engineering, one of the techniques hackers use to attack a targeted system.

Social Engineering

Social engineering is the ability to acquire confidential information about a system after establishing trust with an insider. It is more a human skill than a computer technology, and it is more of an art than a science. People who are very good at manipulating others usually succeed in social engineering. Hackers use this device to establish relationships with the people who have access to confidential information.

Social engineering is one of the most common security threats because it is relatively easy to employ. At the same time, it is considered a low technology break-in tool. By *low technology*, I mean that social engineering uses just the basic tools to hack into a system, rather than any computing skills.

Social engineering uses principles such as trust, respect, fear, and greed to set a trap to manipulate people who have system access privileges. People who employ social engineering skills always remain undercover, so they are very difficult to identify. A successful social engineer is a smooth operator who obtains the desired system access without raising suspicion.

Social engineering works in most cases because it is a human trait to trust other people. Human beings are the most vulnerable components of any security model. No matter how secure the system is, this security is compromised if a user is tricked into giving up the password.

A skilled hacker knows that humans are the weakest link within a security model. Hackers try to use their social engineering skills before employing any other methods of attack on a system. Social engineering is a skill that is hard to gain; once mastered, though, its ill effects are almost impossible to counter with any security strategy.

There are two common types of social engineering—human-based and computer-based. Human-based social engineering refers to a direct person-to-person interaction, while computer-based social engineering refers to using a computer to retrieve the desired information. The following sections discuss these two types of social engineering.

Human-Based Social Engineering

There are different types of human-based social engineering skills, including

◆ **In-person**. An in-person hack occurs when a social engineer physically enters or uses the system. For example, a social engineer might enter the premises of the organization as a guest or as marketing personnel. Then, he or she might try to sell a service or pretend to meet an employee of the organization. Once the social engineer gains access to the premises, he might try to move around the work desks or the cubicles where people work to gain access to information or eavesdrop on employee conversations to obtain relevant information. Social engineers can also use other devices, such as microphones, to overhear conversations.

◆ **Dumpster diving**. Dumpster diving is a process in which a social engineer goes through an organization's trash to find valuable information. Dumpster diving usually works because many businesses forget to destroy valuable information before throwing it in the trash. Notes, confidential mail, and important files might be available in the trash.

◆ **Third-party authorization**. A social engineer might obtain relevant information about an important member within an organization using in-person or dumpster-diving techniques. Once the social engineer gains such information, he or she can manipulate other people in the organization to share key information. For example, a social engineer might obtain information about the vice president of a company and then call help-desk personnel to request access to sensitive information, claiming that the vice president has authorized him to obtain the information. This usually works if the social engineer is effective in manipulating and playing on people's psychology or when the vice president is not around.

◆ **Impersonation**. Impersonation is more advanced than third-party authorization. Using this skill, a social engineer gains details about an employee in an organization. Once the social engineer obtains the necessary details, he or she impersonates that employee by calling the help desk or another employee to obtain sensitive information. Impersonation requires greater skill than third-party authorization.

◆ **Technical support**. A social engineer might routinely check on the employees of a given organization by stating that he is from the organization's technical support group. This way, the social engineer gains access to the sensitive information of the organization one step at a time. The social engineer might not obtain all of the information within one call, but he or she definitely plans to obtain the necessary information in a limited number of calls.

◆ **Shoulder surfing**. Shoulder surfing is a continuation of the in-person technique. After gaining access to the organization's premises, the social engineer tries to look over people's shoulders when they are entering sensitive information, such as a password, on a computer.

Computer-Based Social Engineering

There are different types of computer-based social engineering skills, some of which include

◆ **Using Web sites**. A social engineer might set up a Web site through which he or she might claim to offer cash prizes or sweepstakes. In this situation, people would have to participate in events that are sponsored through the Web site to win. Many such events require an e-mail address (as a user name) and a password. Unfortunately, many people use a single password for multiple accounts because it is easy to remember. The hacker knows that the person who wants to participate in the sweepstakes will probably use the same password that he uses to access the network in his organization. Using this technique, the social engineer can gain access to many passwords without any effort.

◆ **Using e-mail attachments**. An e-mail attachment is another computer-based technique hackers employ to obtain information. E-mail attachments often contain viruses that affect a system. The infected system might send back sensitive information to the social engineer, who in turn might send an e-mail with a catchy or relevant subject line. This increases the probability that the recipient will open the e-mail attachment, which will activate the virus and infect the system. Some examples of such viruses are the I Love You virus and Anna Kournikova virus.

◆ **Using pop-ups**. A pop-up window is another computer-based social engineering skill that a hacker might use to obtain sensitive information. For example, a pop-up might appear while you are on the Internet, stating that the connection to the network has been lost. The pop-up might suggest that you have to enter your user name and password to reconnect. If you do so, the information is sent back to the social engineer.

Application and Operating System Attacks

Application and operating system attacks include attacks that are performed on an application running within a system or on the operating system that drives the operating environment. Generally, hackers use different techniques to identify the application or the operating system of a host within a target network, which can include a ping sweep combined with war dialing and social engineering skills. Once a hacker identifies an application or an operating system, he or she usually footprints a system profile. This makes it easier to enumerate information, such as user accounts, group names, and other confidential data.

Once an application or an operating system is identified, the hacker can use different techniques to gather intelligence from the target. Targeted applications often include FTP servers, mail servers, Web servers, and application servers. Once the hacker obtains the operating system details, many kinds of applications are subject to attack. Almost all operating systems are vulnerable to different kinds of attacks. The following section describes the different techniques hackers employ for application and operating system attacks.

Stack-Based Buffer Overflow Attacks

Stack-based buffer overflow attacks are general attacks that advanced and experienced hackers use to exploit a given system. A buffer overflow attack requires a detailed understanding of a system-level language (assembly language) and the internal details of the operating system. Buffer overflow attacks exploit the lack of bounds checking on a given size of input that is about to be stored in a buffer.

A buffer is a contiguous memory area within the RAM. Contiguous memory areas can be data structures such as arrays and vectors. A hacker usually tries to manipulate the operating system or a running application by exploiting a lack of bounds checking. The hacker gains control by writing past the buffer of an application. A stack is the most common data structure that is targeted for such an attack. A stack is a data structure in which information is stored using a LIFO (*Last In First Out*) technique. Many applications written in C are vulnerable to such buffer overflow attacks. Figure 2.5 displays a stack as a data structure.

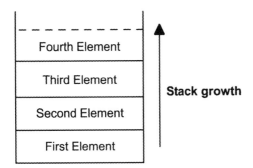

FIGURE 2.5 *A stack as a data structure*

To understand how a stack works, you must understand the execution of an application. Different operating systems usually execute applications in different ways. I will explain a generic application execution scenario that is commonly used by applications. As I mentioned a moment ago, a stack is a LIFO-based data structure, which is used extensively by the operating system to store the executing functions within a given application. For example, if Application X is executed on an operating system, the operating system allocates address space in the memory for the application to execute. The execution of the application begins with the first entry point of the application being called. This entry point is almost always a main function. A main function is a procedure or a method (in other words, an object-oriented term) with the name main. You can also denote the main function as main().

The main() function is the first function to be executed within an application. It starts executing the code written within the scope of the function. In languages such as C, a function has the ability to call other functions from within the current context. For example, the main() function can call a second() function, which in turn can call a third() function. Figure 2.6 shows the sequence of these functions.

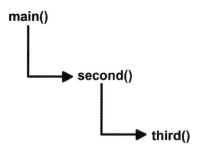

FIGURE 2.6 *A list of function calls*

Whenever an application is in the active state (in the process of execution), a stack for the function calls is maintained. The first function to be executed within an application is main(). Therefore, an entry for the main() function is created within the stack region, as shown in Figure 2.7.

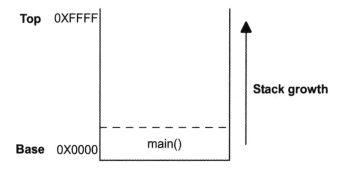

FIGURE 2.7 *The* main() *function within the stack*

Entries made within the stack are called *frames*. The frame region within the stack contains the executable code for the current function. The executable code is a native binary code that is specific to the system's architecture. The frame region also contains other placeholders for the different data types that the operating system supports. One of these data types is a buffer, which can be an array. Arrays are stored within the frame allocated for a given function.

If an application has a number of functions calling each other, a stack is created for the calls. To revisit the previous example, if there are three functions (main(), second(), and third()) within Application X, and if these functions call one another, a calling stack is created, as shown in Figure 2.8.

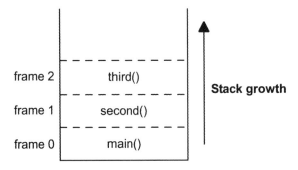

FIGURE 2.8 *A stack with many frames*

Figure 2.8 shows that the currently executing function is always on the top of the stack. When the function completes its execution, the frame for the respective function is folded, which results in the program control falling back on the function that called the recently executing function. The function that folds has a return address that points to the place from which it was called. Therefore, when the function is folded, the program control jumps back to the place to which the return address points (see Figure 2.9).

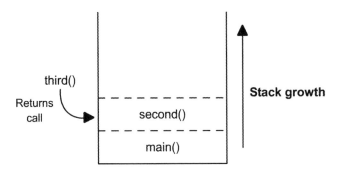

FIGURE 2.9 *A function folding back to its caller*

This way, the last function that was called is the first to complete its operation. The function that calls another function is termed the *caller*, while the function that is being called is the *callee*. Whenever the callee finishes its operation, the program control is returned to the caller, as shown in Figure 2.9.

In a stack-based buffer overflow attack, which is also called a *stack smashing attack*, the hacker has three objectives.

◆ **To target a stack buffer**. The hacker targets a specific buffer within a targeted frame for attack.

◆ **To inject the attack code**. The hacker tries to overflow the buffer by filling in extra binary code as an input string for the buffer. This binary code is executable native code.

◆ **To modify the written address**. The hacker modifies the return address of the callee function to point to the code that he or she injected. After the callee finishes its operation, the function returns to the extra code that the hacker inserted instead of returning to the place from which it was called (within the caller). Thus, the hacker's code gains control of the system and can direct the execution of the application.

Figure 2.10 shows the mode of attack within the stack smashing attack technique.

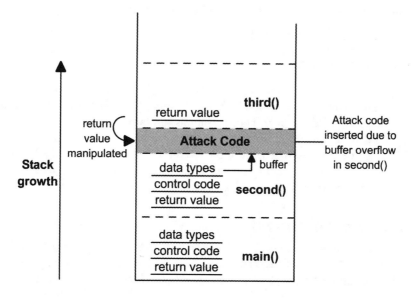

FIGURE 2.10 *A stack smashing attack*

Hackers mainly target applications running in some privileged mode. For example, the applications that execute with the root privilege have access to all of the internal resources of an operating system. The code injected by the hacker within such a privileged application can spawn a child process that can carry on the attack as a separate process without affecting the attacked application. Thus a person using the application will not notice any difference in the application's program flow.

One of the main advantages of this type of attack is that a hacker can inject the attack code into a privileged application from a local account. The hacker need not have any information about the root account. The only thing he or she has to do is gain entry to the privileged process that is executing within the target operating system.

Password Attacks

Password attacks occur on a user account that exists within the system. Before a hacker tries to use this technique, he or she must obtain the name of the account that is being targeted. In general, the hacker needs to use other techniques to obtain the account information, and then he or she can employ the password attack technique.

In a password attack, the hacker tries to use brute force techniques to guess an account password. This type of technique is also known as a *dictionary-based attack*. In a password attack, the hacker uses an automated program that tries to log on to a user account by trying out different passwords from a predefined list, also called a *dictionary*.

The success rate for password attacks is surprisingly high because most people use a common password such as their name or birthday. The hacker creates a list of all of these commonly known passwords.

Web sites are more vulnerable to such attacks. For example, mail accounts on the Internet can be subject to attack because the Web site usually requires a user to submit the account name and the password through an HTML submission form. A hacker can easily recreate a program that submits the HTML data to the appropriate URL. The submission can occur either on a GET or a POST request of the HTTP protocol. This way, the hacker can write automated scripts that iterate through a list of passwords and try to submit the HTML form with the current password in the list.

Web Application Attacks

The Internet is a common place for Web servers, which deliver Web pages to Web clients. HTTP (*Hypertext Transfer Protocol*) is the typical communication protocol between a Web client and a Web server. The Web server serves an HTML page to the requesting client.

A Web server typically listens to the well-known port 80. This is a sitting duck for hackers, because a hacker need not scan any other port to check for an entrance. Even if there are some security measures established on the Web server, ports 80 (HTTP) and 443

(SSL) are rarely blocked. The hacker can penetrate the firewall by exploiting these open ports. Some of the common Web application attacks include

◆ Changing or defacing Web sites
◆ Stealing sensitive client information
◆ DoS (*Denial of Service*) attacks

Hackers exploit the common security holes within such Web application frameworks, some of which are explained in the following list.

◆ **Hidden form fields**. Hidden form fields are embedded within an HTML source. These fields are not displayed on the Web client's browser. Hidden form fields contain sensitive information such as passwords and session IDs. Hackers can gain access to sensitive information about the server application by manipulating the values of the hidden form fields and sending alternative content.

◆ **Backdoors**. Backdoor entries are purposefully kept open by many application programmers to debug a Web application. To better understand this concept, consider a Web site with the address http://www.someorg.com. Suppose this Web site has recently loaded a Web application that is still under run-time tests. The application developers who are testing the Web site might use a backdoor URL, such as http://www.someorg.com/runtime/debug.jsp, which would allow them to control and modify a portion of the application that is executing on the Web site. They might use this backdoor to debug the running application and modify some parts of it. If a hacker stumbles upon such a backdoor, he or she can literally exploit it to directly control and modify the application.

◆ **Known security holes and server misconfigurations**. Known security holes are a vulnerability of the executing environment, which might contain the operating system, Web servers, and applications running within the Web servers. Hackers can exploit any known vulnerabilities of the executing environment to their advantage. Also, many misconfigured applications are subject to exploitation. For example, allowing anonymous logins to FTP and some HTTP-based applications leaves them open to exploitation.

◆ **Stealing cookies**. Stealing a cookie is another way hackers can gain access to user accounts. A cookie is a piece of information that is stored on a Web client and can contain information such as a client's user name and password. Web applications generally use cookies so users do not have to enter their user names and passwords when they visit the site. Hackers can use several techniques to steal a cookie from a client system and deploy it within their own system. If the hacker succeeds, he or she can automatically sign in as the user from whom the cookie was stolen. Eventually, the hacker can gain access to sensitive information about the user. Some techniques that a hacker can employ to steal cookies include sniffing; session hijacking; and breaking into a client's system using remote logins, sweeping, and port scans.

◆ **Parameter manipulation**. Web applications accept input parameters to allow access to different parts of the application. These parameters might contain control code that generates special events on the server side. A hacker can obtain a list of such control codes and manually manipulate the input parameter of an HTTP request. It is relatively easy to manipulate the input parameter; the hard part is obtaining the control codes.

◆ **Buffer overflow.** Hackers can also exploit buffer overflows on a Web application because when a large amount of input is sent to a Web application, the server usually crashes. In other cases, a hacker might use a smashing stack attack to compromise the security of a poorly written Web server. In other words, a hacker can send a large amount of input to the Web application, which causes a buffer overflow. The input might contain control codes to take over the application and redirect the program flow to a newly spawned process at the server end.

Network Attacks

Network attacks are carried out over a network. When a network has many vulnerabilities or when its security model is not strategized satisfactorily, the likelihood of a network attack increases. A hacker, as an external component of the network, will try to break into the network to gain access to its internal components.

In a network attack, a hacker can use different techniques, such as sniffing, spoofing, or session hijacking, to gain control over the network. Obviously, the hacker must footprint the network before trying to break in. The hacker might use many enumeration methods to gain information about important resources within the network. The following sections provide details about the different techniques used in network attacks.

Sniffing

As I mentioned earlier, sniffing is a process in which a hacker breaks into a relatively easy component of a network to eavesdrop on the network traffic. The hacker remotely configures the host that he breaks into so he can read all of the information that is traversing the network.

Many technologies use sniffing for legitimate purposes. For example, a network analyzer is a legitimate sniffer that helps a network administrator diagnose problems in the network. However, a hacker can break into a system and install a sniffer on it. It is difficult to detect systems that are configured remotely by hackers to sniff the network. In a network like the Ethernet, virtually all network interfaces have access to the traffic that traverses the network.

Every network interface has a hardware address called an *Ethernet address*, which is unique from the other addresses belonging to different network interfaces. Whenever information is sent from one host on the network to another host, the sender's and receiver's hardware addresses are encapsulated in the frame that carries the information across the network.

Usually a network interface only reacts to those frames that have the receiving hardware address in their destination field and ignores all of the other frames that do not belong to the network interface. However, you can put the network interface in the promiscuous mode, in which the interface picks up every frame that passes by it, even if the frame does not belong to it. This is exactly what a network analyzer that diagnoses the network would do. A hacker who has gained control over a vulnerable internal component within a network can remotely configure the network interface to the promiscuous mode. This way, the hacker can access confidential network information for his own advantage. Some of the information that the hacker can gain by sniffing a network includes

- ◆ Account information
- ◆ Account passwords
- ◆ Low-level protocol information

Spoofing

Spoofing is a process in which a hacker impersonates or uses impersonation attack methods to gain control over a network. Spoofing can occur on all layers of a protocol suite. The following sections address some examples of spoofing that can occur on different layers of a protocol suite.

Hardware Address Spoofing

At the hardware layer, the network interface card has a unique hardware address. When information is sent from this network interface, the sender's field in the frame that leaves the network interface contains the sender's hardware address. All of the frames that traverse the network contain the sender's and the recipient's hardware addresses, which are used at the hardware layer.

Hackers can manipulate the frames to replace the sender's field content with any other available hardware address. Hardware address spoofing is a process in which a hacker releases frames in a target system by impersonating a legitimate network user. The hacker can achieve this impersonation by changing the hardware address in the sender field that he or she releases on the network. If there is any host in the network that identifies only the hardware address to authenticate a valid user, the hacker can easily gain sensitive information from other systems.

Many of the current systems do not authenticate only the hardware address. Therefore, trying to hack a network by just spoofing the hardware address is nearly impossible. The prerequisite for hardware address spoofing is that the hacker should know a valid 48-bit hardware address of a legitimate host within the network environment. He or she can gain such information through different techniques such as sniffing, sweeping, and port scanning.

IP Spoofing

IP spoofing is a process in which a hacker changes the sender's IP address to a different address so the receiving system thinks the packet arrived from a legitimate system within the network. A hacker can use IP spoofing by releasing packets on the network that contain the IP address of a trusted system within the sender's IP field. If the receiving system authenticates the packets by checking the system's IP address, it will definitely be fooled because the IP address is legitimate.

Many hackers use IP spoofing to gain access to sensitive data within a network. Using IP spoofing, a hacker can mount a critical network file system on a server from a remote workstation and then send requests to obtain sensitive information from the file system. The server might respond by sending the information back to the IP address contained in the packet. The packets won't reach the hacker if the IP address of the hacker is different. However, if the hacker has carefully placed a sniffing utility on any of the hosts within the network, it is relatively easy to sniff out the information from the network.

Session Hijacking

Session hijacking is the same concept as sniffing the network. In a session hijack, a hacker hijacks the network traffic using different techniques such as TCP hijacking. A TCP session hijack occurs when a hacker acts as an intermediary between two systems that have TCP interactions. The hacker who is between the two systems literally can take over the TCP session and interpret or modify the information that is sent between the systems.

TCP session hijacking is possible because most session authentication occurs only at the start of a TCP session. The hacker takes advantage of this to hijack the session, often using source-routed IP packets. In a source-routed IP session hijack, the hacker gains control over the session and routes the packets that are traversing between the two end points through the hacker's system.

To understand session hijacking, you need to understand the basic workings of TCP. It is a reliable connection protocol between two communication end points, which uses a full-duplex reliable stream for a communication channel. Generally, every packet sent across a TCP connection is made up of a TCP header that contains information such as the source port number, destination port number, sequence number, acknowledge number, checksum, and other fields that make up the first 20 bytes of the TCP header.

TCP is considered a reliable protocol because it promises to deliver the information that is sent from the source machine to the target. It is also considered a connection-oriented protocol, which means that an active connection is required between the communication end points for a conversation to occur. TCP sends a packet from a source to a target. The target should acknowledge the package receipt to the sender; otherwise, the sender must resend the packet to the recipient. This is a brief explanation of how communication over a TCP network occurs.

There is a *desynchronized state* within a TCP connection. When a TCP session is in this state, data exchange between the communication end points is not possible even if the connection exists. A hacker utilizes this concept for session hijacking by creating a desynchronized state on the communication end points so that data exchange between the end points is no longer possible. The hacker then involves a third-party host machine (such as his own machine), which acts as an intermediary. This machine in the middle creates an acceptable state for the communication end points to send data to each other. Thus the hacker effectively hijacks the session between two communication end points and is in total control of the session. Using TCP session hijacking, the hacker can eavesdrop on the session and modify the conversation between two communication end points.

Denial of Service Attacks

DoS attacks, which are sometimes referred to as *cyber attacks* or *nukes*, totally disrupt a system so that it cannot perform. They can create major problems on the Internet. Such attacks bring down the host machines, network terminals, or in some cases the entire network. The name is derived from the fact that when such an attack occurs on any system, the system denies services requested by any other client.

A DoS attack is usually a malicious attack that is performed by a vandal who is interested in disrupting communication, sessions, transactions, or any other kind of business activities on the network. DoS attacks are designed to flood the network with useless traffic. They usually exploit the limitations in the TCP/IP suite of protocols. The different types of DoS attacks are categorized under two major sections.

- **Operating system attacks**. An operating system attack exploits known bugs and vulnerabilities within a given operating system.
- **Network attacks**. Network attacks take advantage of the known vulnerabilities in the TCP/IP suite within a given network. A network attack causes a victim's computer to disconnect from the network. Another type of network attack involves a huge amount of data flooding a known site, such as Hotmail or Amazon.com. Network attacks are usually spoofed.

The following section explains some general types of DoS attacks.

Resource Starvation

Resource starvation is a DoS attack in which the hacker consumes the system resources of the victim to prevent the victim from offering any services. The system resources that are consumed in such attacks are

- CPU
- Memory
- Hard disk space

The attack strategy involves many elements such as worms, trojans, and port scans.

Bandwidth Consumption

Bandwidth consumption is another type of DoS attack in which the network is flooded with a huge amount of data to consume the complete bandwidth. Generally, a hacker uses worms that can replicate and flood the network. The hacker can use many strategies, such as distributed DoS attacks, to incapacitate a network. In a distributed DoS attack, the hacker involves many systems dispersed across the Internet to flood a particular site. The hacker might use such an attack if he or she does not have enough bandwidth to flood useless data onto the victim's network to consume the victim's bandwidth. In other words, if a hacker is using a 56 kbps network, and if the victim's network is a T1 line (1.5 mbps) or T3 line (45 mbps), it is virtually impossible for the hacker to flood the victim's network. In such a scenario, the hacker would use multiple systems on the Internet to participate in a distributed DoS attack to flood the victim's network. In a distributed DoS attack, it is harder to pinpoint the hacker.

Routing Attacks

In a routing attack, the hacker manipulates the network routing tables in such a way that they start denying services to the legitimate network hosts. The hacker utilizes his intricate knowledge of the routing protocols used on the network to poison the entries in the routing table. If the routing protocol of the network has very little security, poisoning the entries is relatively easy.

DNS Cache Poisoning

Networks use DNS to look up the IP address of a host name that is provided to the DNS server. A DNS server contains the mapping of host names to IP addresses. A hacker can gain control of a DNS server and poison the entries. Generally, the hacker alters the mapping between a host name and an IP address to include an invalid address. Whenever a lookup is performed on the DNS server, the client retrieves a wrong IP address and therefore is redirected to an invalid address. Thus the hacker effectively denies a specific site's service to clients because every client who tries to connect to the site is redirected to some other site or a black hole. A *black hole* is an IP address that does not exist.

Malicious Software

There is a lot of malicious software on the Internet, ready to claim a victim every second. There are different types and flavors of such malicious agents called viruses, trojans, worms, and backdoors. These agents have different objectives, but they are malicious nonetheless.

◆ **Viruses**. Viruses are software programs that are purposefully written by hackers to affect a victim's system. The general purpose of a virus is to crash a victim's system, consume the system resources, or send sensitive information back to the hacker. A computer virus is designed to replicate itself and spread to affect the

Internet. Viruses can affect applications, binary files, word-processing documents, boot sectors, master boot records, or any conceivable program that can execute.

◆ **Trojans**. A trojan horse is a software program that infects the victim's system to cause harm. Trojans masquerade over the Internet as useful programs, so victims are lured into downloading and using them. The victim is not aware that a malicious trojan infests the downloaded program.

A trojan provides a perceived benefit for the victim while performing malicious activities in the background, so the victim never suspects the program. As an example, while surfing the Internet you might come across a very cool screensaver. After looking at the reviews for the screensaver, you might want to give it a try, so you download it and implement it on your system. If this screensaver is infected by a trojan, it can eventually harm your system by crashing it or sending sensitive information that is stored on the system back to the hacker without your knowledge.

◆ **Worms**. Worms are software programs that are written to replicate themselves on a desired medium. Although worms might not be directly harmful to your system, they are used extensively in DoS attacks. Worms can be written to consume bandwidth by flooding the network. Once a worm infects the target system, it can very rapidly clone itself and consume other system resources such as memory, hard disk space, the CPU, and network bandwidth. Worms are an effective tool for DoS attacks. They can be spread across the Internet using different media such as e-mail or chats, or even as a trojan.

◆ **Backdoors**. A backdoor is a computer program that is written to infect the victim's system and open a secret door for the hacker. A secret door can be a registered port of which the user might not be aware. Once such a backdoor program infects a system, the hacker can immediately gain control of it and set up multiple entries to the system. Even if the backdoor program is detected and eradicated from the system, the hacker still has other entry points that are set up prior to the eradication of the program. Closing all of the doors for such attacks is a tedious and annoying task for the victim.

The preceding sections explained the various security threats for a system. Now I'll explain how to identify and assess the vulnerabilities of the system.

Assessing Vulnerability

Vulnerabilities are weaknesses within the system. The more vulnerabilities a system has, the higher the risk of a successful attack on the system. You can assess vulnerability before or at the same time as you evaluate threats, but you definitely cannot do so after you have evaluated threats. Vulnerability assessment is important to provide proper mitigation strategies while performing threat modeling. Therefore, it would not make much sense to conduct an assessment after you have evaluated the threats. When performing a vulnerability assessment, it is a good idea to start with a homogenous listing of vulnerabilities.

 NOTE

Threat modeling is the first step in determining all possible threats to a system.

Vulnerabilities can exist within a system for the following reasons.

◆ **An internal component is of low quality**. For example, the operating system might have a lot of bugs, and the services running on the operating system might have a lot of security holes. Most vendors regularly supply product security patches for known threats. If these patches are not implemented, then the system is more prone to attack.

◆ **An internal component is poorly designed**. For example, the operating system might not be written with enough security measures in mind. Or, the hardware infrastructure might be implemented using an inappropriate topology.

◆ **A component is misconfigured**. A DNS server of high quality and a good design can still be vulnerable if you do not configure it properly at the time of installation.

Based on the preceding list, you can conclude a simple categorization for a vulnerability assessment. For example, one such categorization follows.

◆ Quality
◆ Capability
◆ Configuration

The classification system for vulnerabilities is not very standardized, but efforts are being made in the industry to group and name the vulnerabilities under a standard schema. Although there are many confusing classifications available, there is one standardized classification scheme called the CVE (*Common Vulnerabilities and Exposures*) list. CVE is a standardization sponsored by the Mitre Corporation. The CVE list provides a naming convention for vulnerabilities to make it easier for security experts to converse with each other using a common vocabulary. The standard can be downloaded from http://cve.mitre.org/cve/index.html.

Once you identify a standard classification, you can eventually detail all of the listed vulnerabilities using one of the following structures.

◆ **Vulnerability ID**. This uniquely identifies the vulnerability in the homogeneous listing.

◆ **Description**. This is a description of the vulnerability in a few sentences.

- ◆ **Category**. This is the categorization of the vulnerability based on quality, capability, or configuration. The vulnerability can fall into more than one category.

- ◆ **Severity**. The severity is explained on a predefined scale such as a scale of 1 to 10, in which 1 is the least severe and 10 is the most severe.

- ◆ **Protective measure**. This explains how to tackle vulnerability. Some examples of protective measures include installing patches for the operating system, upgrading the operating system to a new version, and reconfiguring the network.

Once you have made a proper assessment of all of the vulnerabilities, it is a good idea to evaluate the threats.

Evaluating the Threats

As explained in the initial sections of this chapter, before you draft a security model you need to understand all of the internal and external components of a system. The system in question can be a PC, a network, building premises, a bank, or even a nation. The most important items to identify are the things that belong to the system. This is important to establish a crisply defined boundary between items that make up the system and components that are external to the system.

Once a crisply defined boundary is established, you should prepare a homogeneous listing of all of the conceivable threats without any prioritization. Once you have this homogeneous listing, you can easily evaluate the threats and prioritize them accordingly.

Whenever you plan to apply a security model for a system, you must know the threats for the system because establishing a security model without identifying the potential threats creates a false pretense of security. There is no security model that can have countermeasures for all kind of threats. Unfortunately, a security model is always tailor-made for a system, based on the conceivable threats that can compromise the security of the system.

Analyzing Threats

Threat analysis is a process that helps you evaluate the threats from the homogeneous list. It is an iterative and time-consuming process. Even if you establish a security model after you have identified all of the threats, the process of evaluating the new threats for the current model is always iterative and incremental. The *STRIDE* model is the common industry model used for threat analysis. This model categorizes threats in the following manner.

- ◆ **Spoofing**. Spoofing is a technique hackers use to change the sender's identity within a packet. It can occur on any layer of the OSI protocol suite.

- ◆ **Tampering**. In tampering, also referred to as *integrity threats*, the hacker tampers with the system data. Examples of integrity threats include cookie poisoning, router table poisoning, and DNS cache poisoning.

◆ **Repudiation**. Repudiation threats cannot be logically or theoretically proven, such as when an attack has occurred on a system and there is no way to trace it.

◆ **Information disclosure**. Information disclosure is a threat that occurs when a hacker compromises the security of confidential information. An information disclosure threat occurs when an external component can access confidential information within a system.

◆ **Denial of Service**. DoS incapacitates the system by preventing it from servicing legitimate clients.

◆ **Elevation of privilege**. In an elevation of privilege threat, an unprivileged user tries to access the resources with privileged access control. A stack buffer overflow attack is an example of an elevation of privilege attack.

Threat Modeling

Threat modeling is a process in which you categorize every threat on the homogeneous list based on the characteristics of the threat. Technically, you have the categories that are suggested by the STRIDE model. In other words, you can map the threats from the homogenous listing to any of the categories in the model. Threat modeling uses the following structure for detailing the threats.

◆ **Threat ID**. This provides an ID to the threat to uniquely identify it within the homogenous listing.

◆ **Threat description**. This briefly describes the threat in few sentences.

◆ **STRIDE category**. This categorizes the threat based on the STRIDE model. A threat can belong to more than one STRIDE category.

◆ **Threat target**. This specifies which internal system component is targeted for attack. You can also categorize the internal components based on the context of the system. For example, if the system in question is a network, you can categorize the internal components as follows.

- Hosts
- Servers
- Users
- Groups
- Services
- Connectors
- Sensitive data objects (router tables, file systems, databases, accounts)

◆ **Threat severity**. Establishing the severity of a threat by itself is an intricate process and might include several other processes such as threat prioritization and risk analysis. Usually, you use a scale of 1 to 10 to represent the threat severity. You assign a number after you analyze the criticality, cost, countermeasures, infrastructure, and risks.

◆ **Mitigation techniques**. The mitigation techniques provide different mechanisms to counter an attack. This is an intricate process that requires expertise to identify the correct mitigation technique for a given threat. This technique takes into account the different modalities of attack that belong to the same threat category and how to effectively install a proper security model to counter a threat using the minimum resources.

After you complete the threat analysis, it is much easier to build a security model to safeguard the system. As stated, the process of evaluating threats always evolves with the security model. New mitigation techniques are identified for the existing threats, and new threats are identified as the system is implemented. The severity level might affect the mitigation technique based on the cost of infrastructure. Many of the elements in the process of evaluating threats are dynamic. This in turn alters the status of a threat from one severity level to the next. A good security model should acknowledge the dynamics involved in evaluating a threat and accordingly resolve an appropriate security policy to accommodate this.

In this section, you learned how to identify the threats that can exist for a system. The threat analysis can be followed by different strategies for the system's security model.

Security Strategies

You use security strategies to create a security model for a system. There are different strategies that you can use to apply a proper and successful security model. The following sections detail the various security strategies that you can consider when creating a security model.

Least Privilege

Least privilege is a security strategy that is based on the concept of providing the least amount of privilege, while still enough for any internal component to perform without a hitch. This is a very thoughtful strategy because it provides no loose threads for any component to act beyond its capacity. Providing the least privilege narrows down the amount of exposure for a component so it is safe from exploits. In this strategy, the possibility of attacks is limited because even if a hacker breaks into a component, there are only a limited number of things that he is allowed to do.

Assigning the least privilege is also a very cost-effective strategy because you can concentrate on providing costly security measures for the most privileged components rather than for components with less privilege. A component with high privilege, like an administrator, should have heavier security than a component with less privilege.

One example of the least privilege security strategy is the grouping of accounts in operating systems such as UNIX or Windows NT. In such operating systems, different user groups are created and a security privilege is assigned for the group. The users who belong to the group obtain the privilege assigned to that group. You can have groups with different privilege levels, and a user account can belong to many groups at the same time. If a user belongs to more than one group, the user obtains the collective privileges of the groups to which he or she is assigned. For example, there can be groups for administrators, backup operators, power users, and guests. The privilege for every group is assigned accordingly. Thus a user account that belongs to a particular group has access to only the resources that are allowed for the group.

Defense In-Depth

Defense in-depth is a strategy that secures a system using a security mechanism among multiple layers. The defense in-depth strategy concentrates on securing the Link, Transport, Application, and Network layers to make it hard for a hacker to break in. In the defense in-depth strategy, you use different types of technologies, mechanisms, and techniques to provide in-depth defense against any outside attacks.

In this strategy, the main objective is to deter the hackers from even trying to hack into the system by using a mixture of security mechanisms such as perimeter security, network security, host security, and also human security at the location of the infrastructure. This is an expensive strategy. The idea behind it is to make the hacker think that it is not worth the effort to hack into the system because it is too risky or too expensive to bring down the system. In a defense in-depth strategy, you need to ensure that you have a backup plan if any of the security measures fail. A defense in-depth strategy is like having a Plan A, Plan B, and Plan C that back up each other.

Choke Point

Choke point is a security strategy in which you create a purposeful bottleneck between the local network and the Internet. This bottleneck is called a choke point, and it actually narrows down the channel of attack for a hacker. The idea behind this strategy is that it is easy to monitor the choke point.

The theory behind the choke point is not to reduce the bandwidth of communication, but to limit the number of access points to the network. For example, you can have only one gateway between your local network and the Internet. You can install a firewall on the gateway, which will help you to monitor and control all of the traffic that flows through it. This way, you effectively create a choke point to the network because there is no other access point from the Internet. In such a strategy, you need to ensure that there is no backdoor for the network and that the gateway is the only true access point for the network.

Weakest Link

The *weakest link* security strategy tries to analyze the complete system and identify the weak points. The identified weak points should be eliminated. In a complex network, it can be difficult to eliminate certain internal components due to the effect caused by that component's absence on the entire network. Such components can likely turn out to be the weakest links in the network. Since the components are essential, it might be hard to eliminate them altogether. The best you can do is try to reduce the vulnerability of the component by using the measures suggested at the time of the vulnerability assessment.

If an internal component still compromises the security of the network despite all of these measures, it is important to provide special attention to it. The weakest link strategy advises that closely monitoring the activities of the weakest links in the network is essential for the health of the network. Setting up a good defense for the weakest links is a must.

Fail-Safe Stance

The *fail-safe stance* is a security strategy that is based on the concept of fail-overs. In a complex network, you cannot expect that the internal components of the network will always be healthy and active. It is always a good idea to plan for failures. Within a network, even if you have a high-quality component that never fails, the power that drives the component might fail. The fail-safe stance takes into account that the components are going to fail. If they do fail, they should neither compromise the security of the system nor jeopardize the running state of the system.

You should plan fail-overs for the major components within a system. Some of the networks components within a network for which you need to plan fail-overs include the servers that employ perimeter security, network gateways, DNS and mail services, databases, application servers, Web servers, and electrical power. In the fail-safe stance security strategy, there are fundamentally two stances that a security model can adopt.

♦ **The default deny stance**. By default, the security model prohibits access to the system except to permitted users.

♦ **The default permit stance**. By default, the security model permits access to the system except to denied users.

Between these two stances, the default deny stance is the best choice because you can permit only those services that you trust and deny access for everything else. In the default permit stance, the attitude of the security model is to permit everything and distrust only those services that you think pose a threat. The default permit stance is unsafe because it is presumptuous for the security model to think that the model is aware of all of the threats that are posed to the system.

Universal Participation

Universal participation is a security strategy in which all of the internal components of the system are ordered to participate in the security model. This makes sense because if one of the network hosts does not choose to participate in the security model, a hacker can easily attack that host first and then employ the host to attack other systems. It is very important to have a strong security policy so that people who belong to and use the system understand the reason behind participating in the security model.

You should implement a security model in such a way that the users of the system cannot opt out of the model. If they do, they should not be able to take advantage of the services available in the system. It is easy to state the preceding concepts, but it is very difficult to deploy such security measures. As an example, a user within the system can easily install a new modem and hook up to the Internet through an ISP. As soon as the user hooks up through a different channel than the one provided by the security model, he or she has already compromised the security of the entire system. This strategy requires management and personal relations skills to convince people to participate in the security model.

Diversity of Defense

The *diversity of defense* security strategy is an extension of the defense in-depth strategy. You learned that the defense in-depth strategy provides multiple layers of security to act as a deterrent for hackers. In the diversity of defense strategy, the security model uses a diverse base of technologies and mechanisms to put up a strong defense. In diversity of defense, a network can use firewalls from different vendors to secure different gateways. In addition, the packet-filtering system architecture can be different.

The idea behind providing such a diverse architectural and technological base is to increase the amount of work the hacker needs to do if he or she wants to hack into the system. The amount of work increases because the hacker needs to footprint a diverse base of architecture rather than a homogeneous group. Footprinting, scanning, and enumerating a security model with a diverse base of architecture is more difficult and time consuming than footprinting, scanning, and enumerating a security model with a homogeneous base.

Diversity of defense can prove costly in the long run due to the cost of integrating diverse architecture. Additionally, the maintenance cost for such a diverse base might be high because you need to pay the specialists who excel in all aspects of the architecture or you need to pay different people with different skills to support the system.

Simplicity

Simplicity is a security strategy that is based on one major theme—keeping things simple. In this strategy, the security model concentrates on simplifying all of the internal components of the system to the most basic level. The idea behind this strategy is that the more complex the system is, the more difficult it is to understand and the harder it is to devise a game plan for the security model. The harder it is to devise a security model, the greater the chances of overlooking some key security concepts of the model. You can avoid going through this hassle if you can simplify the system as much as possible. Consequently, you will increase your chances of deriving a better security model.

Security through Obscurity

Security through obscurity is a principle based on the concept of hiding or concealing things. *Obscurity* is the ability to hide the internal resources of the system from the external environment. Security through obscurity is not a very acceptable strategy because it is based on the hope that others will not be able to trace the objects that you have purposefully tried to hide. For example, you can create your own proprietary firewall and not provide the architectural details to the outside world. If the inherent details of the architecture are different from any other architecture, you have successfully achieved security through obscurity because hackers will not know anything about the architecture. However, just because you have achieved security through obscurity does not mean that your system is impenetrable; hackers will surely figure out some way to break in, given enough time. Security through obscurity should be used with other strategies to be effective. By itself, it is not a very effective strategy.

Summary

This chapter provided an in-depth overview of network security. It explained the fundamental elements of network security and some basic security concepts used in current systems to provide effective defense mechanisms. You learned about the common threats faced by the current network systems and how to perform vulnerability assessments and evaluate threats. The chapter also presented different security strategies that you should consider when you are creating a security model. The next chapter will introduce a very popular technology in network security—firewalls.

Check Your Understanding

Multiple Choice Questions

1. Identify the elements used in qualitative risk analysis.

   a. Threats

   b. Measures

   c. Probability of event occurrence

   d. Vulnerabilities

2. Which of the following is not an incremental phase of a security model?

   a. Establishing a security policy

   b. Identifying a security threat

   c. Performing audits

   d. Implementing network security

3. A public key cipher is _____ algorithm that uses a pair of keys to secure data.

   a. An asymmetric encryption

   b. A symmetric encryption

   c. A hash

   d. A cryptography

4. Which of the following is not a human-based social engineering skill?

   a. Dumpster diving

   b. Impersonation

   c. Shoulder surfing

   d. Using pop-ups

Short Questions

1. What is cryptography?

2. What is footprinting?

Answers

Multiple Choice Answers

1. a, b and d. Threats, measures, and vulnerabilities are the elements used in qualitative risk analysis.

2. b. Identifying a security threat is not an incremental phase of a security model.

3. a. A public key cipher is an asymmetric algorithm that uses a pair of keys to secure data.

4. d. Using pop-ups is a computer-based social engineering skill.

Short Answers

1. Cryptography is the science of encryption and decryption of data. Encryption is the process of converting the raw data (clear text) into a form that is secure (cipher text). Decryption is the process of converting the cipher text to its original format (clear text).

2. Footprinting is the process in which a hacker plans extensively to obtain information about the target system by using a systematic approach of profiling the details of the target environment.

Chapter 3

In the era of the Internet, the need for securing data can never be underestimated. Information is power. If your organization is unable to secure confidential information from competitors and hackers, the survival of the organization in this competitive world is at stake.

The need to secure information was well understood when the world moved from single-PC computing to distributed computing. The devices and methods used for securing computers and networks have kept pace with the new methods employed by hackers to retrieve confidential information. One such method that is commonly used by organizations and individual users is firewalls.

A firewall allows you to prevent security threats to your personal computer as well as to the computers on a network. It provides a layer of security between your internal network and the Web service that is exposed to the Internet.

This chapter provides an introduction to firewalls. It begins with a description of the origin and use of firewalls. Next, it covers the types of firewalls and which firewall you should select to address the security needs of your organization. Finally, the chapter discusses the limitations of firewalls and the possible future developments in firewall technology.

The Origin and Need for Firewalls

Firewalls have long been used to guard networks against unwanted intruders. This section begins with a brief write-up on the history of firewalls. Next, it delves into the functions of firewalls and the role of firewalls in securing a network.

The History of Firewalls

The figurative meaning of the term *firewall* is not much different from the literal meaning of the word. Firewalls provide the first level of defense for the computers that exchange information over a network.

The first firewalls that were similar to present-day firewalls came into existence in the late 1980s. In those days, when a network in an organization was spread over multiple departments, routers were used to separate these departments into smaller LANs. This approach provided flexibility to the management of the departments because each department could deploy its custom applications. These applications did not affect the performance of the applications deployed in the other departments because a router shielded each department.

Firewalls were first put to their present-day use in the early 1990s. These firewalls were IP routers that employed filtering rules to control the flow and access to information. They usually allowed all traffic within a network to communicate freely with the traffic outside the network but not vice versa. This ensured that the internal network was shielded from the traffic on the external network.

The next league of firewalls was more sophisticated than the earlier versions. The new league was capable of using filters and application gateways, and it provided a GUI (*Graphical User Interface*) for managing the policies on the firewall.

The firewalls in use today are derived from this second league of firewalls. However, firewalls today are much more sophisticated and enable you to control access to data that is in multiple formats, from HTTP to audio- and video-streaming data. As newer types of data are exchanged on the Internet, the need for newer firewalls that can detect and filter the new types of data will increase.

The Functions of Firewalls

A firewall is a security system that is deployed on a network to prevent unauthorized access. The use of a firewall is not restricted to a network; you can even use it to secure a personal computer that regularly accesses the Internet.

Further, a firewall can be a physical device or software. When you want to deploy a firewall on a physical device, you can use a router that connects the internal network to the Internet. Similarly, when you want to deploy a software-based firewall, you can use a proxy server, which has direct access to the Internet and processes all of the requests from the other computers on the network. You will learn more about the two types of firewalls described here in the "Types of Firewalls" section later in this chapter.

There are some basic functions that all firewalls perform, regardless of type. These functions include authenticating users, filtering services and packets, securing a network from network scanning, and performing NAT (*Network Address Translation*). These functions of firewalls are defined in the following sections.

Performing User Authentication

Users who place requests for data need to be authenticated to ensure that they are allowed to access the private network. A firewall can authenticate users to determine whether requests are genuine.

The security policy of an organization determines the level of authentication that is implemented by a firewall. If the security policy states that only the users of the private network can access the Internet, a firewall that validates the user name and the password should suffice.

However, there might be situations in which users who are logged on to an external network should be allowed to access the private network of an organization. For example, the senior managers in an organization might be allowed to access their data using a laptop connected to the Internet. In such cases, the security policy would state that users from a public network should be allowed to log on and access the internal network. However, in such cases, the firewall might implement strong user authentication so that only authorized external users would be able to access the network. Figure 3.1 illustrates strong user authentication on a firewall.

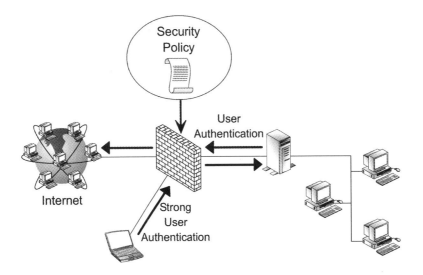

FIGURE 3.1 *Implementing user authentication on a firewall*

Strong user authentication uses cryptographic techniques such as digital certificates to establish the authenticity of a user. Cryptographic techniques are much more reliable than authenticating a user by user name and password.

Filtering Services and Packets

The primary objective of deploying a firewall is to ensure that the data that traverses the network conforms to the security specifications of the organization. For example, an organization might restrict users from downloading executable files or ActiveX controls from the Internet because these might contain harmful viruses and trojan code. Similarly, an organization might restrict users from subscribing to and accessing newsgroups because these might cause undue load on the network.

A firewall enables you to impose such restrictions on the network by using service filtering and packet filtering.

◆ **Service filtering**. Service filtering is used to grant access to selected services on a network. For example, if users are restricted from accessing newsgroups, you can restrict the NNTP (*Network News Transfer Protocol*) that is used by newsgroup services. Similarly, if users should not be allowed to access e-mail services, you can restrict the SMTP (*Simple Mail Transfer Protocol*).

◆ **Packet filtering**. Data is transmitted on the Internet in the form of packets. By filtering the packets of data that are received from the Internet, a firewall can ensure that unpermitted data is blocked at the firewall itself. As I mentioned earlier, firewall administrators can specify a security policy that prohibits the firewall from receiving packets for executable files.

 NOTE

Instead of completely denying access to packets of data, a firewall can send an error message to the sender of the data packet, send an alert message to a firewall administrator, or send the data but retain a copy of it for later analysis.

Preventing Network Scanning

Network scanning is a technique employed by hackers to determine the hosts that are alive on a network and the services that are being run on these hosts. A hacker can gain access to the network by using the services that are made available by the hosts. Network scanning was covered in detail in Chapter 2.

To prevent network scanning, a firewall can block all IP-directed broadcasts at the router. You can also scan your own servers to determine the ports that do not need to be open. You can close these ports so that hackers are unable to access them.

Performing NAT

It is often necessary to ensure that the IP addresses of the computers on your network are not exposed on the Internet. Exposing the IP addresses of internal computers to the Internet poses a security threat because hackers can use these IP addresses to gain access to your internal network.

To avoid exposing the IP addresses of the computers on your internal network, you can implement the concept of NAT, which uses a set of public IP addresses to query all of the data from the Internet. Whenever a computer in the internal network places a request for information, the following transactions take place after the firewall has successfully authenticated the request.

1. The data packet from the computer in the internal network is received at the firewall.

2. NAT translates the IP address in the request to one of the public IP addresses available at the firewall.

3. The request is forwarded to the destination.

If a response is received from the destination, the following sequence of steps is followed to send the response to the computer that placed the request.

1. At the firewall, NAT translates the destination address on the data packet to the IP address of the client computer that placed the request.

2. The response is sent to the client computer.

Figure 3.2 depicts the sequence of steps for making requests and receiving responses from a firewall that uses NAT.

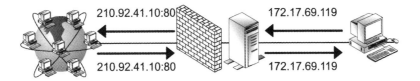

FIGURE 3.2 *Using NAT to hide a network's internal IP addresses*

For a detailed description of NAT, refer to Chapter 4, "Firewall Technologies."

The Role of Firewalls in Network Security

According to Cheswick and Bellovin, who carried out research on Internet firewalls, a firewall has the following characteristics.

◆ **Single point of contact**. A firewall is a single point of contact between two or more networks. All traffic must pass through the single point of contact.

◆ **Controlled traffic**. A firewall can control and authenticate the traffic that passes through it.

◆ **Logged traffic**. The traffic that passes through a firewall is logged.

Although the preceding definition of firewalls was provided in the early 1990s, it still holds true. The following sections will examine each of these three characteristics in detail.

Single Point of Contact

The primary purpose of a firewall is to ensure that unauthorized users from the Internet do not have access to confidential information. To meet this requirement, a firewall administrator needs to ensure that all of the traffic to the Internet is routed through the firewall.

To illustrate the need for a single point of contact, consider the scenario of an organization that has deployed a firewall to secure its network. Further, consider that a user who is connected to the organizational network also has a personal Internet connection. If the user logs on to the Internet using a dial-up modem, he or she bypasses the firewall and is vulnerable to attacks from the Internet. Not only can the user's computer be attacked, all of the computers on the network become susceptible, as shown in Figure 3.3. Therefore, the effectiveness of the firewall is undermined.

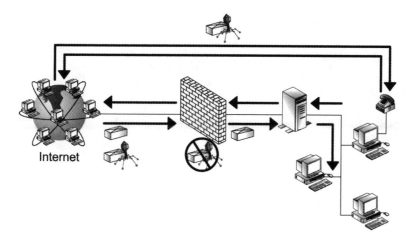

FIGURE 3.3 *The importance of using a firewall as a single point of contact*

Controlled Traffic

The traffic that passes through a firewall is controlled. As discussed earlier in this chapter, a firewall can perform service and packet filtering to enable only the traffic that is permitted by the security policy to pass through the network.

Firewall administrators can also enable user authentication at the firewall to ensure that only the users who are authenticated by a valid user name and password or a digital certificate are allowed to access the Internet.

Logged Traffic

All of the traffic that passes through a firewall is logged. You can examine the logs to determine the details of the requests that the firewall has processed. You can also analyze the log files to determine whether any security breach was attempted on the network.

Firewalls and VPNs

As the name suggests, a VPN (*Virtual Private Network*) enables you to establish a private data network on a network that is publicly accessible, such as the Internet. By establishing a VPN, an organization can tremendously cut down the operational costs that are otherwise involved in establishing a LAN or a WAN (*Wide Area Network*).

Since the data in a VPN travels over a public network, you need to encrypt it before you send it to the destination. These days, firewalls support firewall-to-firewall encryption that allows you to encrypt data, send it over the network in an encrypted form, and decrypt it when it reaches the destination. Figure 3.4 depicts this encryption.

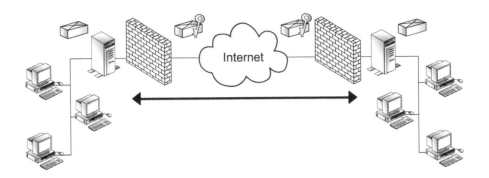

FIGURE 3.4 *Establishing a VPN using firewalls*

Types of Firewalls

Depending upon the layer of the network on which a firewall operates, firewalls can be classified into two categories.

◆ **Network-layer firewalls**. Network-layer firewalls are either built on a router or placed immediately after the router.

◆ **Application-layer firewalls**. Application-layer firewalls are based on programmatic code that is used to regulate the interaction of the users on an internal network with the Internet.

The following sections examine these firewalls in detail.

Network-Layer Firewalls

Network-layer firewalls, as described previously, are deployed on routers, which provide permanent connectivity between an internal network and the Internet. When a firewall is deployed on a router, a network administrator can configure the access control rules on the router to control access to information through the firewall. In this scenario, Network-layer firewalls control Internet traffic with the help of access control lists that are configured on the routers. These firewalls filter traffic on the basis of source address, destination address, type of protocol, and port number of the client that has placed the request. The data packets that match the permitted access control rules are allowed to pass through the network. The firewall either rejects the packets that do not conform to these rules or sends an ICMP message back to the sender of the message.

NOTE

ICMP is an error-reporting protocol that is used by a gateway to inform the server that an error occurred while processing a message.

Figure 3.5 depicts a Network-layer firewall that is built on a router.

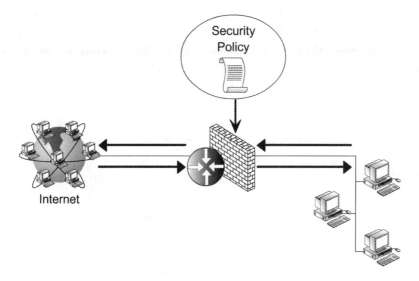

FIGURE 3.5 *A Network–layer firewall*

An important advantage of using Network-layer firewalls is that the speed of data-packet processing is high because very little logging or analysis of data packets is done. These firewalls are also able to support a larger user base than Application-layer firewalls, which I will discuss in the next section.

On the other hand, since the log generated by the firewall is limited, network administrators are unable to make a detailed analysis of the activity on the network. Another disadvantage of Network-layer firewalls is that since they are deployed at the Network layer, they are unable to understand application-level protocols, and are therefore less effective in preventing unwanted data from entering a private network. As you will see in the next section, an Application-layer firewall solves some of the problems associated with Network-layer firewalls.

Application-Layer Firewalls

Application-layer firewalls utilize the application gateways and proxy codes to control access to a network. Since these firewalls are deployed at the application level, they are much more effective in managing the data flow between an internal network and the Internet.

Application-layer firewalls first ensure that a data packet is valid, and then they establish a connection between the client and the server. Since firewalls come in the first line of interaction between the users on the Internet and the private network, they can conveniently provide user authentication.

An Application-layer firewall is usually deployed on a dedicated server that has access to the Internet. All of the other computers access the Internet through the dedicated server. Figure 3.6 depicts an implementation of Application-layer firewalls.

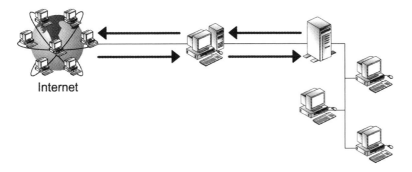

Internet

FIGURE 3.6 *An Application-layer firewall*

An Application-layer firewall is usually accompanied by a set of proxy services and application software. The proxy services control access to Internet services, and the application software configures user authentication, packet filtering, and service filtering on the firewall. The application software that manages the firewall is also referred to as a *proxy server*. One example is Netscape Proxy Server.

The proxy servers on the market today perform more tasks than just managing the flow of data across networks. The new-generation proxy servers, such as ISA (*Internet Security and Acceleration*) Server 2000, enable you to cache data from frequently visited Web sites on the hard disk and provide an elaborate management console for managing services on the firewall. The management console for ISA Server 2000 is shown in Figure 3.7.

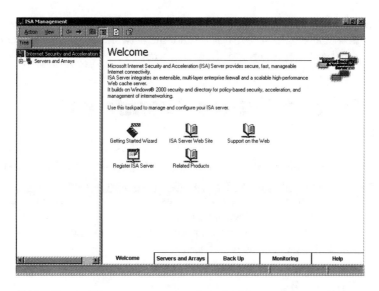

FIGURE 3.7 *The management console for ISA Server 2000*

When proxy servers implement data caching, every time a user requests a Web site for data that is available in the cache, the proxy server retrieves the data from the cache instead of retrieving it from the Web site. This method saves operational costs and speeds up data retrieval.

Proxy servers also maintain elaborate logs of the sites that users have accessed. By examining the proxy logs, network administrators can determine whether there has been a breach in the security of the network. Figure 3.8 shows a sample log file generated by a proxy server.

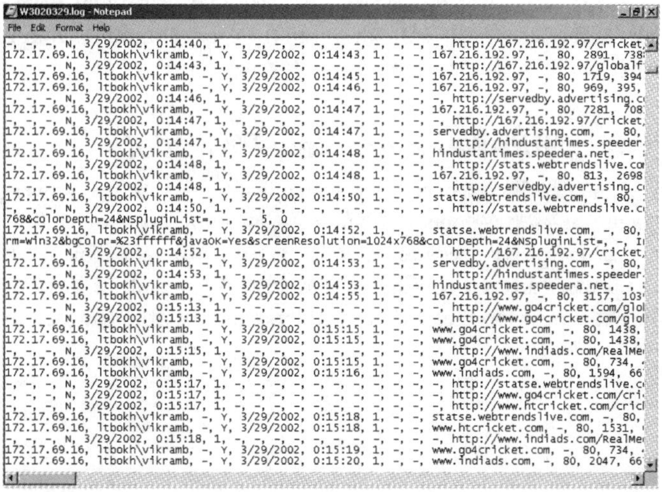

FIGURE 3.8 *A log file generated by a proxy server*

Application-layer firewalls have one distinct disadvantage. Since the information is first processed at the firewall level to ensure that it is valid, the networks running Application-layer firewalls tend to be slower in terms of Internet access.

Constraints and Future Trends of Firewalls

The present-day firewalls suffer from a few constraints. While some of these constraints will be addressed in the near future, owing to the rapid shift toward Internet computing, some constraints are likely to persist for a while. In this section, I will describe the limitations of firewalls and the likely future developments in firewall technology. To ensure that your system remains secure despite firewall limitations, you should make sure that firewalls are the first, but not the only, line of defense!

Limitations of Firewalls

Undoubtedly, organizations that have implemented firewall solutions are better equipped to handle security threats from outside the private network. However, with advances in the attack techniques adopted by intruders, even firewalls cannot ensure complete security of data and networks. In this section, I will list some of the limitations of firewall technologies and how these limitations might affect the performance of a firewall.

Alternative Route to Data Access

The simplest security breach can occur when an alternative method of accessing data on the Internet is available. For example, if a user can use a dial-up modem to access the Internet and bypass the firewall, all of the security policies that you might have implemented on the firewall are rendered useless. In addition, the user's computer compromises the security of the entire network if it is connected to the network.

Reconfiguration of Firewalls for New Protocols

With newer formats of data exchange becoming available on the Internet, newer protocols for data exchange are being developed. When an application-layer firewall needs to support new protocols, a new proxy needs to be coded for the protocol. This process can get cumbersome if the proxies are not configured correctly. As a result of incorrect configuration, firewalls might expose loopholes that intruders can exploit to gain access to the network.

Threats from Virus-Infected Data

The effect of a virus attack on a firewall can be multifold. Since all data exchange within an organization is through the firewall, a virus attack can infect all of the files that pass through the firewall. With new viruses discovered virtually every day, it is becoming increasingly difficult to manage the virus-free operation of firewalls.

Future Developments in Firewalls

The future developments in firewalls will be similar to the developments in the rest of the IT world. Organizations are moving toward integrating their existing businesses and data across different platforms to provide a comprehensive solution to their customers; the trends in firewall development will be similar.

In the future, firewalls will achieve better integration with the security implementation systems that are deployed in organizations. For example, a firewall might be able to communicate with the risk assessment system to guard against a new type of virus that has specific characteristics.

In the future, firewalls might provide faster network speed and enable network administrators to specify organization-level security policies that can be easily customized for the specific departments or employees in an organization. Last but not least, firewalls might be used to incorporate the best features of Network-layer and Application-layer firewalls.

Summary

This chapter covered a brief history of firewalls. It also described the functions of firewalls, such as filtering services and packets, preventing network scanning, and performing NAT. The chapter provided a classification of firewalls based on the layer in which the firewall operates. This classification included Network-layer firewalls and Application-layer firewalls. Finally, the chapter described the limitations of firewalls, such as the inability to control the movement of traffic that bypasses the firewall and the inability of the firewall to function effectively in case of a virus attack.

Check Your Understanding

Multiple Choice Questions

1. Which of the following was one of the first uses of a firewall?

   a. VPN

   b. Internal LAN

   c. Intrusion prevention

   d. Internet connectivity

2. Which of the following characteristics of firewalls is not a direct consequence of the research conducted by Cheswick and Bellovin for Internet firewalls?

   a. Single point of contact

   b. Controlled traffic

   c. Logged traffic

   d. Use for VPNs

3. Which of the following correctly describes service filtering?

   a. Disconnecting intruders from an internal network

   b. Denying internal users access to certain Internet services

   c. Denying external users access to certain Internet services

   d. Making a service call to the server on behalf of the client

4. Which of the following terms is used to denote the ability of a firewall to conceal the IP address of a requesting client?

   a. NAT

   b. Network scanning

   c. Service filtering

   d. Packet filtering

5. On which of the following parameters does a Network-layer firewall score over an Application-layer firewall?

   a. Level of detail for user logs

   b. Ease of administration

   c. Response time

   d. Effective implementation of security policy

Short Questions

1. Compare and contrast Network-layer firewalls and Application-layer firewalls.

Answers

Multiple Choice Answers

1. b. The creation of internal LANs to segregate the departments in an organization was among the first uses of firewalls.

2. d. The use of firewalls for VPNs was envisioned after the research conducted by Cheswick and Bellovin.

3. b. Service filtering is used to restrict the users of an internal network from accessing certain services on the Internet.

4. a. A firewall uses NAT to conceal the IP address of a requesting client on the Internet.

5. c. A Network-layer firewall has a better response time than an Application-layer firewall because it has a lower level of logging and analysis.

Short Answers

1. Table 3.1 shows the comparison between Network-layer firewalls and Application-layer firewalls.

Table 3.1 Comparison of Different Types of Firewalls

Network-Layer Firewalls	Application-Layer Firewalls
Deployed in the Network layer	Deployed in the Application layer
Deployed on a router	Deployed on a stand-alone server
Provide a basic level of packet filtering	Provide an advanced level of packet filtering
Does not provide user authentication	Provide user authentication
Maintain a basic log file	Maintain an elaborate log file
Has high performance because of low level of logging and analysis	Has low performance because information packets are processed by the firewall to ensure that they are valid

Chapter 4

In the previous chapter, I introduced you to the concept of firewalls and provided a brief overview of the types of firewalls and their role in network security. This chapter provides details about different firewall technologies such as packet filtering, proxy systems, NAT, and VPN. This chapter also introduces you to firewall-linked technologies such as Kerberos and IPSec (*Internet Protocol Security*).

Introduction

A firewall is hardware or software that enforces an access control policy between a trusted and a non-trusted network. Basically, a firewall either allows or denies access to the Internet traffic between the internal and the external components of a network. The technologies used to provide secure network access vary widely. However, they are all based on some common firewall features, which include

- Data filtering
- Traffic control
- Perimeter defense
- User authentication
- Access control
- Network monitoring
- Logging activities
- Triggering events based on predefined alerts

A firewall is the most important component within a network that protects the network from intrusions. Usually a firewall is a combination of hardware and software. As the name suggests, the basic purpose of a firewall is to prevent the spread of intrusion from external components into the network by controlling access to internal components. In other words, the firewall decides which external systems can have access to the internal components of the network. Firewalls are generally associated with Internet connectivity, but it is not uncommon to see firewalls deployed on intranets. When a firewall is deployed on an intranet, some parts of the network are safeguarded from components within the same network.

Firewalls come in different flavors and forms. A firewall can just be software running on a host or it can be dedicated hardware that is connected between the Internet and the network gateway. Whatever the form or flavor is, the basic idea of the firewall remains the same.

When you place a firewall on the network gateway that accesses the Internet, the networks are referred to as *perimeter networks*. Perimeter network security is based on the concept of DMZ (*De-Militarized Zones*), which are zones between the Internet and the internal network. The zones belong neither to the Internet nor to the internal network (see Figure 4.1).

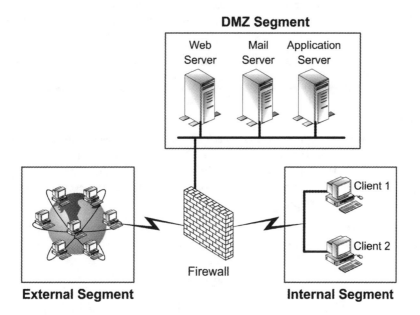

FIGURE 4.1 *Implementing perimeter security with DMZ*

 NOTE

DMZ is a compartmented enclave in which potentially vulnerable public servers, such as Web, DNS, FTP, and e-mail, are kept. This zone is protected by a firewall that filters public traffic coming into the zone. At the same time, this zone protects the trusted private network by filtering incoming and outgoing traffic between the public servers and the trusted network. In such a setup, there is an extra layer of defense that protects the private network in case the public servers are compromised.

Firewalls can be made up of the following technologies.

◆ Packet filtering
◆ Proxy systems

However, before I delve into either of these technologies, it is important for you to understand how a TCP/IP network works.

TCP/IP Networking

As I explained in the previous chapter, the TCP/IP protocol suite is a model based on the OSI architecture. TCP/IP allows many computers running on different hardware and operating systems to communicate with each other. The main theme of the TCP/IP protocol suite is to allow communication among heterogeneous computing platforms. A TCP/IP network uses the TCP and IP protocols to provide a communication channel for heterogeneous systems.

Some of the common concepts associated with TCP/IP are encapsulation, demultiplexing, and IP routing.

Encapsulation

Generally, a networked application that needs to communicate with another networked application has to traverse the layers of a protocol stack. In a TCP/IP protocol stack, the data sent by a TCP/IP application traverses the entire protocol stack, from the Application layer to the Link layer. It travels the network as a bit stream and eventually traverses the protocol stack at the recipient's end.

When data traverses the protocol stack, every layer in the stack adds its own header to the data in a process called *encapsulation* (see Figure 4.2).

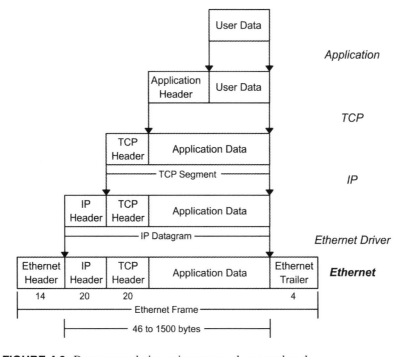

FIGURE 4.2 *Data encapsulation as it traverses the protocol stack*

If the application that sends data is TCP-based, then the information sent from the Application layer to the Transport layer will contain the user data and some application-specific header information added by the application, as shown in Figure 4.2. The Transport layer adds its own header information to the data when the data travels through it to the Network layer. In the current scenario, the Transport layer is using the TCP protocol; therefore, a TCP header will be added to the data. The TCP header and the application data together are referred to as a *TCP segment*.

The Network layer is based on the IP protocol. Therefore, when data passes through the Network layer to the Data Link layer, an IP header is added to it. Together the IP header and the TCP segment are called an *IP datagram* or an *IP packet*. If the Link layer uses Ethernet drivers to connect to the network, as shown in Figure 4.2, then an Ethernet header and an Ethernet trailer will also be added to the packet before it is finally released on the network. Figure 4.3 illustrates the IP header with its different components.

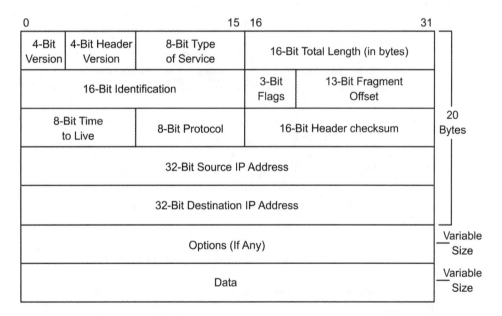

FIGURE 4.3 *Components of an IP header*

Usually, the TCP, UDP, ICMP, and IGMP protocols send their data to the IP layer. The IP layer uses the protocol field in the IP header to distinguish the data sent from each of these protocol types. Table 4.1 lists the protocols and the corresponding protocol field values.

Table 4.1 Protocols and Field Values

Protocol	Protocol Field Value
ICMP	1
IGMP	2
TCP	6
UDP	17

As I stated earlier, many Internet services use TCP or UDP ports for communication. Whenever an application communicates through a TCP or UDP port, either a TCP header or a UDP header is added to the data. Figure 4.4 shows the TCP and UDP headers.

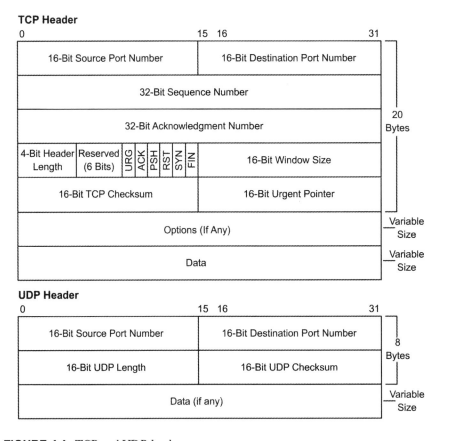

FIGURE 4.4 *TCP and UDP headers*

After data has traversed the protocol stack, it reaches the destination and traverses the protocol stack at the recipient end. This process is known as *demultiplexing*, and it is explained in the following section.

Demultiplexing

Demultiplexing is a process in which the data received from the network traverses up the protocol stack from the Link layer to the Application layer (see Figure 4.5).

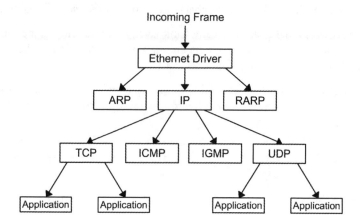

FIGURE 4.5 *Demultiplexing of data*

As shown in Figure 4.5, the following steps are involved in demultiplexing data.

1. Data received by the Link layer is forwarded to the IP protocol in the Network layer.

2. The Network layer reads the protocol field in the IP datagram and forwards the datagram to the respective protocol, which can be ICMP or IGMP in the Network layer or TCP or UDP in the Transport layer.

3. When the data is demultiplexed and forwarded to the TCP or UDP protocols in the Transport layer, these protocols demultiplex the data to the appropriate ports on which the application is listening.

IP Routing

IP routing is an important technology behind the concept of Internet networking. Without it, packets cannot be routed from one node to another on the Internet.

On a basic level, the concept of IP routing is easy to understand. When the host is directly connected to the destination by a point-to-point link, the packets get delivered from one point on the network directly to another point on the same network. However, complexity arises when a host on one network has to deliver the packets to a destination on another network. In such cases the host usually forwards the packet to a default router that routes the packet to the destination on another network. A network router can either be a dedicated router or a computer on the network configured to act as a router. Mostly, it is the IP layer that is configured to act as a router.

The IP layer receives IP packets frequently from the TCP or UDP protocols and occasionally from the ICMP or IGMP protocols. The IP layer also receives IP packets from the network interface to be routed to other destinations. To keep track of the datagrams received, the IP layer maintains a routing table, which it checks every time it receives a datagram.

When the IP layer receives a datagram from the Link layer, it checks the destination IP address and compares it to the routing table. Depending upon the location of the destination host, the IP layer makes the following decisions.

◆ If the routing table states that the destination IP address belongs to one of the hosts within the network, then the datagram is demultiplexed further up the protocol stack.

◆ If the destination IP address does not belong to any of the hosts within the network, then the IP layer acts as a router (if it is configured as a router) and routes the datagram to the appropriate destination.

To get a good grasp of the routing process, you need to understand the entries in the routing table.

◆ **Destination IP address**. This can be the address of a host or a network.

◆ **IP address of the next-hop router**. The next-hop router is an adjacent router that is directly connected to the current one.

◆ **Flags**. There are two flags in the routing table. The first flag identifies a destination IP address as a host or a network ID. The second flag identifies whether the next-hop router is a router or a network interface.

◆ **Interface**. This provides information about the location where the datagram should be sent for transmission.

As you can see from the information in the routing table, the route between a host and its destination is not predetermined. Every routing table provides the details of the next-hop router that is closer to the destination. The following rules are followed when the data packet is forwarded to the next-hop router that is closer to the destination.

1. **Check the routing table for a destination IP address**. When the routing table is checked for the destination IP address, the network ID and the host ID of the destination are included. If the destination IP address is found, then the data packet is transferred to the next-hop router indicated by the routing table entry.

2. **Check the routing table for a destination network ID**. If the network ID is found, then the data packet is transferred to the next-hop router indicated by the entry in the routing table. Such an entry includes all of the hosts on a given network ID.

3. **Check for a default entry within the routing table**. Usually, a default entry points to a smarter router as its next-hop. If such an entry is found, the packet is delivered to the default next-hop router.

4. **Generate an error**. If none of these tasks succeed, then the packet is undeliverable and will generate a host unreachable or network unreachable error.

As you can see from the preceding steps, the router first checks whether a complete destination IP address is in the routing table. If this look-up fails, the router looks for a matching network ID. If this also fails, the router looks for a default entry. If there is no default entry, the router generates an error.

Now that you understand the basics of TCP/IP networking, read on to learn more about firewall technologies.

Packet Filtering

Packet filtering is the most basic form of firewall security. In this process, every packet that is routed between the internal and external components of the network through a firewall is monitored to check whether it should be allowed access to the respective network. Access is either allowed or denied based on the policy that you have set up on the firewall. Packet-filtering systems function according to the packet-filtering rules applied on layer 3 devices.

Routers are layer 3 devices that you can configure to filter data. Such routers, which also filter packets, are known as *screening routers*. Figure 4.6 shows a network with a screening router.

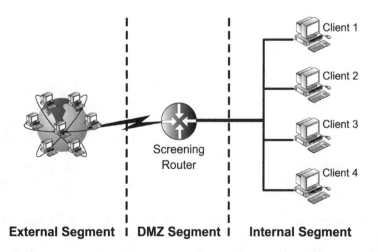

FIGURE 4.6 *A network connected to the Internet using a screening router*

Packet-filtering systems, such as screening routers, screen each packet and its header information to determine its origin, destination, and type and decide whether the packet should be allowed to pass. All packets have a packet header and a payload. The packet header contains the following details.

◆ Source of the packet

◆ Destination of the packet

◆ Type of packet

◆ Any additional details required in the packet

After the packets have been analyzed, the packet-filtering system completes one of following tasks.

◆ It accepts the packet, meaning that it lets the packet pass.

◆ It rejects the packet, meaning that it does not allow the packet to pass, and informs the source of the packet of the rejection.

◆ It denies the packet, meaning that the packet is discarded unbeknownst to the source.

The Filtering Process

As I explained in the preceding sections, an ordinary router routes packets without filtering them, whereas a screening router, which is used in a packet-filtering firewall, screens packets based on the packet-filtering rules that are applied to the router. A router can accept, deny, or reject the packet based on the filtering rules. Apart from these three basic actions, the screening router also logs the information about the packets and, if necessary, triggers an alarm when the security is breached.

The filtering process depends upon the filleting system used. There are three broad types of filtering systems in use.

◆ **Simple packet filtering**. A simple packet-filtering system screens a packet based on the source address, destination address, and ports to which the data is being sent. You can configure simple packet-filtering systems to disallow packets from all sources except those that are specifically listed for this purpose. Such a security strategy is called a *default denial strategy*. Similarly, you can deploy a default accept strategy in which you allow all source addresses except those specifically listed. You can configure the simple packet-filtering system to allow only those packets with certain destination addresses to enter the network. Additionally, you can configure the packet-filtering system to allow access to certain specified application ports and deny access to the rest.

◆ **State tracking**. In more complex packet-filtering systems, the filtering process is based on state tracking, a filtering system in which only those packets that arrive as responses for outgoing packets are allowed to enter the network. To identify an inbound session as a response, all outbound sessions are tracked.

Therefore, all inbound and outbound traffic is tracked by the filtering system. For state tracking, the routers should have more complex features than for simple filtering systems.

◆ **Protocol-based filtering systems**. In addition to the preceding filtering systems, there are packet-filtering systems that you can configure to check the protocol of the packets that are received. Some of the rules that can be set upon such packet-filtering systems can allow HTTP connections but deny FTP and SMTP connections. Packet filters that check protocols can also check to see whether a packet sent to a well-known port is formatted per the protocol expected by the port. For example, you can configure the packet-filtering system in such a way that all SMTP-based packets sent to port 80 can be rejected or denied.

 TIP

Many Internet-based services use the TCP or UDP port to communicate with each other. Some basic Internet applications and their respective ports include

◆ **HTTP**. Uses TCP port 80.

◆ **FTP**. Uses TCP port 21.

◆ **DNS**. Uses TCP and UDP port 53.

◆ **SMTP**. Uses port 25.

You can also find a list of port numbers in RFC 1700, which is an important document used by system architects to design packet-filtering systems.

Advantages of Packet Filtering

Packet filtering has a number of advantages and disadvantages. Some of the advantages follow.

◆ Packet-filtering helps you implement a choke point as a security strategy because it creates a single location in the network where a packet filter can be efficiently installed and monitored.

◆ The packet-filtering system can protect your network against sniffing, port scanning, and some kinds of network sweeping threats.

◆ A packet-filtering system can resolve some of the address-spoofing attacks on the network.

◆ Since packet filters operate at the Network layer, packet filtering eliminates the processing overhead by higher-level firewalls, such as application proxies. Therefore the performance and efficiency of packet filters is high.

Disadvantages of Packet Filtering

Packet filtering has some disadvantages as well.

◆ Packet filters drastically affect the router's performance because the router, besides performing the routing logic, must filter packets based on the rules applied. Therefore, separate resources are used for packet filtering, and the perimeter routers are not configured as screening firewalls.

◆ A packet-filtering system is useful only in networks for which a black-and-white security policy is advisable. In other words, a packet-filtering system does not check to see which user is trying to access the network, but only checks the packets to see what source, destination, or protocol is used within them.

◆ A packet-filtering system cannot protect your network against most address-spoofing, session-hijacking, or password attacks. In addition, viruses, trojan horses, and backdoors can also enter the network through HTTP tunneling protocols. Even stack-based buffer overflow attacks and Web application attacks cannot be effectively prevented using packet filtering.

Proxy Servers

Proxy servers are application-specific relay services. They provide services that control the exchange of data between two networks at the application level instead of at the IP level. They act in lieu of a given network's internal components.

 NOTE

There are different kinds of proxy servers and proxy technologies. Proxy servers are also called *application proxies, circuit proxies, caching proxies,* and *application-level gateways.* Although different vendors of the technology use different names for the proxy service, the underlying concept for all of these different types of services remains the same.

Generally, a proxy server monitors information through an application gateway between the network and the Internet. Using a proxy server, you can disable IP routing between the Internet and the internal components of the network. Once IP routing is disabled, the internal components of the network will not be able to directly interact with any external component of the non-secured network.

Features of a Proxy Server

Proxy servers include several features that make them suitable for managing data flow between networks. Some of the important features include

♦ **Transparency to network components**. Proxy servers are typically transparent. Therefore, neither the internal components of the network nor the external components of the Internet are aware of the existence of the proxy service. For the external components of the network, the proxy server acts as the host for the application service. Similarly, the host of the application service gets a notion that it is interacting directly with the external components on the Internet.

♦ **Application-specific services**. Proxy services are written for a specific application protocol. The application-specific protocol used for the proxy service can be a common protocol such as HTTP, FTP, or Telnet. Since the proxy service is written for a specific application, a service can actively participate to monitor protocol-specific activities for the application. For example, you can configure a proxy server to allow or disallow specific domains on the Internet from accessing the internal components of a network.

 NOTE

A proxy service is offered by any proxy server. In this section, the two terms have been used interchangeably, with each term being used where appropriate.

♦ **Single point of contact**. Proxy services are a single point of contact for the external hosts on the Internet and the internal hosts within the network. The advantage of having a proxy server as a single host that communicates on the Internet is that only the proxy server is assigned a valid IP address. The components of the trusted network can therefore be assigned IP addresses at the discretion of the network administrator.

♦ **Ability to perform user authentication**. A proxy server can act as a user authentication service. You can configure it to only allow certain users on the internal network to access the Internet.

♦ **Execution on a dual-homed host**. Proxy servers require a dual-homed host to execute. A dual-homed host is a host system that has two network interfaces—one exposed to the untrusted network, such as the Internet, and the other exposed to the internal or trusted network. The IP addresses of the two network interfaces are unique. Figure 4.7 illustrates a proxy server running on a dual-homed host.

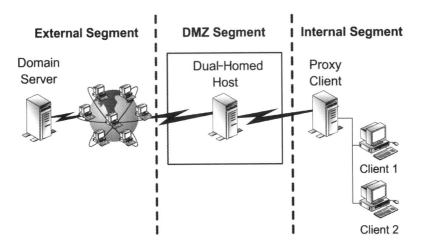

FIGURE 4.7 *A proxy server running on a dual-homed host*

As shown in Figure 4.7, a proxy service includes a domain server, a proxy server, and a proxy client.

◆ **Domain server**. This serves application services, such as Telnet, FTP, or HTTP, for the client.

◆ **Proxy server**. This server transparently manages the information that flows between the domain server and the proxy client. A proxy server, in effect, monitors the requests made by proxy clients and decides whether they should be processed.

◆ **Proxy client**. This is the internal component of the network that sends application service requests to the proxy server.

For the proxy service to work, you do not need any special hardware infrastructure on the network. You need proxy server software installed on the application gateway and you also need to configure the proxy clients to use the proxy server.

Requirements of a Proxy Service

Proxy services can range from caching proxies to generic proxies. Caching proxies cache information that is requested by clients. This helps reduce the load on the network because whenever a proxy client requests information from the Internet, it is served from the cache instead of the Internet.

Generic proxies are services that exchange information without providing any security. In addition to caching and generic proxies, proxy services also come in other flavors in which a proper security policy can be applied to the proxy server. The security policy can either allow or deny access to components of the external network.

For proxy services to work, the basic driving software is a proxy server. The foremost requirement for using a proxy server is that it should be installed on a multi-homed host. Next, you require a proxy-aware client system that can interact with the proxy server. This can be application software such as Telnet, an operating system, or a router.

To work with a proxy-aware application for a specific protocol, you need to configure the application to point to the proxy server that is installed on the network. For example, if your network is set up with a proxy as a gateway to the Internet, and you are planning to use Internet Explorer to browse the Internet, you have to configure Internet Explorer to point to the proxy server. This way, all requests made by the browser will be sent to the proxy server.

You can also use a proxy-aware router so that the client application is not aware of a proxy server. When you use this type of router, the client application can make requests on the network, and the router can intercept the requests and route them to the proxy server, which in turn can provide access to the Internet. A proxy service that uses a router to route the packets to the proxy server is called a *hybrid proxy*.

In such proxy services, the client is unaware of a proxy server. The client does not have to be set up to point to the proxy server. It becomes the router's responsibility to understand the protocol on which the packet is based and to route the packets to the proxy server. There are many routers available that provide smart routing capabilities.

SOCKS

SOCKS (*Socket Security*) is an IETF (*Internet Engineering Task Force*)-approved standard. It is available as an RFC 1928 document. SOCKS is a generic proxy protocol for TCP/IP-based applications. It is a type of proxy system that supports proxy-aware applications and clients and integrates security concepts within the framework. SOCKS can be used as a network firewall, a generic application proxy, or in VPNs. The SOCKS proxy allows many Internet services, including HTTP, chat, and ICQ.

A SOCKS package is typically made up of the following components.

- ◆ A SOCKS server for the specified operating system
- ◆ SOCKS client programs such as Telnet, FTP, or Internet browsers
- ◆ A SOCKS client library

The SOCKS server is implemented at the Application layer, and the SOCKS client is implemented between the Application layer and the Transport layer of the TCP/IP stack. The SOCKS protocol provides access to hosts from one side of the SOCKS server to the other. In other words, the SOCKS protocol allows hosts within a secured network to access services outside the network. However, it does not allow external components to access services within the network.

Within the SOCKS proxy services, the client runs a modified TCP/IP protocol stack to access the SOCKS server that authenticates the request. In other words, the SOCKS protocol provides encapsulation for the information sent from the client to the SOCKS server. The request sent by the client contains details such as IP address, port number, and the protocol that is being used. However, the SOCKS server removes these details from the request and then forwards it to the appropriate domain on the Internet.

The SOCKS proxy server does not forward the client details because it does not want the external network components to gather information about the client that generated the request. This provides a level of anonymity so that an individual trying to gather information about the network is unable to identify the internal network hosts.

Versions of SOCKS

There are two versions of SOCKS available—SOCKS version 4 and SOCKS version 5. The SOCKS version 4 protocol performs three functions.

- ◆ **Establishes a connection**. The protocol obtains a connection to the external network component on behalf of the client.
- ◆ **Sets up proxy circuits**. A SOCKS proxy server enables you to set up proxy circuits, which are created between the external application and the client.
- ◆ **Relays application data**. The SOCKS protocol relays data from the client to the external network host and back.

SOCKS version 5 builds on the features of SOCKS version 4 and adds an additional user authentication feature. Generally, whenever you discuss SOCKS protocols, you should refer to SOCKS version 5 because it is the most recent version.

Advantages of SOCKS

The SOCKS protocol is used primarily because of its simplicity and flexibility. The protocol provides rapid deployment of new network applications, simple network security policy management, transparency for accessing the network across multiple proxy servers, and authentication and encryption methods. Some of the important benefits of the SOCKS protocol are summarized here.

- ◆ **User authentication**. The SOCKS protocol authenticates users before establishing communication. For each TCP or UDP communication, the SOCKS protocol transfers information from the SOCKS client to the SOCKS server, authenticates the user, verifies the communication channel, and guarantees the integrity of the channel.
- ◆ **Application-independent proxy**. The SOCKS protocol manages and protects the channel for an application. A SOCKS protocol is a generic proxy service that can be used by any application without a special proxy configuration.
- ◆ **Bi-directional proxy support**. Unlike many firewall technologies, SOCKS supports a bi-directional proxy protocol. Bi-directional proxy support is the ability

to allow the external network components to establish communication channels back to the proxy server. This way, multiple communication channels can be opened simultaneously on a single SOCKS proxy server, which manages the relay of data that is received through a communication channel to an appropriate client within the internal network.

◆ **Access control policies**. The SOCKS protocol provides the flexibility to manage network communication through access control lists based on diverse parameters such as users, IP addresses, application protocols, and time.

Advantages of Proxy Services

In the preceding sections, I explained the concept and requirements of proxy services. In this section, I will describe the advantages of using proxy services.

◆ **Proxy services provide caching**. All of the clients within an internal network need to go through a single instance of a proxy system. Since most information can be reused, the proxy server can cache the information requested by the clients so that the next time they request the same information, the proxy server can serve the information from the cache. This increases the performance of the network.

◆ **Proxy services provide intelligent filtering**. Proxy services are more intelligent than packet-filtering systems because a proxy service can be set up at the application level, unlike packet-filtering systems. Therefore, proxy services can screen application-specific content more effectively.

◆ **Proxy services provide user authentication**. Packet-filtering systems provide access control policies for packets based on only the source address, destination address, communication protocol, and the respective port being used. In a packet-filtering system, there is no way to identify the user who has requested the information. In a proxy service, you can create an effective access control list to allow or disallow certain users from accessing certain services on the Internet.

◆ **Proxy services provide application-level logging**. Since a proxy service executes on the Application layer, it has the ability to understand the application-level protocols. Therefore, it can log application-level information, which can help system administrators monitor network activity.

Disadvantages of Proxy Services

Proxy services have some disadvantages. For example, the client cannot automatically detect the proxy address and use it to access the external network. Similarly, proxy servers cannot be configured to manage traffic on all protocols. The disadvantages of proxy servers are detailed here.

◆ **Proxy services require client modification**. Proxy services require a proxy client to be configured in such a way that the client is aware of the proxy server.

Although this is not always the case, most of the proxy implementations require some client-side configuration.

◆ **Proxy services are protocol-specific**. Proxy servers are specifically written for a given application protocol because the server needs to understand the specifications of the protocol to effectively relay data between a host on the Internet and a client within the internal network. Although proxies that provide generic protection and features are also available, they are not as effective as a protocol-specific proxy services. If a network administrator needs to implement different types of proxy services, such as HTTP or FTP proxy, then the maintenance of all of these different servers is an additional overhead.

◆ **Proxy services have low performance**. Proxy services do not have very good performance because of the application-level overhead that is involved in processing the information that arrives at the Application layer.

User Authentication

Authentication and auditing services are the most basic technologies that must be used in any security model for a system. Securing networks using firewalls definitely requires authentication to identify the user and auditing to monitor the network. There are different technologies available for authentication, authorization, and auditing. Kerberos is one such technology. In this section, I will discuss the Kerberos technology for user authentication.

Kerberos

Most of the services on the network need to abide by a security policy to ensure that a proper security model is applied. You need to ensure that only authenticated users are using the services available on the network.

Kerberos is a technology that provides centralized authentication and authorization for the network. It enables authentication based on user identity to allow or disallow use of the system. Kerberos also provides authorization—that is, access control based on user identity. For example, after a user is authenticated, he or she might be authorized to access HTTP and SMTP services, but blocked from accessing FTP services.

Kerberos implements secure communication by enabling cryptographic keys within the model. It is based on the TCP/IP protocol stack and is used primarily in application-level protocols such as Telnet or FTP. It can also be used on Transport and Network layers such as TCP, UDP, and IP.

How Kerberos Works

Kerberos is a network authentication system that is mainly used for securing physical networks to avoid eavesdropping or replay attacks. It provides data stream integrity and secrecy by using cryptographic systems such as DES. It is based on third-party authentication protocols that are trusted by the Kerberos model.

Typically, the model works by introducing the concept of tickets that clients or services on the network can use to effectively identify themselves. A ticket is a sequence of a few hundred bytes that can be embedded in any network protocol, thereby allowing the protocol to ensure the identity of the principals involved. Tickets are also used to identify the user to other principals.

In a Kerberos model, a specific administrative host on the network performs primary tasks that conform to the Kerberos model. Such a host provides administrative features and centralized key management for the model. The host is also named as a Kerberos authentication server that maintains a list of all of the users' secret keys. The Kerberos model also generates keys based on specific sessions between two communication end points to secure the connection from sniffers.

To understand the workings of Kerberos, you need to understand the concept of *realms*. A realm is a security domain that has its own authentication server, for which it has its own security policy. Realms can accept or reject authentication from other realms. They are also hierarchical—they contain child realms and parent realms (see Figure 4.8).

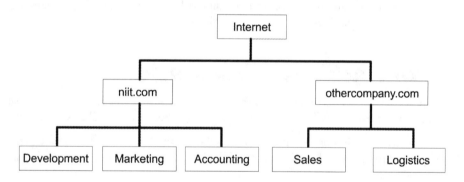

FIGURE 4.8 *The hierarchy of realms in the Kerberos model*

The hierarchical structure shown in Figure 4.8 enables realms to share authentication information with other realms that have no direct contact with each other. For example, if a network uses a Kerberos model with a realm posed as niit.com, the realm might have child realms, such as Development and Marketing. If a user has been authenticated to a child realm, marketing.niit.com, and wants to use information from another child realm, development.niit.com, you do not need to reauthenticate the user because his or her identity is passed between the child realms through the parent realm.

The child realms of the parent realm trust each other. If sales.othercompany.com, a child realm of othercompany.com, wants to share information with realms under niit.com, then Kerberos authenticates the user before sharing any information.

Goals for the Kerberos Security Model

The three primary goals of the Kerberos security model are as follows.

◆ **Authentication**. Authentication is a process in which the identity of the user is verified to determine whether he or she should be allowed to access the realms of the Kerberos model. Kerberos provides many authentication techniques. A user can use a smart card or some kind of a hardware token to identify himself or herself to the computer. Some enhanced versions of authentication also use biometric measures to identify a user.

◆ **Authorization**. Authorization is a process in which the Kerberos model determines the user's access privileges to allow access to only those resources that fall within the access control list for that particular user.

◆ **Accounting and auditing**. The Kerberos model assigns user quotas and other accounting criteria for the user to limit the use of resources. The Kerberos model also audits the user transactions with the computer, which makes it easy to trace a particular action to a specific user.

Network Address Translation

As more systems begin connecting to the Internet, the number of IP addresses available is being reduced every day. There is a shortage of IP addresses in the Class C address space.

In the current version of the IP addressing schema, an IP address of 4 bytes represents a unique identity for a host on the Internet. The address is represented in a dotted-quad format, such as:

```
140.253.14.40
```

Since there are only 4 bytes to represent the IP address, the total number of IP addresses available is 2^{32}. In other words, 4,294,967,296 IP addresses can be assigned to hosts on the Internet. Although this is the theoretical limit, the actual limit is much smaller. Therefore, all of the estimated 4 billion addresses cannot be used. According to an estimate, only about 2 billion of these addresses can be used for practical purposes. Considering the ever-increasing number of hosts connecting to the Internet, these 2 billion addresses will be completely used up in the near future.

A way to solve the problem of the IP address shortage must be found. Certain protocols, such as IPv6, are emerging to solve this problem. Meanwhile, NAT is a quick fix to resolve the problem.

NAT is a routing scheme created to provide a solution for the shortage of IP addresses and to facilitate proper security on a given network and flexibility in network administration. In other words, NAT provides a means for private networks to connect to the Internet without worrying about the security risks involved or about using valid IP addresses for the internal network hosts.

NAT allows a network administrator to use a set of IP addresses for the internal hosts, which might not be valid in the sense that these IP addresses have not been assigned by any controlling authority and do not necessarily represent unique addresses on the Internet. NAT uses one set of IP addresses for the internal network components and a different set for communicating on the Internet.

NAT does not provide its own security per se, but it helps hide the internal components from the external network components. NAT enables a network administrator to connect multiple computers to the Internet using a single IP address. Not only is this a choke-point strategy, but it is also cost effective for small businesses and home users.

How NAT Works

Assume that an ISP assigns only one IP address to a small business organization, and the organization wants to connect more than one computer to the Internet. By using NAT, the organization can share the IP address among multiple local computers within the network. All local computers can connect to the Internet at the same time. Moreover, the Internet will not be aware of this division within the internal network.

NAT provides firewall-style security without any specific setup for the network because only the local computers within the network can access the Internet. NAT uses a router to provide firewall security. The computers on the Internet are unable to reach the local computers because they are not even aware that these local computers exist.

 TIP

Although there are many ways to provide basic access for an outside host to connect to an internal component, it is not advisable to open the internal components to the Internet.

When an internal network component sends some information to a host on the Internet, NAT modifies the source address of the packets to make them look as if they have been sent from a valid IP address. When an external component on the Internet wants to send a packet to any of the internal components, the packet is first sent to the NAT system, which in turn modifies the destination address of the packet and directs it to the internal host. Figure 4.9 illustrates the concept of NAT.

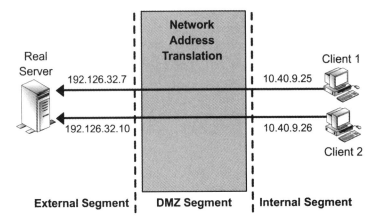

FIGURE 4.9 *The NAT system*

> ### NOTE
>
> At any given point in time, there are relatively few users within the local network who will be accessing the Internet. NAT takes advantage of this fact and provides the process-switching feature, which modifies the source address of the packets that are going outside the network so that they are directed to the appropriate next-hop router in the external network.

Figure 4.10 depicts the actual process by which the IP addresses on the local network are exposed to the registered IP address on the Internet.

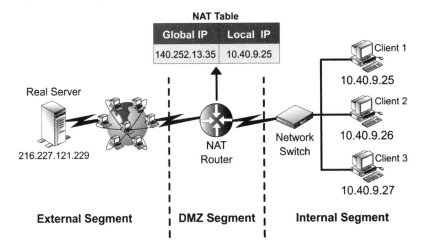

FIGURE 4.10 *The NAT process*

TRAFFIC TYPES SUPPORTED BY NAT

NAT supports only specific protocols. Before you implement NAT, you need to know which protocols are supported so that you configure it only for those protocols. NAT supports the following traffic types.

- ◆ HTTP (*Hypertext Transfer Protocol*)
- ◆ FTP (*File Transfer Protocol*)
- ◆ TFTP (*Trivial File Transfer Protocol*)
- ◆ TCP (*Transmission Control Protocol*)
- ◆ NTP (*Network Time Protocol*)
- ◆ NFS (*Network File System*)
- ◆ Telnet
- ◆ ICMP (*Internet Control Message Protocol*)
- ◆ NetBIOS over TCP (datagram and name service only)
- ◆ DNS (*Domain Name Service*)
- ◆ DNS "A" and "PTR" queries
- ◆ Archie, which provides lists of anonymous FTP archives
- ◆ rlogin, rsh, rcp ("r" services)
- ◆ Finger, a software tool for determining whether a person has an account at a particular Internet site
- ◆ Progressive Networks RealAudio
- ◆ H.323
- ◆ VDOLive
- ◆ NetMeeting

However, NAT does not support the following traffic types.

- ◆ IP Multicast
- ◆ DNS zone transfers
- ◆ SNMP (*Simple Network Management Protocol*)
- ◆ Routing table updates
- ◆ Talk
- ◆ BOOTP
- ◆ Netshow

The process depicted in Figure 4.10 encompasses several steps.

1. The host 10.40.9.25 attempts to connect to a valid IP 216.227.121.229.

2. The NAT system checks to see whether there is an entry for the source address that matches a global IP, which is an IP address of the inside host after the translation for the NAT system. This global IP is used to represent a valid source IP on the Internet.

3. When a match is found, the NAT system translates the local address to the global address. If a match is not found, the NAT system uses any IP from a pool of legal addresses that it maintains. Because the match is found in the current scenario, the local IP address 10.40.9.25 is translated to 140.252.13.35.

4. The NAT system sends the packet with the translated source address to the Internet.

5. The Internet host that has the IP address 216.227.121.229 receives the packet and responds to the same global IP address, which in this case is 140.252.13.35.

6. The NAT system again checks the mapping table and retrieves the local IP address, which maps to the destination address of the receiving packet. NAT translates the destination IP to the local IP. In the current scenario, the destination IP 140.252.13.35 is translated to 10.40.9.25.

NAT also uses many other address translation schemes to translate an internal address into an external address. The following section describes one such addressing mechanism.

Overloading Global IP

In the overloading global IP addressing schema, the NAT system allocates many local addresses to a single global IP address. When you overload a global IP address within the NAT system, it is the NAT system's responsibility to maintain high-level protocol information within the NAT table based on the port numbers for TCP or UDP. In other words, when many local addresses are mapped to a single global IP address, the NAT system uses the inside host's port numbers to maintain unique network addresses. Figure 4.11 shows this address translation schema.

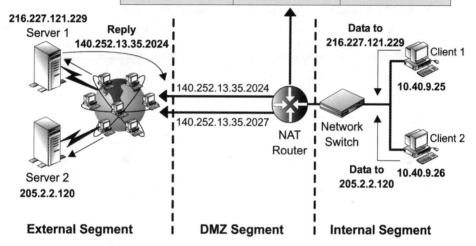

NAT Table

Inside IP and Port	Inside Global IP and Port	Outside Global IP and Port
10.40.9.25: 2024	140.252.13.35:2024	216.227.121.229:80
10.40.9.26: 2027	140.252.13.35:2027	205.2.2.120:80

FIGURE 4.11 *Overloading a global IP address*

In the process depicted in Figure 4.11, the network translation schema used by NAT encompasses several steps.

1. The host 10.40.9.25 tries to connect to 216.227.121.229.

2. When the first packet from 10.40.9.25 reaches the NAT system, the system checks the NAT table to look for a mapping. No translation entry is found for the local address. The NAT system will reuse the same global address for translation because overloading is enabled.

3. The NAT system uses the global IP address 140.252.13.35, but with a unique port number that is assigned to the global IP. In other words, the NAT system uses a unique IP 140.252.13.35: 2024 as the source address.

4. The receiving system 216.227.121.229 responds to the host 140.252.13.35: 2024.

5. The NAT system receives the packet from 216.227.121.229 and checks the destination IP in the NAT table. The NAT table provides a local IP address for the unique IP and port number combination that exists on the current packet. In the current scenario, the lookup retrieves the local IP address 10.40.9.25, and the NAT system replaces the destination IP with the retrieved local address.

Advantages of NAT

From the preceding section, it is clear that NAT is a mechanism to provide economy of usage for valid IP addresses that can be used on the Internet. In addition to this advantage, NAT also provides some security benefits.

◆ NAT enables the incremental increase or decrease of valid IP addresses without having to change the host switches or routers within a network.

◆ NAT helps hide the internal components of a network from the hosts on the Internet. This feature is a security advantage because it becomes difficult for a hacker to identify the numbers of internal systems within a network.

◆ NAT can be used for static address translation or configured for dynamic mapping, which allows flexibility in system configuration.

 NOTE

Static translation occurs when the system administrator manually configures an address table; dynamic translation occurs when the NAT system resolves the mappings using a specified schema, such as by overloading a global IP.

◆ NAT systems help restrict incoming network traffic. They can provide efficient restrictions on incoming traffic compared to other technologies, such as packet-filtering systems, because using dynamic translation schemas within an NAT system makes it very difficult for external networks to initiate any valid connection without the NAT system's knowledge.

Disadvantages of NAT

NAT also has several disadvantages, which are listed here.

◆ Since the NAT system hides the IP addresses of the true communication end points, some applications that use physical addresses will find it very difficult to relate with the NAT translation schema. However, if these applications can be rebuilt to use domain names instead of physical addresses, this disadvantage can be overcome.

◆ Since address translation occurs within the NAT system, many of the network-monitoring tools based on IP tracing will fail to provide realistic reports about the network because the tools do not yield the required results when translation occurs.

◆ NAT systems increase network latency because of the translation for every packet in an information stream. Since there will be thousands of packets traversing the NAT system at any given point in time, some delay in communication will result from the CPU usage to translate every packet.

◆ NAT systems interfere with network authentication schemes because these schemes, in a way, tamper with (or modify) the information contained within a packet. When this happens, NAT systems will violate the integrity check involved in many authentication systems. In such scenarios, the communication between the two end points fails.

◆ The dynamic address allocation involved in NAT systems generates reports that are difficult for those systems that monitor and audit the network to analyze. This is because after the address has been translated, the auditing log will contain the translated IP addresses, which would make sense only at the time of the session. The same translated IP address could be used to represent some other local host at a later time. Therefore, using the log reports to trace the involvement of the local host at any given time is very difficult.

Virtual Private Networks

A VPN is an extension of a local network that encompasses links across global networks such as the Internet. In a point-to-point link between two communication end points, you can ensure that the connection can be configured for high bandwidth and is secure because it is not shared by any other external elements. However, in a VPN, you are trying to connect two communication end points over a publicly shared network such as the Internet.

When you use the Internet as your media for information sharing, you are risking the integrity of the information. A VPN provides security for the information that is shared between two communication end points over the Internet. All VPNs allow users to obtain a remote connection to any host on the Internet and provide a point-to-point connection between the user and the host in a secure manner.

A VPN is based on the point-to-point private link model, where two communication end points across the Internet can share data with each other. A VPN encrypts the data that is shared between two communication end points for the sake of confidentiality. Packets that are sniffed by a hacker over the network are difficult to decrypt without the keys that were used to encrypt the data. This link, in which the communication data is encapsulated and encrypted, is known as the *VPN connection* (see Figure 4.12).

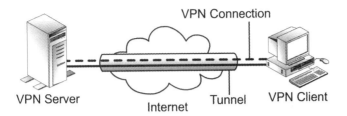

FIGURE 4.12 *A VPN connection*

The VPN depicted in Figure 4.12 enables encryption and integrity protection of the information that travels through the link. VPNs can be used to connect geographically separate nodes to interact with each other. This concept, called a *dedicated WAN link*, is based on a routed VPN connection across the Internet. The basic principle behind the VPN is to provide

◆ A point-to-point private link

◆ Information encryption and encapsulation

◆ Data integrity

VPN technology is designed to address various communication trends in the current era, which include

◆ Wireless distributed processing

◆ Field agents trying to telecommute back to a centralized database

◆ Globalized operations

◆ Increased security consciousness among home users

◆ Increased traffic flow of e-commerce

◆ Higher reliability on the Internet as a broadcasting and messaging medium

All of these types of information requirements need a secure communication channel for sharing information. To service all of these existing needs, you can use VPN technology in combination with an ISP and an existing networking infrastructure. Technically, VPNs are not a firewall technology. However, they cannot be ignored when you strategize a proper security model based on a firewall technology. You can use VPNs elaborately to provide remote access to centralized resources over the Internet, as depicted in Figure 4.13.

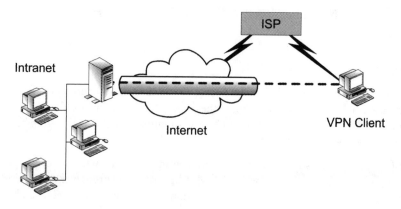

FIGURE 4.13 *Remote access using a VPN*

Figure 4.13 depicts the concept of using a local ISP to access a remote centralized database without worrying about the security or the cost that would have been incurred if any other methods were used.

VPN Requirements

VPNs are generally used in a remote-networking environment in which a remote client needs to access a centralized database over the Internet. When you implement a remote networking solution, you must ensure that only authentic users can access the network. The solution must allow geographically dispersed offices or roaming clients to connect to the centralized resource and share information. To provide such a solution in a secure mode, VPNs should provide the following functionality.

◆ **User authentication**. The VPN should establish a user's identity.

◆ **Authorization and auditing**. The VPN should enable restricted access to the resources and also monitor and audit access for the sake of traceability.

◆ **Data encryption**. The VPN should encrypt data transported across the Internet for its security.

◆ **Key management**. The VPN should constantly generate and refresh encryption keys for the client and the servers of the system.

◆ **Multi-protocol support**. The VPN should handle the common protocols that are used over the Internet, which typically include TCP/IP.

VPNs can include technologies such as IPSec to provide this functionality. There are also other enhanced VPN solutions based on PPTP (*Point-to-Point Tunneling Protocol*) or L2TP (*Layer 2 Tunneling Protocol*). These solutions are more enhanced than IPSec because they meet all of the requirements and provide all of the functionalities explained in the preceding list.

To understand VPN solutions based on PPTP or L2TP, you first need to understand the concept of tunneling.

Tunneling

Tunneling is a process in which data between two communication end points is transferred through a tunnel. This process includes the concepts of data encapsulation, data transmission, and data decapsulation. A tunnel is a communication channel to transfer data for a given network over another network.

The information that is transferred through a tunnel is initially of the originating network's protocol type. However, the final payload transferred through the tunnel is of the network type used to transfer data. This transition in protocol type is achieved by adding additional headers to the frame that was produced by the originating network. In other words, the originating frame will be encapsulated to the transit network type, which is the intermediate network.

The additional headers are used to route the payload over the intermediate network. The path through which the encapsulated payload travels is called a *tunnel*. Figure 4.14 illustrates the process of encapsulating a payload and tunneling it.

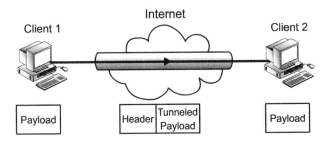

FIGURE 4.14 *Tunneling between communication end points*

The transit network shown in Figure 4.14 can be the Internet. After the payload reaches the appropriate destination, it is decapsulated and forwarded to the respective target on the other side of the network.

Following are some examples of the tunneling protocol.

◆ **PPTP**. This protocol enables the traffic of other protocols, such as IP and Net-BEUI, to be encrypted and encapsulated in an IP header that will be sent across the Internet.

◆ **L2TP**. This protocol enables the traffic of other protocols, such as IP and Net-BEUI, to be encrypted and sent over any medium that supports point-to-point datagram delivery, such as IP, X.25, Frame Relay, or ATM.

◆ **IPSec tunnel mode**. This protocol enables the IP packets to be encrypted and encapsulated in an IP header to be sent across the Internet.

The tunneling protocol requires the client and the server (the two communication end points) to use the same tunneling protocol at each end. Some of the tunneling protocols are listed in the preceding section. These protocols work on frames (layer 2) or on packets (layer 3). PPTP and L2TP are layer 2 protocols. They work on the frames that are generated by the Link layer (OSI layer). The IPSec tunnel mode works on IP packets that are generated at the Network layer (OSI layer).

Point-to-Point Protocol

PPP (*Point-to-Point Protocol*) is designed to work on slow-serial links. PPP is based on the concepts of SLIP (*Serial Line IP*) and contains the following components.

◆ A process to encapsulate IP packets over a serial line

◆ An LCP (*Link Control Protocol*) to create and monitor the data link

◆ Multiple NCPs such as IP, OSI, DECnet, and AppleTalk

The following phases illustrate the negotiation process within a PPP dial-up session.

◆ **PPP link establishment**. PPP uses LCP to establish, maintain, and end a physical connection.

◆ **User authentication**. In this phase, the client system provides the user's credentials to the remote access server. An authentication scheme at the server end authenticates the user's credentials. The following authentication procedures can be used at the server end.

  • **PAP (*Password Authentication Protocol*)**. PAP is a clear-text authentication scheme in which the server receives a user name and password, and PAP returns them in clear text.

  • **CHAP (*Challenge-Handshake Authentication Protocol*)**. CHAP is an encrypted authentication mechanism that sends a challenge to the remote client. The challenge consists of a session ID and an arbitrary challenge string. The remote client must use the MD5 one-way hashing algorithm to return the user name and an encryption of the challenge, session ID, and the client's password.

◆ **Invoking Network-layer protocol(s)**. After the previous two phases are sucessfully completed, PPP invokes various NCPs, such as IP or AppleTalk, which were selected during the link establishment phase.

◆ **Data transmission**. Finally, if all of the preceding phases are successful, PPP will start transmitting the data across the communication end points. The payload will have an additional PPP header before transmission.

Point-to-Point Tunneling Protocol

PPTP is a tunneling protocol that is based on the Link layer. In other words, it is a layer 2 protocol. PPTP uses the PPP frames within IP packets so that the packets can be transmitted over the Internet. RFC 2637 provides the architectural details of PPTP. If data has to be transmitted over the Internet (TCP/IP network), PPTP uses TCP to maintain the tunnel for communication. PPTP also relies on the GRE (*Generic Routing Encapsulation*) protocol to provide encapsulation for the PPP frames over the Internet. Figure 4.15 illustrates a PPTP packet.

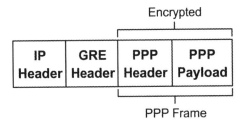

FIGURE 4.15 *The PPTP packet structure*

Layer 2 Tunneling Protocol

L2TP is also a tunneling protocol based on the Link layer. In other words, it is also a layer 2 protocol. It is a mixture of PPTP and the L2F (*Layer 2 Forwarding*) mechanism that has been created by Cisco Systems. In general, L2TP provides PPP encapsulation over IP, Frame Relay, ATM, and X.25. RFC 2661 provides the architectural details of L2TP. If data has to be transmitted over the Internet (TCP/IP network), L2TP will use UDP and a series of other L2TP messages to maintain the tunnel of communication. Figure 4.16 illustrates an L2TP packet.

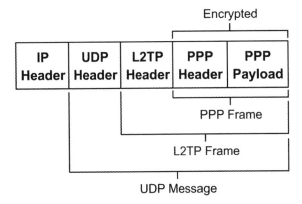

FIGURE 4.16 *The L2TP packet structure*

Internet Protocol Security (IPSec) Tunnel Mode

IPSec is a tunneling protocol that is based on the Network layer, which is layer 3 of the OSI model. IPSec tunnel mode is used to transfer information from one communication end point to another in a secure manner.

IPSec provides encryption mechanisms for the traffic on the Internet. In general, it provides a definition for the IP packets that are transferred over the tunnel. IPSec tunnel mode provides encryption and encapsulation for the IP packets that need to be sent across a private or a public network. When a tunnel server receives the encapsulated data, it will decapsulate the payload and eventually decrypt it to obtain the original IP packet. Once the original IP packet is obtained, the packet is routed to the appropriate target within the network.

 NOTE

IPSec is defined in a series of RFCs, such as RFC 2401, RFC 2402, and RFC 2406. These RFCs define the architectural details of IPSec, such as authentication headers, encapsulation, data integrity, and data encryption.

The main constituents of the IPSec protocol as defined by IETF are data encryption and data integrity. IPSec uses the concept of security keys for encryption and decryption of data. The features of IPSec are as follows.

◆ IPSec allows only IP packets for communication. No other protocols are supported.

◆ IPSec is based on a security policy that establishes the encryption and tunneling mechanisms to be used.

Since IPSec is a layer 3 protocol, it provides security for the complete network. This implies that any layer above the Network layer (until the Application layer) is covered under the IPSec security. IPSec tunnel mode uses the following mechanisms to ensure data integrity.

◆ **Negotiated Security Association**. The first packet that is triggered between two communication end points will initiate a negotiation process for a security association between the two end points. The negotiation is based on a standard protocol called IKE (*Internet Key Exchange*). The IKE negotiation provides data security mechanisms between the two end points and generates a security key that is shared by the end points for data encryption. Once this security association succeeds, the transmission of the payload, whose integrity and encryption is ensured by IPSec, can be initiated.

◆ **Authentication Header (AH)**. IPSec uses the AH to provide authentication and integrity for the source without using encryption. The AH contains a sequence number and the authentication data that is used to verify the identity of the sender and the integrity of the data. It is located between the IP header and the transport header.

◆ **Encapsulating Security Payload (ESP)**. IPSec uses ESP to provide authentication and integrity along with encryption. Unlike AH, ESP provides a mechanism to encrypt the IP payload. ESP is used whenever confidentiality of data is required.

IPSec uses many security algorithms based on cryptography to secure the information over the network. These algorithms include

◆ DES

◆ RSA crypto system

◆ Hashed message authentication code

◆ Diffie-Hellman key agreement

Advantages of Virtual Private Networks

VPN allows you to create a virtual network for your enterprise. Using VPN, you can implement a cost-effective solution for connecting your enterprise on a public network. The advantages of VPN are

◆ **Internet as a communication medium**. A VPN uses the Internet as its communication medium. This provides an economical measure to connect geographically dispersed systems using secure tunnels.

◆ **Secure access to protocols**. VPNs provide security for many protocols that do not inherently support security features. For example, protocols based on SMB do not easily participate in packet filtering and proxying for secure communication. However, VPN provides remote access for these protocols in a secure way.

◆ **Overall encryption method**. VPN provides overall encryption for the network traffic because it conceals the information for the internal components of the network that need to be revealed within the payload. VPN achieves this by encrypting all of the information about the source addresses and the protocol headers within the payload.

Disadvantages of Virtual Private Networks

Some of the disadvantages of VPN are

◆ **Security limited to communication**. Since VPN relies on another existing network as its communication medium, the host that connects to the transition network, such as the Internet, is still vulnerable to attack by other openings on the network. VPN only guarantees security and integrity of data that travels between the client and the server. After the client obtains the information, it is the client's responsibility to secure it, and VPN does not guarantee security beyond communication.

◆ **Possible security threat**. If a host using the VPN is hacked, the hacked system can take advantage of the VPN connection on the host and attack other connected systems by using the VPN itself. Securing such remote ends from external attacks is the most important thing that you must consider before enabling VPN on remote systems.

Summary

This chapter provided a detailed overview of different firewall technologies such as packet filtering, proxying, NAT, and VPNs. It also explained user authentication using Kerberos as the security model and provided a detailed explanation of different types of tunneling technologies, such as PPTP, L2TP, and IPSec. The next chapter, which explains firewall architectures, will build on the concepts that you learned in this chapter.

Check Your Understanding

Multiple Choice Questions

1. Which of the following are common features of a firewall?
   a. Data filtering
   b. Access control
   c. Snooping
   d. Social engineering

2. Which of the following can be considered firewall technologies?
   a. Packet filtering
   b. TCP/IP
   c. Network Address Translation
   d. Network switch

3. On which of the following ports does an SMTP service execute?
   a. Port 80
   b. Port 53
   c. Port 21
   d. Port 25

4. Which of the following protocols can be used to construct VPN tunnels?
   a. PPTP
   b. PPP
   c. L2TP
   d. NAT

Short Questions

1. List the common features of a firewall.
2. What is the main advantage of using a proxy server instead of a packet-filtering system?

Answers

Multiple Choice Answers

1. a and b. The common features of a firewall are data filtering and access control.
2. a and c. Packet filtering and Network Address Translation are firewall technologies.
3. d. The SMTP service executes on port 25.
4. a and c. The PPTP and L2TP protocols can be used for VPN.

Short Answers

1. Some of the common features of a firewall are

   - Data filtering
   - Traffic control
   - Perimeter defense
   - User authentication
   - Access control
   - Network monitoring
   - Logging activities
   - Triggering events based on predefined alerts

2. Unlike packet-filtering systems that only provide a black-and-white security policy, a proxy service can provide authentication based on users. Packet-filtering systems provide access control policies for packets based on only the source address, destination address, communication protocol, and respective port being used. A packet-filtering system has no way of identifying the user of the application. However, a proxy service uses an effective access control list to allow or disallow certain users access to certain services on the Internet.

Chapter 5

*Firewall
Architectures*

As a network administrator, you are responsible for securing your organization's network. By now you know that a firewall is a very good option that you can use. However, just knowing what firewalls are and how they work will not empower you to build secure networks.

When you build a house, why do you consult an architect? You might have all of the components to build a house, but the architect tells you where to put each component so that you have a safe, secure, and comfortable house. Similarly, to build a secure network, you need to know the architectural details—you need to know where to put each component. Just as the architect might design your house differently than your friend's house, the architecture and design of each network might be different. The design of the network and the placement, structure, and configuration of the firewall will differ based on various factors including the size of the network, the network traffic, and your specific network requirements.

In this chapter, I'll discuss various firewall architectures that you can use to secure your network. Analyzing the different architectures will help you decide which one to implement in your network.

You can categorize firewall architectures based on the firewall placement and the network (or data) that needs to be protected. The primary architectures are dial-up, single router, screened, and screened subnet architectures. They are all described in this chapter.

Dial-Up Architecture

If you are using a dial-up service, such as an ISDN line, you might use a third network card to provide a filtered DMZ. In such a configuration, your local area network and ISDN line use the first and second network cards.

You use a DMZ if you want to host your own Internet services without sacrificing unauthorized access to your private network. The DMZ is placed between the Internet and your internal network's line of defense, which is usually a combination of firewalls and bastion hosts. Typically, the DMZ contains devices that provide access to Internet traffic such as Web servers, FTP servers, e-mail servers, and DNS servers. A DMZ provides full control over your Internet services but keeps them separate from your regular network.

Figure 5.1 illustrates the dial-up architecture.

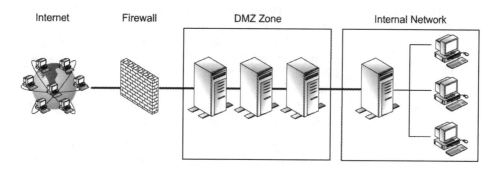

FIGURE 5.1 *Dial-up firewall architecture*

Single Router Architecture

Single router architecture is one of the simplest firewall architectures. In this design, you can place a single router at the end of the network, and all traffic will pass through it. You can apply filters on the router to ensure secure and authentic communication.

In the single router architecture, you can use a cable modem to accomplish the authentication and security functions performed by a router. Figure 5.2 illustrates the single router architecture.

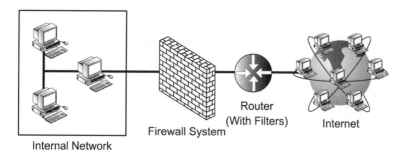

FIGURE 5.2 *Single router architecture*

Dual Router Architecture

Dual router architecture is an addition or variation to single router architecture. In this architecture, two routers filter network traffic. Dual router architecture might be implemented by using one router to filter network traffic from the internal network to the perimeter network, and the other router to filter traffic from the perimeter network to the Internet.

To understand dual router architecture, consider a common setup in which two routers can provide better security than one. Suppose you have a firewall that protects more than one network, say LAN A and LAN B. Assume that the firewall allows specific application-level access to LAN A and provides access to services such as Telnet and FTP on LAN B. In such a scenario, you can use the first router to secure communication to LAN A and the second to prevent TELNET, FTP, and other unauthorized access to LAN B. In such a configuration, even if the firewall is compromised due to misconfiguration or any other reason, the second router will ensure that LAN B is secure.

It is important to remember that the dual router architecture does not automatically provide greater security. You need to carefully consider the implementation and placement of the routers to derive security.

Dual-Homed Host Architecture

The *dual-homed host architecture* is based on the concept of a dual-homed host computer. Such a computer has two network interfaces—the Internet or any external network and the internal network. The host can route IP packets between the networks to which these interfaces are attached.

To implement the dual-homed host firewall architecture, you need to disable the routing function so that IP packets from one network are not directly routed to the other network. When that happens, systems inside the firewall (within the internal network) and systems outside the firewall (on the external network) can communicate with the dual-homed host. However, these systems cannot communicate with each other directly.

Figure 5.3 illustrates the network architecture for a dual-homed host firewall.

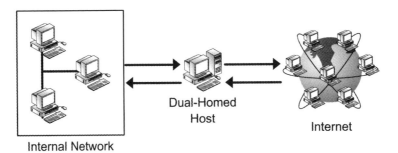

Dual-Homed
Host

Internet

Internal Network

FIGURE 5.3 *Dual-homed host architecture*

Screened Host Architecture

Unlike the dual-homed host architecture, in *screened host architecture*, a host that is connected only to the internal network provides all network services. A screening router acts as the interface between the internal and external networks. This router provides the primary security by filtering all of the data packets.

The host on the internal network is a bastion host. The screening router is set up in such a way that hosts on the Internet can only open connections to the bastion host. The bastion host can then permit or reject connections to the Internet, thus maintaining a high level of security.

Packet filtering done by the screening router can allow internal hosts to open connections to the Internet for certain services or reject all connection attempts from internal hosts to the Internet, forcing the internal hosts to route their connection requests through the bastion host.

Figure 5.4 illustrates the screened host architecture.

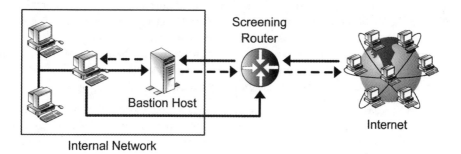

FIGURE 5.4 *Screened host architecture*

 NOTE

A bastion host acts as a gateway between internal and external networks. The bastion host is designed to defend against attacks aimed at the internal network.

The screened host architecture provides better security than the dual-homed architecture because it is easier to configure and manage a router than a host. However, the screened host architecture is not foolproof. If an attacker manages to break into the bastion host, the internal network is open. Also, if the screening router is compromised, the attacker can gain access to the internal network. The screened subnet architecture offers higher security to overcome this threat.

Screened Subnet Architecture

The *screened subnet architecture* offers added security to the screened host architecture. In addition to the bastion host and the screening router, this architecture adds a perimeter network to the design, further isolating the internal network from the external network.

In this architecture, the bastion host is placed on the perimeter network. Instead of one screening router that acts as the interface between the internal and the external networks in the screened host architecture, there are two routers—the interior router and the exterior router. The interior router, also called the *choke router*, acts as the interface between the internal network and the perimeter network. The exterior router, also called the *access router*, acts as the interface between the perimeter network and the Internet (or any other external network).

This architecture is more secure that the dual-homed host and screened host architectures because the bastion host, by nature, is an enticing target for intruders. In the case of the screened host architecture, access to the bastion host leaves the entire network vulnerable to attack. However, in the screened subnet architecture, the bastion host does not have direct access to the internal network. As a result, if an attacker compromises the bastion host, the internal network is not automatically exposed.

You can make the screened subnet architecture as simple or complex as you need. In its simplest form, this architecture has a single perimeter network with a bastion host and two screening routers. You can add as many layers of perimeter networks as you want to secure your network. However, make sure that you set different levels of security at each perimeter network to make it difficult for intruders to invade the network. An architecture that consists of multiple perimeter networks (for increased levels of security) is called a *multiple screened subnet architecture*.

Figure 5.5 depicts the screened subnet architecture in its simplest form.

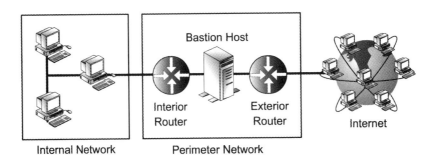

FIGURE 5.5 *The screened subnet architecture*

NOTE

A perimeter network acts as an additional layer of security between your internal and external networks. In an Ethernet-based network, you can view all network traffic from a bastion host. If an intruder breaks into a bastion host, it is very easy to intercept all traffic. A perimeter network offers an added level of security because the bastion host does not directly interact with the internal hosts, so traffic between two internal hosts does not pass through the bastion host. Even if an intruder accesses the bastion host, the internal traffic, which is presumably sensitive, is not visible to the intruder. The intruder can only view traffic flowing from the Internet and some internal host to the bastion host and back. Therefore, the internal traffic is secure from the intruder.

Variations to the Screened Subnet Architecture

In the previous section, I discussed the ideal screened subnet architecture. However, you can make variations to this architecture to match the requirements of your network.

Multiple Bastion Hosts

So far, I have described screened subnet architecture with a single bastion host. You generally use this configuration when you set up your firewall with screened subnet architecture. However, you can set up a firewall with multiple bastion hosts to improve performance, introduce redundancy, and separate data and servers.

Network performance is an important criterion that can influence your decision to have more than one bastion host. The following scenarios depict some cases in which you might have more than one bastion host.

♦ You are hosting certain services, such as SMTP, for internal users and certain other services, such as FTP, for external users. In such a scenario, you can have one bastion host that provides services to internal users and another that supports services on the Internet. This way, the internal users are not affected by the traffic generated by the Internet users.

♦ You are using network-intensive services, such as newsgroups. You can dedicate one bastion host to such services so that other services can work without being affected.

♦ You want to introduce redundancy in your network, so that if one bastion host fails, the others can continue to provide services to the network. However, this condition is only true for specific services, such as DNS or SMTP.

◆ You want to separate data from servers. For example, suppose you offer HTTP services to your internal users as well as to users on the Internet. You can have one host serve the internal users and another serve the external users. Therefore, you can provide different data to the different user sets without the risk of compromising confidential data. This configuration not only enhances the performance of your network, but also the security of data.

Figure 5.6 depicts a firewall structure with two bastion hosts.

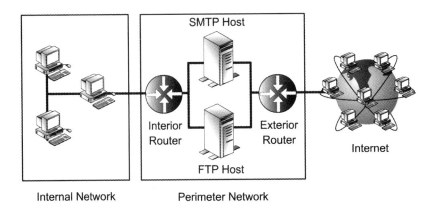

FIGURE 5.6 *Screened subnet architecture with two bastion hosts*

One Router Acting as the Interior and Exterior Router

This is another variation to the screened subnet architecture. Instead of having two routers, you can use a single router that acts as the interior and exterior router. To configure your firewall in this manner, you need to use routers on which you can specify both inbound and outbound filters on each interface. The routers that you select must be capable of supporting this kind of packet filtering.

This variation does not necessarily have many advantages, but it is definitely an option. One advantage to this option is that it saves the cost of acquiring multiple routers. However, the main disadvantage is that to access your internal network, attackers now need to break into only one router instead of two, as in the case of the traditional screened subnet architecture. Therefore, weigh the pros and cons before you decide on the implementation of the screened subnet architecture.

Figure 5.7 depicts the screened subnet architecture with a single router acting as both the interior and exterior routers.

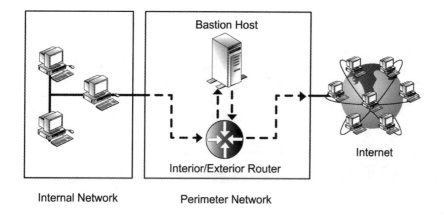

FIGURE 5.7 *Screened subnet architecture with a single router*

A Bastion Host Acting as the Exterior Router

You can use a single dual-homed computer as both your bastion host and your exterior router. However, as in all situations, you must carefully consider your requirements. For example, if you only have a single dial-up PPP connection to the Internet and you are running a PPP package on your bastion host, you might use the bastion host as the exterior router as well because you don't need the exceptionally good performance or flexibility of a dedicated router for a single low-bandwidth connection.

This configuration is functionally equivalent to the interior router/bastion host/exterior router configuration for the traditional screened subnet architecture. In this configuration, you might or might not have the ability to use packet filtering, depending on the operating system and software that you use. However, because the exterior router does not have to do much packet filtering anyway, using an interface package that does not have good packet-filtering capabilities is not a serious problem.

This configuration is slightly more vulnerable than the traditional architecture because the bastion host is exposed to the Internet without the protection of the exterior router. The only protection is the packet-filtering capabilities that the host's own interface package offers.

Figure 5.8 depicts the use of the screened subnet architecture with the bastion host acting as the exterior router.

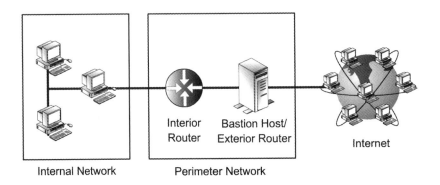

FIGURE 5.8 *Screened subnet architecture with the bastion host acting as the exterior router*

Multiple Exterior Routers

There are some situations in which you might decide to use multiple exterior routers in the same perimeter network. The most common situation is probably when you have multiple connections to the Internet. You can also have multiple exterior routers if you have connections to the Internet and parallel connections to other sites, such as the site of your partner organization.

Multiple exterior routers increase the performance of your network. They do not pose any significant security threat because they work the same way as a single exterior router. The only point that you might want to remember is that when you have two exterior routers, you double the chance of an intruder breaking into one of the routers. However, a break-in on an exterior router is not a major security risk for your network. Determine what information the intruder can access and then decide on the firewall configuration.

Figure 5.9 illustrates a firewall configuration with two exterior routers.

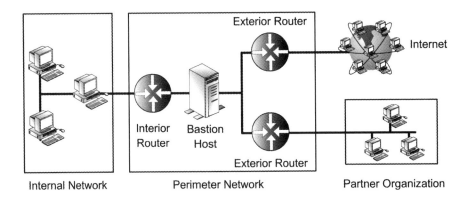

FIGURE 5.9 *Screened subnet architecture with two exterior routers*

Multiple Perimeter Networks

If you have concurrent connections to external networks, you can have multiple perimeter networks complete with the works—interior router, bastion host, and exterior router. This configuration, shown in Figure 5.10, provides some advantages, including redundancy in case any component of the perimeter network fails and privacy and separation of data that is transmitted between the Internet and other confidential networks.

However, this configuration has its share of disadvantages. Most important, there are multiple interior routers that are doorways to your internal network. If you do not monitor and manage these routers carefully, you might end up exposing the network to a serious security risk.

Figure 5.10 illustrates the screened subnet architecture with two perimeter networks.

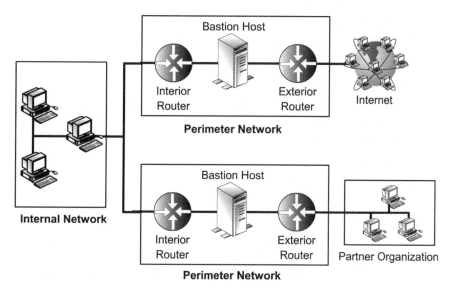

FIGURE 5.10 *Screened subnet architecture with two perimeter networks*

Summary

Firewalls provide security to your network; how you configure them depends on your specific network requirements. The primary ways in which you can configure your firewalls include dial-up architecture, single router architecture, dual-homed host architecture, screened host architecture, and screened subnet architecture.

There are many variations to the screened subnet architecture that you can apply to suit your specific network requirements. Common variations include multiple bastion hosts, single interior and exterior routers, bastion hosts as exterior routers, multiple exterior routers, and multiple perimeter networks.

This completes the description of firewall architecture. In the next chapter, you will learn how to create a security policy and derive a firewall design on the basis of that policy.

Check Your Understanding

Multiple Choice Questions

1. Which of the following architectures uses a host that is connected only to the internal network and is responsible for all communication between the internal network and the external network?

   a. Single router architecture

   b. Dual-homed host architecture

   c. Screened host architecture

   d. Dial-up firewall architecture

2. Which of the following architectures would you recommend to an organization that wants to implement a high performance architecture that segregates the internal and external requests made by users?

   a. Single router architecture

   b. Screened host architecture

   c. Dual-homed host architecture

   d. Screened subnet architecture

3. A large enterprise uses an Internet connection from four ISPs and has also established direct network links with its partner organizations. The enterprise uses its communication links for running mission-critical applications. In order to ensure high security as well as high performance, which firewall architecture would you recommend?

   a. Dual router architecture

   b. Screened host architecture with two perimeter networks

   c. Dual-homed host architecture

   d. Screened subnet architecture with multiple perimeter networks

Short Questions

1. Explain the role of a perimeter network in the security of the internal network.

2. List the variations of the screened subnet architecture with a brief description of each variation.

Answers

Multiple Choice Answers

1. c. The screened host architecture uses a host that is connected to the internal network and is responsible for routing communication between the internal and external networks.

2. d. The screened subnet architecture can be used to implement a high performance architecture that segregates the internal and external requests made by users.

3. d. The screened subnet architecture with multiple perimeter networks can be used when an enterprise wants to use high performance concurrent connections to the external network.

Short Answers

1. A perimeter network is as an additional layer of security between an internal and external network. When you use a perimeter network, the bastion host does not directly interact with the internal hosts. Therefore, traffic between two internal hosts does not pass through the bastion host. Even if an intruder accesses the bastion host, the internal traffic is not visible, and the intruder can only view the traffic flowing from the Internet and internal hosts.

2. The variations of the screened subnet architecture are as follows.

   - **Multiple bastion hosts**. A bastion host functions as a gateway between the internal and external networks. You can use multiple bastion hosts in the firewall architecture if you want to improve performance, introduce redundancy, and separate data and servers.

   - **One router acting as an internal and external router**. To save your organization the cost of acquiring additional routers, you can use a single router as an internal and external router. However, this variation is vulnerable to security breaches.

   - **Bastion host acting as an exterior router**. You can use a single dual-homed computer as a bastion host and external router. However, this configuration does not produce the exceptional performance or flexibility that a dedicated router provides.

   - **Multiple exterior routers**. You can use multiple exterior routers when you want to manage multiple connections to the Internet and increase the performance of your network. This configuration, however, is costly.

   - **Multiple perimeter networks**. You can use multiple perimeter networks to provide high security to the internal network and impart high performance in data communication between an internal network and multiple external networks.

Chapter 6

The need for Internet firewalls has increased tremendously over the years. Enterprises are looking for the best firewall solutions to protect the internal components of their networks from threats and network intrusions. If the needs of the organization are not well defined, then it is almost impossible to identify the best firewall solution. Therefore, you must first determine the needs of your organization and then design a firewall solution that best meets those needs. In this chapter, you will get a detailed overview of Internet firewall design to help you design a firewall solution for your organization.

This chapter explains how to build firewalls using different technologies that are available. It also presents the evaluation criteria you should apply when choosing the most appropriate firewall.

Firewall Design Overview

The primary objective of a firewall is to secure access between the local network and the Internet. Different vendors accomplish this objective using different strategies and mechanisms. Although the architecture of firewalls varies, the underlying principle in their implementation is common. All firewalls generally use well-known security schemes to secure the network.

Choosing the right firewall from among the ones supplied by different vendors is partly science and partly art. As I stated earlier, the first step in choosing an appropriate firewall for an organization is to carefully determine its security needs.

A large variety of both hardware and software products are presently available on the market. This might make the task of choosing a suitable product mix difficult unless you have a clear picture of the security requirements of the specific organization.

To design a firewall, you must first understand the boundaries between the *security domains* in your network. A security domain is a region of a network that is controlled by one uniform security policy. As an example, the internal network as a whole is a security domain that needs to be secured from the external components on the Internet. To secure this domain, you must select a basic security architecture that includes hardware, software, connectivity issues, and the distribution of functionality among components.

Chapter 4 described in detail the firewall technologies available on the market. As a review, there are three firewall technologies available—packet filters, application proxies, and circuit gateways.

◆ **Packet filtering**. Packet filtering is a process in which the firewall router examines the TCP or UDP packet that contains the source and destination IP addresses and forwards it to the ports on the network. Packet filtering is implemented on routers using ACLs (*Access Control Lists*). However, packet filters cannot differentiate between different types of users to determine whether they should be allowed to access the information requested.

◆ **Application proxy**. An application proxy can be used to secure the network. It controls and monitors application-level data access on the network and can deny access to certain applications within the local network.

◆ **Circuit gateway**. A circuit gateway provides the concept of tunneling, which can connect two known systems across the Internet and secure the communication between them.

To select the right firewall technology, you must first perform a needs analysis, which is based on identifying a proper security policy for the organization.

Firewall Security Policy

A firewall allows you to implement a security policy to ensure security within an organization. It generally provides centralized access control to the local network and divides the network into two separate parts, one which is trusted and one which is not. Such a black-and-white approach helps the firewall effectively manage the resources within the trusted network and safeguard them from the untrusted or "evil" network.

Before you decide on the security architecture for the organization, you have to cast its security policy, which will lay down each person's duties for securing the organization from external threats.

Need for a Security Policy

A security policy aims to generate security consciousness among organization personnel. It is a set of rules and guidelines that are clearly stated for implementation by all personnel. A security policy provides the following services.

◆ **Assigns responsibilities to computer users in an organization**. It is very important that you explicitly state every user's responsibility within the security policy.

◆ **Identifies the controlling authorities to whom all of the users are must answer**. A security policy guides administrators and system managers to make informed decisions about controlling and monitoring the system in the most secure possible manner based on the resources available to them.

◆ **Determines the consequences of breaking the policies in terms of social and legal implications**. A security policy should clearly define the legal and social implications of violating the rules defined by the security policy. For example, if a rule states that users should not send offensive content by e-mail, then the policy should also state the penalties that might be imposed for violating the rule. For instance, the user account might be disabled for a month if the user sends offensive e-mail.

Guidelines for Designing a Policy

A security policy should include rules that clearly stipulate the dos and don'ts for the organization's personnel. The policy statement should also include justification for each rule. Following are some common guidelines that can help you design a security policy.

◆ **Create user groups**. If it is not feasible to assign responsibilities to every employee, then responsibilities and rights should be assigned to groups of users. When a user belongs to a group, then the appropriate group policy will be applied automatically to the user.

◆ **Use simple language**. It is important that you draft the security policy in everyday language, avoiding legal jargon and phrases. However, you must also ensure that the language will not cause ambiguity or generate casualness.

◆ **Determine how the policy will be implemented**. It is very important to enforce the policy within the organization. The policy administrator should also determine how violations of the policy will be handled. This should cover both the adverse effect of the violation and the violator's conduct.

◆ **Determine the course to alter a policy**. A policy needs to be altered when you determine new security needs. Therefore, the policy should be written so that you can easily make alterations and additions. You should also define a process map for revising the policy when it is required.

Policy Design Checklist

Before you decide on a security policy, you should properly map the organization's existing network topology. This section provides a sample checklist that you can use to design a firewall policy.

◆ Who are the computer users?

◆ What are the users' account names?

◆ Does the organization need account-based rules?

◆ Who keeps track of user accounts?

◆ Does the organization have user groups?

◆ Does the organization need group-based policies?

◆ Does the organization have guest accounts for miscellaneous users?

◆ What are the rules that govern such accounts?

◆ Can accounts be shared among different users?

◆ Are passwords reusable?

◆ Do user accounts expire?

◆ Does the organization have a lease period for user accounts?

◆ Are any efforts made to ensure that employees select strong passwords?

◆ What if an unauthentic user obtains the password of a valid user? Are there additional barriers to entry, such as hardware keys?

◆ Can users use laptops in addition to the computers assigned to them? How does the organization control such hot docking?

◆ What are the security constraints for a computer to connect to the local network?

◆ What are the security constraints for a computer to connect to an external network?

◆ How are user accounts safeguarded from external threats?

◆ How is confidential and sensitive information safeguarded from external threats?

◆ What types of content can the users download from an external network?

◆ Which internal components should be visible on the Internet?

◆ What services should be made available on the Internet?

◆ What connections from the Internet should be allowed to access the internal network?

◆ How are connections authenticated?

◆ Who has access to the externally visible computers or other devices (mobile users, remote administrators)?

◆ Who is responsible for changes to such devices?

◆ What type of information is allowed to pass to the external network?

◆ How is information secured so that it does not leave the perimeter of the organizational network?

◆ Can users set up connections to ISPs using personal modems? Are dial-in connections allowed? If they are, how are users authenticated?

◆ What level of access to the internal components of the network do the dial-in connections provide?

◆ Are users allowed to carry secondary storage media such as CDs or tape drives in and out of the organization?

◆ Is any physical checking performed to detect the transfer of information?

◆ Are all systems physically protected from outsiders?

◆ Are important computers adequately secured from insiders?

◆ To what systems does each user have access? Are critical systems restricted?

◆ What type of administrative control does each user possess?

◆ Can users install executable files themselves? These files could include games, operating systems, productivity tools, or other software.

◆ Are users allowed to access an e-mail server?

◆ Do users understand the policy regarding e-mail privacy, inflammatory mail or postings, and mail forgery?

◆ What are the resource consumption guidelines?

◆ What actions are taken to prevent information theft or malice? Are these actions explained to every user? Is there a contract?

◆ Can users share resources, such as files and printers, with each other?

◆ Can users share accounts with other users?

◆ When does an administrator examine a user's account?

◆ Does the administrator monitor network traffic? What type of traffic should be monitored?

◆ Who has the authority to approve new accounts and access related services?

◆ Who can use supervisory access? Is there a record of who has this access?

◆ How does the organization handle threats and break-ins? Is the network immediately shut down, or is an attempt made to monitor the intruder?

◆ How are employees informed about such events?

◆ Does the organization involve lawyers and legal agencies at the time of intrusion detection and tracking?

◆ What if an employee with high-security access leaves the organization?

◆ Is there a document that lists the inventory of the internal components?

◆ How is information backed up? How are the backups verified?

◆ How are backups safeguarded?

◆ Does the system require information logging?

◆ What type of information is logged?

◆ How are logs secured?

◆ What are the alerts and triggers for raising an alarm in the case of a break-in?

◆ Who sets up these triggers?

◆ Who monitors the logs?

◆ What security measures are taken against viruses, trojans, and Internet worms?

◆ What type of security policy do mobile users implement?

◆ What type of data is made accessible to remote users?

♦ What type of security is implemented for communication channels?

♦ What measures are taken to secure the internal components of the network, such as routers, switches, important system files, and other operating environments?

♦ How is the security policy advertised to the users of the system?

♦ How are users convinced to abide by the policy?

♦ What are the cultural changes required within the organization?

You should consider the preceding questions when designing an appropriate security policy for your organization. The security policy is also influenced by other factors such as legal requirements or the existing organizational policy.

Some organizations also need to safeguard sensitive information from the general public. For example, a school should ensure that it safeguards a student's records, such as his or her classes, grades, and reviews. Similarly, a financial corporation should safeguard the credit details, account details, and transactions of its clientele. Certain countries also have policies in which an employee's personnel records should be safeguarded from others within and outside the organization. All such obligations determine newer security constraints when deriving a security policy.

Finalizing a Security Policy

Writing a security policy requires involving different personnel in the organization. Before you determine a security policy, you should consult all of the key players in the organization. To do so, you could set up multiple meetings that involve

♦ Top-level managers

♦ Representatives from different organizational groups, such as sales, distribution, marketing, and logistics

♦ System administrators, lawyers, and accountants

Multiple sessions of meetings help when you are brainstorming an appropriate and practical security policy for the organization. They help the organization understand the concerns of different types of users and the different aspects of the system under consideration. It is a good idea to document all of the decisions that are made in the security meetings so that you can refer to these decisions while framing the policy. Documentation also provides a framework upon which to work and proof that the users have agreed to these decisions.

After the security policy is in place, you should perform a feasibility analysis, which should include important questions such as:

♦ What type of information is available within the organization?

♦ What type of information needs to be secured within the available list?

♦ What level of security is required to safeguard such information?

- What is the cost-benefit ratio for different security considerations?
- What is the best security architecture for a given cost?
- What type of security stance does the organization need to pose?
- Can the existing infrastructure support the security strategy?
- Is there a need for additional infrastructure?
- Can the existing personnel (system administrators and security experts) within the organization effectively implement the security strategy, or do you need to hire external contractors and security consultants?
- Have you already chosen the firewall vendor? Are there any existing contracts that, if broken, will be an added cost to the organization?
- What is the timeline allocated to implement the security strategy? Are all of the participants available within this timeline?

After you have conducted all of the policy questions and feasibility studies, you can identify and evaluate the available products on the market. As you might notice, defining the requirements makes it easier for you to identify the right products that will fit the constraints that you have set up in your policy file.

Firewall Products

Different firewall architectures are available on the market. Some have router-based architectures and some are more advanced. Advanced firewalls are usually workstation-based and are deployed on specific hosts. In this section, I will describe some of the common router-based and workstation-based firewalls.

Router-Based Firewalls

The firewalls based on router architectures provide functionality such as packet filtering or NAT. Most firewall vendors who provide routers implicitly include these functionalities within their routers. Some of the major vendors who provide router-based architectures include

- Cisco Systems
- 3Com Corp
- Livingston Enterprises
- Network Systems Corporation
- Bay Networks

These routers provide interfaces to set up the rules for filtering TCP and UDP packets based on the application ports. They provide a generic system that can filter packets sent across to different application protocols.

There are many well-known router-based firewalls on the market. Specifically, some routers such as the Cisco 2500 series are very common in the current marketplace. There are also routers for small offices, such as SonicWall from Sonic Systems or Intel 8100/8200 from Intel Corporation.

Some routers provide lower-level IP filtering based on ICMP. Routers provide filtering rules, but in a vendor-specific manner. For example, Cisco provides packet-filtering rules called Access Lists that require the use of Cisco's configuration language. The Livingston Firewall IRX provides packet-filtering rules called Filters. Although both the Cisco router and the Livingston router provide the same functionality, they express it using different mechanisms.

Router-based architectures can be used as firewalls only when the number of hosts within a network is very small or the network is very decentralized, where an access control domain cannot be effectively configured. Generally, router-based architecture does not support functionalities such as logging or stateful packet filtering. Although this is not true of all routers, most of the low-end routers that I discussed do not support such functionalities.

There are also many advanced router-based architectures such as the Cisco 12000 series that are only used by ISPs to provide very high security and bandwidth services for optical networks. The cost of implementing such routers is prohibitive for small- to medium-sized organizations.

Workstation-Based Firewalls

Most organizations prefer more advanced features than what a router-based firewall can provide, such as stateful packet filters and application gateways. These features provide data protection for the internal network.

Such advanced features can be implemented on a particular host that can act as a firewall. These hosts are not dedicated hardware, like the router, but they are dedicated computers that provide workstation-based packet filtering. Such workstation-based firewalls can provide stateful packet filtering and also act as application gateways.

Workstation-based firewalls can provide advanced logging, monitoring, and tracking capabilities compared to router-based firewalls. The following list names some of the workstation-based firewalls on the market.

- ◆ Check Point Next Generation FireWall-1 from Check Point Software
- ◆ Sun Screen from Sun Microsystems
- ◆ RealSecure family from Internet Security Systems
- ◆ Gauntlet Firewall for Solaris from Secure Computing
- ◆ eTrust Firewall for Windows from Computer Associates International
- ◆ Cisco PIX Firewall Family from Cisco Systems, Inc.

- Internet Security and Acceleration Server 2000 from Microsoft Corporation
- UniRo-Secure from UniSoft Co., Ltd
- Access Point Family from Lucent Technologies
- Springtide IP Service Switch from Lucent Technologies
- Avaya VPN Gateways from Avaya, Inc.
- AltaVista Firewall from Digital Equipment Corp.
- Eagle from Raptor Systems Inc.
- SonicWALL Family from SonicWALL, Inc.
- BorderGuard from StorageTek Network Systems Group
- SecuwayGate 1000 from Future Systems, Inc.
- BorderWare Firewall Server from BorderWare Technologies, Inc.
- Gauntlet Firewall from Trusted Information Systems, Inc.
- NetScreen Family from NetScreen Technologies
- WolfPac Firewall from NetWolves Technologies
- IBM Firewall for AIX from IBM
- CyberGuard Firewall from CyberGuard Corporation
- SecuiWALL from SECUi.COM
- CyberwallPLUS-IP from Network-1 Security Solutions, Inc.
- NETASQ F100-3 from NETASQ
- StoneGate from Stonesoft Corporation
- Portus from Livermore Software Labs
- InterJak 200 from Filanet Corporation
- NetStructure VPN Gateway from Intel
- Raptor Firewall Family from Symantec Corporation
- SecureIT from SLMsoft
- Ascend SecureConnect from Ascend Communications, Inc.
- GNAT Box GB-100 from Global Technology Associates, Inc.
- Microsecure Firewall from Microsecure
- 3Com Firewall Family from 3Com Corporation
- iGateway Family from Intoto, Inc.
- WatchGuard SOHO from WatchGuard Technologies, Inc.
- IM Firewall from Elron Software

Evaluating Firewalls

The preceding section provided an overview of different firewalls available on the market. In this section, I will explain the criteria on which the firewalls should be evaluated. I will first list the parameters on which firewalls should be evaluated and then discuss some additional features that merit consideration before you purchase a firewall.

Parameters for Evaluation

It is important to consider products that work on different operating environments, such as Solaris, UNIX, Windows, or Macintosh, because there is no one product that can work on all of the operating systems. Firewall products need to be evaluated on the following scale.

◆ **Reliability**. A firewall is a device to enforce security. The network must be able to safely rely on the firewall. The firewall by itself should be secure from external attacks. The implementation of the firewall should be robust, and the configuration should be efficient.

◆ **Scalability**. The firewall architecture should be flexible in scaling to different requirements. If the current user base is small, then the implementation of the firewall should accommodate this without demanding excessive support infrastructure. If the number of hosts within the network exponentially increases, the firewall should be able to scale accordingly to manage the hosts. You should also be able to configure the firewall to work with higher bandwidths or to provide more memory so that it scales based on the requirements.

◆ **Configuration and interface**. The user interface of the firewall should be user-friendly and simple. A firewall can be configured effectively only if the system administrator can easily understand and manipulate the configuration syntax and the user interface. You should be able to reconfigure the existing setup without drastically affecting the configuration of other host systems on the network.

◆ **Availability**. A firewall should be highly available. You should consider redundant architecture and backup procedures when you are installing a firewall. To ensure high availability of the firewall, you should consider fail-over, clustering, or any other 24-hour-per-day strategy at the time you build the firewall solution.

◆ **Audits and logs**. The firewall should support efficient logging and auditing services for the sake of monitoring the network traffic. It should support an extensive reporting mechanism to trigger alarms and events generated by the internal components of the firewall, such as packet filters, intrusion detection systems, or circuit gateways. The firewall should also provide easy-to-manipulate graphs and other alternative graphical representations about the current status of the network.

◆ **Cost**. The total price of all of the components within a firewall strategy is a significant influence in determining which product to use. The following components account for the cost of a firewall.

- The hardware components, such as routers, switches, workstations, backup devices, and UPS (*Uninterrupted Power Supply*)
- The software components, such as the operating system, backup software, application servers, and other advanced firewall architectures
- Allied costs, such as for installation and administration, licensing, product support, and upgrade

Additional Criteria for Selecting Firewalls

The preceding section provided the evaluation criteria for identifying the right firewall based on your organization's needs. There are some additional criteria that you should consider when determining the appropriate firewall solution for your organization.

◆ What types of technologies does the firewall support?

◆ What types of protocols does the firewall support?

◆ What types of encryption and tunneling mechanisms does the firewall support?

◆ Does the firewall come with any built-in remote management capabilities? If so, how are the remote services by themselves secured?

◆ What are the performance index and throughput for the firewall? This information should be based on the reviews conducted by public journals.

◆ How complex is the firewall architecture?

After you identify all of these criteria, you should maintain proper documentation that explains in detail why you selected a particular firewall to match the needs of your organization.

Firewall Configuration

A firewall gateway is the primary tool that protects your confidential information within a trusted network. Depending on the security policy, you can increase or decrease the effectiveness of the firewall. After you select a firewall and define a security policy, it's time to work on a simple firewall configuration.

Any firewall that you buy will have proprietary features built in by the firewall vendor. The implementation and configuration of the firewall is completely vendor-dependent. Therefore, it's difficult to explain the configuration details in a completely generic manner. However, I have made an effort to explain the generic configuration and administration concepts of the screened subnet architecture. Hopefully, this will help you avoid getting into the vendor-specific implementations and details of the firewall architecture.

Moreover, the screened subnet architecture is relatively simple to understand compared to other firewall architectures presented earlier in the book. Remember that the configuration presented here is generic and simple. A real implementation will be more complex and vendor-specific.

Split-Screened Subnet Architecture

This section provides a basic network layout for the split-screened subnet architecture. It is not necessary to use a similar layout; however, understanding the basic features of the layout will help you design your network effectively.

I assume that you have a local network that you need to safeguard. The network layout is segmented on the principle that there are technically 255 host IPs (in a class C), and I have configured the network by segmenting the network using 63 host IPs per subnet. Therefore, the subnet mask used is 255.255.255.192, which is generated by subtracting 63 from 255.

To configure the network, you need to know the configuration of the domain, subnets 1 through 3, and the firewall. These details are given in the following sections.

Domain Configuration

Table 6.1 lists the configuration of the domain.

Table 6.1 Domain Configuration

Parameter	Value
Domain	niit.com
Net ID	Class C (209.130.78)
Host IP address range	209.130.78.0 to 209.130.78.255
Architecture	3-layered (external, DMZ, internal)
Broadcast address	209.130.78.255
Netmask	255.255.255.0

Subnet Configuration

Table 6.2 lists the details of subnet 1, which is the external network or perimeter 1.

Table 6.2 Subnet 1 Configuration

Parameter	Value
IP address range	209.130.78.0 to 209.130.78.63
Network address	209.130.78.0
Netmask	255.255.255.192
Gateway to the Internet (router)	209.130.78.1

Subnet 2 includes the DMZ network, also referred to as perimeter 2. Table 6.3 lists its configuration.

Table 6.3 Subnet 2 Configuration

Parameter	Value
IP address range	209.130.78.64 to 209.130.78.127
Network address	209.130.78.64
Netmask	255.255.255.192
Gateway to the external network (firewall)	209.130.78.65
Gateway to the internal network (router)	209.130.78.126
Web server	209.130.78.70
Mail server	209.130.78.71
FTP proxy server	209.130.78.72
FTP server	209.130.78.73
External DNS server	209.130.78.74

Subnet 3 represents the organization's internal network. Table 6.4 lists its configuration.

Table 6.4 Subnet 3 Configuration

Parameter	Value
IP address range	209.130.78.128 to 209.130.78.191
Network address	209.130.78.128
Netmask	255.255.255.192
Gateway to the DMZ subnet (router)	209.130.78.129
Internal DNS server	209.130.78.130

Firewall Configuration

Table 6.5 lists the details of the firewall configuration.

Table 6.5 Firewall Configuration

Parameter	Value
Architecture	Split-screened subnet architecture
Type	Dual-homed
NIC 1	209.130.78.2 (external)
NIC 2	209.130.78.65 (DMZ)
Host name	fw.niit.com
IP address	209.130.78.2

Figure 6.1 illustrates the network layout diagram based on the configuration discussed in the preceding sections.

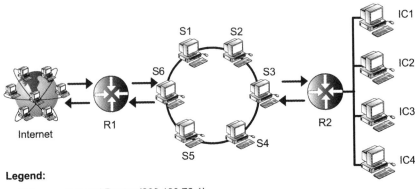

Legend:

R1 = External Router (209.130.78.1)
R2 = Internal Router (209.130.78.126 , 209.130.78.129)
IC1, IC2, IC3, IC4 = Internal Clients
S1 = Web Server (209.130.78.70)
S2 = Mail Server (209.130.78.71)
S3 = FTP Proxy Server (209.130.78.72)
S4 = FTP Server (209.130.78.73)
S5 = Internal DNS Server (209.130.78.130)
S6 = External DNS Server (209.130.78.74)

FIGURE 6.1 *Split-screened subnet architecture*

Figure 6.1 provides a basic layout that can be used for different firewall configurations. The layout presented is the split-screened subnet architecture with two perimeter layers—external and DMZ.

Perimeter layer 1 is an external perimeter because it is the part of the network outside the firewall. You can secure the perimeter 1 network by securing the exterior router. Often an ISP provides the external router; therefore, you might not have the necessary privileges to fully configure it. In such cases, it is best to use the split-screened subnet architecture with a dual-homed host for providing layered security. This architecture is an extensive security measure that protects hosts on the DMZ and the internal network.

In most cases, the exterior router is configured to packet-filter the source-forged IP packets from the Internet. Even though the ISP that hosts the exterior router generally provides a security policy, relying on the exterior router alone might compromise the hosts on the DMZ. Therefore, you should install a dual-homed host between the exterior router and the DMZ to provide an additional layer of security.

You should extensively configure the firewall for your specific needs. You can assign bandwidth for different types of traffic. For example, you can use the firewall to assign bandwidths for customer traffic and other administrative traffic separately. You can also use an extensive security policy to configure packet filtering on the firewall.

There are multiple variations of firewall architecture that you can arrive at using the preceding layout. Some of the variations are

- ◆ **Packet filtering configuration (screening router).** This configuration makes some changes to the existing layout. You can create it by removing the interior router and combining the exterior router with the firewall.

- ◆ **Bastion host configuration (screened subnet architecture).** In a bastion host configuration, which is based on the screened subnet architecture, an interior and exterior router are used with a bastion host in the DMZ. All of the public servers (DNS, WWW, and SMTP) are within the internal network, not the DMZ. The bastion host acts as an advanced proxy to forward the protocol-specific details to the public servers within the internal network. This configuration and other variations of the bastion host will be explained further in Chapter 7, "Bastion Hosts."

- ◆ **Application gateway firewall (dual-homed host).** In this configuration, the exterior and the interior routers are removed, and a single firewall system protects the internal network. This architecture is not recommended because it provides a single point of failure.

This chapter explains only packet-filtering configuration. Bastion host configuration is explained in Chapter 7.

Configuring a Packet-Filtering Architecture

This section provides details for configuring a packet-filtering architecture. The network layout for the architecture is made up of details of the domain, firewall, and internal network. Table 6.6 lists the details of the domain.

Table 6.6 Domain Configuration

Parameter	Value
Domain	niit.com
NetID	Class C (209.130.78)
Host IP address range	209.130.78.0 to 209.130.78.255
Architecture	2-layered (external, internal)
Network address	209.130.78.0
Broadcast address	209.130.78.255
Netmask	255.255.255.0
Gateway to the Internet (Internet router) address	209.130.78.1

Table 6.7 lists the firewall details.

Table 6.7 Firewall Details

Parameter	Value
Host name	fw.niit.com
IP address	209.130.78.1

Finally, Table 6.8 lists the details of the internal network.

Table 6.8 Internal Network Details

Parameter	Value
Web server	209.130.78.70
Mail server	209.130.78.71
FTP proxy server	209.130.78.72
FTP server	209.130.78.73
DNS server	209.130.78.74

Figure 6.2 illustrates the network layout diagram.

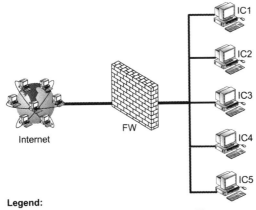

Legend:
FW = Firewall (fw.niit.com [209.130.78.1])
IC1 = Web Server (209.130.78.70)
IC2 = Mail Server (209.130.78.71)
IC3 = FTP Proxy Server (209.130.78.72)
IC4 = FTP Server (209.130.78.73)
IC5 = DNS Server (209.130.78.74)

FIGURE 6.2 *Packet-filtering architecture*

As I explained earlier, the best place for a packet-filtering system is between the internal network and the Internet, as shown in Figure 6.2. This provides a choke-point strategy to your network security. A choke-point strategy emphasizes a single point of contact between the Internet and the internal network.

Service Configuration

There are different services that you can add to the packet-filtering firewall. Some of these services are described in the following list.

◆ **Spoofing rule.** This is a security rule that detects and prevents network-spoofing attacks. When you add a spoofing rule to the firewall, it prevents inbound packets that internal source addresses from passing.

◆ **Ping.** The ping service is allowed only for the internal users. It prevents external systems from profiling and enumerating the internal hosts.

◆ **HTTP.** Generally, HTTP traffic is allowed for inbound and outbound traffic. No filtering rule is applied to this protocol. Typically, an HTTPS port is also open so that you can establish secure communication for the exchange of sensitive information.

◆ **FTP.** All outgoing FTP connections are allowed. Inbound FTP connections are also permitted on the anonymous FTP server, using PASV mode. The reason behind passive mode configuration is that inbound connections for normal-mode FTP require a port number greater than 1023. Allowing ports greater than 1023 through the firewall can compromise the security for network-scanning attacks. Therefore, the only usable options are passive mode FTP using the packet-filtering system or normal mode using a proxy system. In addition, you can add a denial rule for all outbound normal FTP connections to prevent security holes.

◆ **Telnet.** You can implement a security rule that allows only trusted external hosts to connect to the internal systems. Telnet from internal systems to external hosts is allowed.

◆ **Mail.** The SMTP and POP protocols are generally permitted without any rules in the case of the screened subnet architecture. Although this is not a very safe security stance, usually no packet-filtering rules are applied to these protocols. If you consider a bastion host configuration or the split-screened subnet architecture, the configurations for SMTP and POP are very secure and use proxy systems.

◆ **DNS.** You can establish an internal DNS system to manage all of the DNS requests.

Packet-Filtering Rules

In this section, I will establish the packet-filtering rules for the preceding configuration. The security stance under consideration is a default-deny stance that will deny access from the external systems to the internal systems. The packet-filtering rule will presume that it can identify all of the inbound and outbound packets. Based on this presumption, the packet filter can filter all of the packets on different parameters, such as the source address, destination address, port number, and protocol (TCP or UDP).

Table 6.9 presents all of the rules applicable to the packet filter.

Table 6.9 Rules for the Packet Filter

Rule	Direction	Source IP	Destination IP	Protocol	Source Port	Destination Port	ACK	Action
Spoofing— Incoming	In	209.130.78.*	Any	Any	Any	Any	Any	Deny
HTTP— Outgoing	Out	209.130.78.*	Trusted	TCP/IP	>1023	80	No	Permit
HTTP— Outgoing	In	Trusted sites	209.130.78.*	TCP/IP	80	>1023	Yes	Permit
HTTP— Incoming	In	Trusted sites	209.130.78.70	TCP/IP	>1023	80	No	Permit
HTTP— Incoming	Out	209.130.78.70	Trusted	TCP/IP	80	>1023	Yes	Permit
FTP— Outgoing	Out	209.130.78.*	Any	TCP/IP	>1023	21	No	Permit
FTP— Outgoing	In	Any	209.130.78.*	TCP/IP	21	>1023	Yes	Permit
Normal FTP— Outgoing	In	Any	209.130.78.*	TCP/IP	20	>1023	No	Permit
Normal FTP— Outgoing	Out	209.130.78.*	Any	TCP/IP	>1023	20	Yes	Permit
PASV FTP— Outgoing	Out	209.130.78.*	Any	TCP/IP	>1023	>1023	No	Permit

Rule	Direction	Source IP	Destination IP	Protocol	Source Port	Destination Port	ACK	Action
PASV FTP— Outgoing	In	Any	209.130.78.*	TCP/IP	>1023	>1023	Yes	Permit
FTP— Incoming	In	Trusted sites	209.130.78.73	TCP/IP	>1023	21	No	Permit
FTP— Incoming	Out	209.130.78.73	Trusted	TCP/IP	21	>1023	Yes	Permit
PASV FTP— Incoming	In	Trusted sites	209.130.78.73	TCP/IP	>1023	>1023	No	Permit
PASV FTP— Incoming	Out	209.130.78.73	Trusted	TCP/IP	>1023	>1023	Yes	Permit
Telnet— Outgoing	Out	209.130.78.*	Any	TCP/IP	>1023	23	No	Permit
Telnet— Outgoing	In	Any	209.130.78.*	TCP/IP	23	>1023	Yes	Permit
Telnet— Incoming	In	Trusted sites	209.130.78.*	TCP/IP	>1023	23	No	Permit
Telnet— Incoming	Out	209.130.78.*	Trusted	TCP/IP	23	>1023	Yes	Permit
SMTP— Outgoing	Out	209.130.78.*	Any	TCP/IP	>1023	25	No	Permit
SMTP— Outgoing	In	Any	209.130.78.*	TCP/IP	25	>1023	Yes	Permit
POP— Outgoing	Out	209.130.78.*	Any	TCP/IP	>1023	109, 110	No	Permit
POP— Outgoing	In	Any	209.130.78.*	TCP/IP	109, 110	>1023	Yes	Permit
SMTP— Incoming	In	Any	209.130.78.71	TCP/IP	>1023	25	No	Permit

continued on next page

Table 6.9 Rules for the Packet Filter (continued from previous page)

Rule	Direction	Source IP	Destination IP	Protocol	Source Port	Destination Port	ACK	Action
SMTP—Incoming	Out	209.130.78.71	Any	TCP/IP	25	>1023	Yes	Permit
POP—Incoming	In	Any	209.130.78.71	TCP/IP	>1023	109, 110	No	Permit
POP—Incoming	Out	209.130.78.71	Any	TCP/IP	109, 110	>1023	Yes	Permit
DNS—Outgoing	Out	209.130.78.*	Any	TCP/IP	>1023	53	No	Permit
DNS—Outgoing	In	Any	209.130.78.*	TCP/IP	53	>1023	Yes	Permit
DNS—Outgoing	Out	209.130.78.74	Any	UDP/IP	53	53	N/A	Permit
DNS—Incoming	In	Any	209.130.78.74	TCP/IP	>1023	53	No	Permit
DNS—Incoming	Out	209.130.78.74	Any	TCP/IP	53	>1023	Yes	Permit
DNS—Incoming	In	Any	209.130.78.74	UDP/IP	>1023	53	N/A	Permit
DNS—Incoming	Out	209.130.78.74	Any	UDP/IP	53	>1023	N/A	Permit
DNS—Incoming	In	Any	209.130.78.74	UDP/IP	53	53	N/A	Permit

Once you have set up the rules, you have successfully configured the packet-filtering system. You can then analyze the network in real time to see how it performs. You can also try performing a normal scan from the external network to search for any loopholes in the configuration.

As far as the packet-filtering system is concerned, it is the simplest and cheapest option that you can utilize for firewall security. As I explained, the split-subnet architecture requires careful consideration at the time of setup and is more complex than the packet-filtering system. The bastion host configuration will be explained in the next chapter.

Summary

In this chapter, you learned about the rationale for establishing a firm security policy within the organization. You also learned how a security policy should be derived, and you were shown a sample checklist that can be used to design the policy. Next, the chapter provided a list of router-based and workstation-based firewall technologies available. It emphasized the criteria for evaluating a firewall architecture that is suitable for your organization. Finally, the chapter presented a scenario to configure a packet-filtering architecture on a local network with class C address. The next chapter will explain Windows and UNIX-based bastion hosts in detail.

Check Your Understanding

Multiple Choice Questions

1. Identify the questions that influence the creation of a security policy.
   a. How do you set up an NAT router?
   b. What is the configuration syntax used on the router?
   c. What type of administrative power does the user possess?
   d. Who uses your computers?

2. Which of the following personnel should be involved in determining a security policy?
   a. Group representatives
   b. Ordinary system users
   c. Top-level managers
   d. System administrators

3. Which of the following questions should be considered in a feasibility analysis?
   a. Are any efforts made to ensure that employees choose strong passwords?
   b. What is the cost-benefit ratio for different security considerations?
   c. Do you need additional infrastructure?
   d. What is the timeline allocated to implement the security strategy?

4. Which of the following criteria are used in evaluating a firewall?
   a. Scalability
   b. Packet filtering
   c. NAT
   d. Cost

5. What are the firewall architectures in the following list?

    a. Screened subnet

    b. NAT

    c. VPN

    d. Application-gateway

6. Which of the following architectures is the simplest to configure?

    a. Screened router architecture

    b. Dual-homed architecture

    c. Screened subnet architecture

    d. Split-screened subnet architecture

7. Which of the following architectures uses a bastion host?

    a. Screened subnet architecture

    b. Packet-filtering architecture

Short Questions

1. List the evaluation criteria for selecting the right firewall.

2. Explain the difference between a packet-filtering architecture and an application gateway.

Answers

Multiple Choice Answers

1. c and d. The computer users in the organization and their administrative powers influence the creation of a security policy.

2. a, c, and d. Group representatives, top-level managers, and system administrators should be involved in designing a security policy.

3. b, c, and d. You should consider the cost-benefit ratio, the need for additional infrastructure, and timelines for the security strategy in a feasibility analysis.

4. a and d. Scalability and cost are involved in evaluating a firewall.

5. a and d. The screened subnet architecture and the application gateway architecture are both firewall architectures.

6. a. The screened router architecture (also called the packet-filtering architecture) is the simplest to configure.

7.   a. The screened subnet architecture typically uses a bastion host to forward the packets related to the public servers implemented within the internal network.

Short Answers

1.   The evaluation criteria for selecting a firewall are

- Reliability
- Scalability
- Configuration and interface
- Availability
- Audits and logs
- Cost

2.   A packet-filtering architecture or screened router architecture is based on a single router that filters all of the packets (inbound and outbound). A screened router routes the traffic between the external and internal networks. In an application gateway architecture or a dual-homed firewall, routing between the two networks (internal and external) is disabled, and a single point of contact is used for security enforcement. An application gateway also acts as a proxy system to ensure security.

Chapter 7

In the previous chapters, you leaned about firewalls. In this chapter, you will learn about a well known security mechanism—bastion hosts. I will start with an introduction to bastion hosts and then move on to the various requirements for setting them up. Next, I'll discuss Windows NT- and UNIX-based bastion hosts.

Introduction to Bastion Hosts

By now you must be eager to know what bastion hosts are, so let's get started. A *bastion host* is a computer on the internal network that is intentionally exposed to attack. It is designed in such a way that the public network knows of its existence. Generally, most of the firewall architectures use extensive mechanisms to secure bastion hosts. Whenever a host on the Internet wants to connect with any of your internal systems, the request is routed to the bastion host so it can forward the request to the internal systems.

In Chapter 5, I discussed different variations of firewall architectures that you can implement on the internal network. In most of the firewall architectures, bastion hosts play an important role in establishing a secure perimeter for the internal network. Due to their prolonged exposure to outside networks, bastion hosts face a great risk of malicious attacks. Firewall designers spend much time and effort designing and configuring bastion hosts so that such risks are minimized. A bastion host is typically used to provide public services such as:

◆ Firewall gateways
◆ World Wide Web services
◆ DNS
◆ Mail servers
◆ FTP
◆ Web application services

The process of configuring a bastion host is also called *hardening*. To configure a bastion host, turn off the unnecessary protocols, ports, and services. The hardening of the host depends on many factors, including

◆ The operating system used on the host
◆ The software running on the host
◆ The role intended by the host

While hardening the bastion host, you should pay careful attention to the logging of the security events. It is important to constantly monitor and secure all of the logs so that the attacker does not erase the evidence of his visit to your network. In addition, you should secure the password lists and ACLs from the attacker.

A bastion host is isolated from the internal network. Therefore, it is not aware of any system details of other hosts on the internal network. For example, details such as the authentication services and other programs that are executing on the internal hosts are not exposed to the bastion host. The rationale behind this design consideration is that an attack on the bastion host must not compromise the security of the internal network.

There are many types of bastion hosts, and there can be more than one bastion host securing a network. Following is a list of different types of bastion hosts.

- ◆ **Internal bastion hosts**. This is a configuration in which the bastion host is set up to communicate with internal systems to forward information (such as mail and news) obtained from the external network. Such bastion hosts have more services enabled on them and generally have a higher number of ports open to satisfy the applications.

- ◆ **External bastion hosts**. This is a configuration in which the bastion host is set up to provide public services, such as WWW, SMTP, or DNS, to the Internet. It does not forward any request to the internal systems; it handles the requests itself. There are very limited services that are set up with limited ports open to satisfy such services. An external bastion host needs more fortification and is well guarded. Any access to the internal systems is cut off.

- ◆ **Victim hosts**. These are like sacrificial lambs that you offer to the attacker. If at any point you are not sure about what type of security configuration is required for a particular service, you can set up such a service on a victim host. The victim host will not contain any sensitive information or any other data that could compromise the safety of the internal network. It will only contain the bare minimum service configuration to run the appropriate service. Sometimes victim hosts are also set up to deliberately expose the system to attacks, to gain time to facilitate tracking such attacks on the network.

No matter what type of configuration you have in mind, a bastion host is always exposed to security threats. Invariably, the number of attacks on an external or a victim host is always higher than the number of attacks on an internal bastion host. This does not mean, however, that a bastion host will always be attacked. A high intensity attack is a constant threat to a bastion host. Such an attack poses a grave threat to the safety of the network, which is why security architects and experts spend considerably more time fortifying the bastion hosts than they spend on other systems in the network. In most network configurations, the internal hosts are configured not to trust the bastion host.

Typically, a bastion host is configured with simplicity in mind. You should not complicate the configuration of bastion hosts because it can introduce unintended security holes. Also, complexity increases the chance of host misconfiguration. In such cases, it is hard to maintain or monitor the bastion host at run time. The administrator will find it difficult to analyze the performance and security details of the host.

When configuring bastion hosts, make sure that you perform the following tasks.

◆ Remove all unnecessary ports and non-critical services.

◆ Modify the ACLs of the system objects.

◆ Remove the internal network information.

◆ Disable the daemons running on the bastion host.

◆ Apply newer versions of service packs or patches when they are released.

Now that you have an understanding of bastion hosts in general, take a look at the system requirements for bastion hosts.

System Requirements

The primary components of any machine are the hardware and software. It is important to choose your hardware and software carefully to meet the system requirements of an effective bastion host. This section provides details on what type of operating system and hardware you should select to build an appropriate bastion host.

Before you look at the hardware and software requirements for bastion hosts and identify the system configuration, you need to address the following key factors.

◆ **Robustness**. The hardware and software configuration that you select for a bastion host should be fail-safe. You should be able to fully rely on the bastion host for your network's security. Most of the time, bastion hosts are a single point of failure. If the configuration of this system is compromised, then the security of your entire network will be in jeopardy.

◆ **Availability**. The availability of your bastion host is quite important. There should not be any downtime of the bastion host for scheduled maintenance. Instead, you should build in full redundancy. You should configure the secondary bastion host to completely take over the job of the primary host in case the primary host fails. The transition from the primary host to the secondary host should be transparent. You should make available appropriate backup power arrangements using UPS in case of power failures.

◆ **Scalability**. You should choose the hardware and software carefully, based on how well they scale. There might be times when you want to scale down the host because you want to set up an independent host for every service. At other times, you might want to scale up the services and speed of the host without compromising the simplicity. In such cases, the sum-total scalability factor (including hardware, operating system, and the software services running on the host) plays a major role in choosing the bastion host.

◆ **User interface**. The configurability of the bastion host is also quite important. The administrator should be able to configure, monitor, and maintain the host easily. The user interface of the software services, operating system, and other features (such as tools and daemons) plays an important role when setting up a bastion host.

Now take a look at the hardware and software configuration requirements for bastion hosts.

Hardware

To start with, choose the hardware specifications for your host. When you choose the hardware components of the bastion host, remember that the newest technology is not the criteria because certain recent hardware technologies might not be industry-matured. In such cases, you would not know the compromises that you might have to make, since such technologies might not have been tried and tested. The hardware configuration you choose can be a fairly new technology, but not necessarily the latest. When you are deciding on a hardware configuration, consider the following factors.

◆ **Architecture**. The architecture of your hardware makes an important distinction in the quality of your bastion host configuration. Hardware architecture is vendor-specific. In other words, you have a wide variety of architectures to choose from, including Intel, Apple, Sun, HP, and IBM. You have Intel x86 architecture, Sun Sparc architecture, and the Apple PowerMac (G4) architecture. You also have a host of other system architectures based on Compaq (digital), HP, IBM, and several other vendors. The hardware architecture can be further broken down into the chipsets and the type of processor used on the motherboard. Typically, Intel architecture with a PCI (*Peripheral Component Interconnect*)-based chipset should do. Also, a Pentium class processor (PII or higher) is a good CPU architecture to consider. Your hardware architecture should also support RAID (*Redundant Array of Inexpensive Disks*). This is good for fail-over services.

◆ **Speed**. This is the speed of the sum-total of the system, not just the clock speed of the processor. Generally, a well-designed CPU architecture with a lower clock speed on the processor is faster than a not-so-well-designed CPU with a higher clock speed. You should consider your choices carefully when you select a processor. The bus speed of the system is also an important criterion when choosing a system. If you compare a 2 GHz processor with 100 MHz bus to a 1.4 GHz processor with a 400 MHz bus, the performance of the latter will be higher. Bus speed plays a vital role on many server systems. Also, the speed of the memory (RAM) should be synchronous to the bus speed of the system. The speed of the hard disk also counts most of the time. You don't need to have the fastest system; however, considerable speed is required because the bastion host needs to simultaneously process many services and network connections at any given time. A system that is too fast could also be a threat in itself. If an attacker breaks into the bastion host, he or she can use the speed of the hardware to easily launch other brute force attacks on the internal system. Therefore, you should get just enough speed to run the services. Some security experts believe that a bastion host does not need to be fast at all. They claim that there is not much processing power required to execute most of the standard services, such as DNS or SMTP. This holds true if you are running standard services. However, if you want to execute any other services, such as a Web server, an application server (which would be very rare), or other services that require heavy compression or decompression, then you need a faster processor. Either way, a processor speed between 400 MHz and 1 GHz is advised.

◆ **Primary memory**. As I explained earlier, a bastion host needs to be efficient enough to run many services simultaneously with multiple connections open on the network. Although the speed of the processor does affect the performance of the system, the more important factor is memory. To execute many services at the same time, your system should be able to provide a vast amount of memory. How much is vast enough is a context-specific question. Typically, a memory size higher than 512 MB is recommended. It is good to have memory up to 1 GB on the RAM. Also, the cache size (L1, L2) of the system matters when choosing a configuration. Note that memory speed is also a criterion.

◆ **Secondary memory**. The hard disk size is important if you are considering a bastion host that can also act as a proxy system because it is good to cache the pages to reduce the traffic on your network. Caching the pages that are used by the clients on your internal network will also increase the performance of your network. To do so, you need to have a substantial amount of hard disk space. Typically, the cache size will not be bigger than 2 GB, but this can vary widely based on the network activity and the number of users on your network. Lately, hard disks up to 100 GB have become very common. A bastion host does not require that large of a hard disk because you do not store any information on your host. Anything between 5 GB and 20 GB is good enough—it will allow the installation of any OS and software that are necessary to run the bastion host. CD-ROM drives and tape drives are also advisable for installing software and backing up logs and other information from the bastion host. An IDE architecture that supports RAID is a good choice.

◆ **Display**. The bastion host's display is not very important. Usually you can execute many operating systems with a simple VGA card with a standard monitor. The resolution is not a criterion. Also, most of the UNIX- or Linux-based hosts don't even require a GUI operating system to run on the bastion host. In such cases, a basic VGA card with normal display capabilities should suffice.

◆ **Chassis**. You should keep in mind the mounting and chassis of the system because many bastion hosts can be set up in such a way that scaling the hardware should not be a problem. In other words, the chassis of the system should be such that mounting extra disks or removing disks is easy. Also, having hardware architecture that allows *hot-swapping* of certain components at run time is not a bad idea. Hot-swapping is the ability to add another hardware component (such as a hard disk) at run time without bringing down the system. This is helpful when you are performing certain maintenance work at run time.

◆ **Network**. A good NIC is essential for networking. Typically, a 10/100 Mbps card is used. This can take the entire network up to T3 speed (shared). Make sure that you have a non-promiscuous mode network adapter. That way even if the security of your bastion host is compromised, the attacker will not be able to read all of the traffic that travels on the perimeter network, provided that you have more than one bastion host. Sometimes a non-promiscuous mode network adapter might not be compatible with other network devices, such as routers or bridges. Make sure that you read the vendor documentation before venturing into such cards. Also, some cards provide a wake-on LAN feature. This feature allows the administrator to remotely start the system for maintenance. This feature is not of much use because the bastion host rarely shuts down. Moreover, this feature might compromise the security of the host because an attacker can also manipulate the NIC remotely if such features are present.

Operating System

Once you have selected the appropriate hardware configuration for your bastion host, you should install the operating system on the hardware. As a matter of fact, you should base your identification of the right hardware configuration and the appropriate software on the operating system that you will install. The operating system that you will install on the bastion hosts should also satisfy the following criteria.

◆ Scalability
◆ Reliability
◆ Configurability
◆ Robustness

Most of the UNIX-based operating systems satisfy all of the preceding criteria. In the Microsoft world, Windows NT and Windows 2000 machines can also be configured as bastion hosts. Most of the time, either a Windows NT-based system or some type of UNIX variant is used as the operating system on a bastion host because Windows NT and UNIX are stable, time-tested platforms. There are other operating systems, such as Macintosh, which you can configure as bastion hosts, but the problem with such systems is that there are not enough tools available on the market for such platforms.

The UNIX operating system has been around for quite some time. As such, there are a variety of tools available on the market for such systems. UNIX or Linux operating systems are the preferred operating system for bastion hosts by many of the security experts. Windows NT also fits the bill, but it is considered more complex. However, Windows NT servers can be used as bastion hosts when you are using the Windows platform on other internal clients, which makes the configuration of the bastion host much easier. Whenever you are selecting an appropriate operating system, the basic criterion should be that the operating system supports a networking environment.

In the later sections of this chapter, you will learn how to set up a UNIX or Linux box as a bastion host. You will also learn how to set up a Windows NT or Windows 2000 box as a bastion host. If you are planning to use any other operating system, make sure that the operating system supports the following criteria.

◆ Networking
◆ Multi-user environment
◆ Stable file system
◆ Threading
◆ Support for RAID
◆ A 32-bit or higher word size, if possible

A list of other possible operating systems includes

◆ SUN Solaris
◆ Mac OS X
◆ VMS
◆ HP UX
◆ IBM OS/2

Services

Once you have set up the hardware and the operating system of the bastion host, you need to set up the other services that the bastion host intends to provide to the Internet. Typically, a bastion host exposes all of the publicly accessible services. A list of some publicly accessible services includes

◆ Domain naming using DNS
◆ Web servers using HTTP
◆ Mail servers using SMTP
◆ News servers using NNTP
◆ File transfer using FTP
◆ Telnet

A bastion host should not expose any services that will compromise the security of the internal network. It is important that the bastion host provides the DNS service in order to host other services, such as FTP and SMTP. Figure 7.1 shows the services that are exposed by a bastion host.

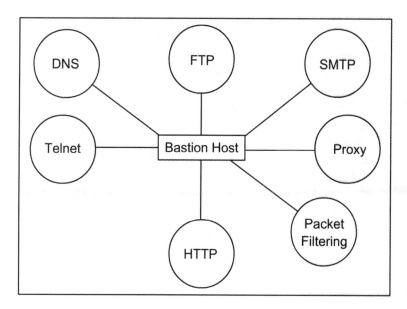

FIGURE 7.1 *Services of bastion hosts*

A single bastion host can provide all of the services listed previously, or you can establish every service on a separate bastion host. The latter choice keeps the bastion host very simple. In that case, the bastion host needs to concentrate on only one service rather than several. This also simplifies the configuration the bastion host, but it brings in an administrative overhead in terms of managing all of the different systems. Although the design consideration of a single service on a single host is a logical, simple model, the administrative and financial constraints overcome the benefits of such a model.

After you establish all of the services, it is important to set up the access control for them. None of the user accounts on the internal network should be able to log on to the bastion host because of the vulnerabilities that user accounts bring to it. In other words, a user account always uses a reusable password that can be broken by an attacker (by brute force). After the user account is compromised, the bastion host can be easily compromised. Therefore, you should keep the number of user accounts to a bare minimum or have only administrator accounts for the bastion host.

Location

Now that you have finalized the hardware, operating system, and services of the bastion host, your next step is to identify the appropriate physical and network location. Physically, a bastion host should be in a secure place. Most of the time, it is set up in an administrator's room behind locked doors. The physical security of the bastion host is important to prevent social engineering attacks such as physical break-ins or shoulder surfing.

The network location of the bastion host is also important due to its amount of exposure on the Internet. If the bastion host is located on the internal network and an attacker breaks in, the security of the entire internal network is at risk because the attacker can usually sniff the traffic on the network by forcing the NIC card of the bastion host into promiscuous mode. For this reason, a bastion host is generally placed on a separate network at a DMZ or the perimeter security.

Because a bastion host is configured as an extremely restricted system and is placed on the perimeter security, the risk to the internal network is drastically reduced if the bastion host is compromised. Usually on a perimeter security, there is no system that contains sensitive information that might be of use to the attacker. As a result, even if an attacker forces the NIC card of the bastion host into promiscuous mode, he will not gain much information by sniffing on the perimeter network traffic. You can also limit further exposure of your internal network to the bastion host by setting up packet filtering on the interior router that separates the internal network from the perimeter security. Figure 7.2 illustrates the location of the bastion host on the perimeter security.

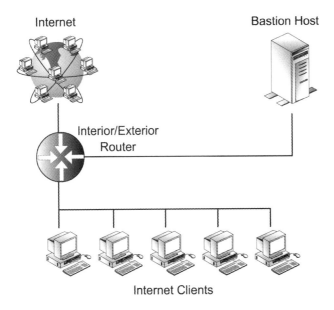

FIGURE 7.2 *The bastion host on a perimeter network*

After you have identified all of the required components, you need to harden the bastion host for final implementation.

Hardening

Hardening is a process in which you configure the bastion host so it can withstand attacks on the system. You must take extreme precautions when you configure your bastion hosts because they are the most exposed systems in your network.

You must harden the bastion host even before you connect the host to the network. In other words, you should first configure and test the bastion host services on a separate network. When you are finally convinced that the bastion host is totally safe, you can put it into use.

It is very important to document every process that you use when you harden a specific bastion host. That way, you can keep track of the process involved in rebuilding the host. Documentation also helps you identify all of the services and software that you set up on the host. Typically, you must document the following information when you harden the bastion host.

◆ **Information about hardware configuration and drivers**. This includes the following information.

- CPU
- Motherboard
- Chipsets
- RAM
- Hard disk
- Peripherals
- NIC
- Display

◆ **Information about the software**. This includes information about:

- Operating system
- Local services (printing, file sharing)
- DNS
- FTP
- WWW
- SMTP
- Daemon processes
- Applications and tools

The preceding list provides initial documentation of what needs to be created for the bastion host. Based on this list, you must document the following details for the drivers, services, and tools that are installed on a bastion host.

◆ Vendor information

◆ Version information

◆ Service packs

◆ Hot patches

◆ Build information

◆ Licenses

Also, keep a backup copy of all manuals, CDs, tapes, or any other disks that you have at the time of installation because they might be a useful resource at a later time. This level of detailed documentation is useful in analyzing the aftermath of an attack. In other words, if a hacker succeeds in attacking your bastion host, you can use the documentation to identify the attack modalities and try to fix the problem. For example, if the software driver of your NIC card had a bug, and the hacker used the bug in the driver to launch the attack, you can report the bug to the driver vendor. The vendor can verify the bug, write a new update patch for the driver, and immediately mail the update back to you. In most cases, if you have all of the information about the system readily available, you will be able to get help very quickly. The following sections provide a detailed explanation of hardening a bastion host.

Hardware Setup

Having identified the hardware configuration of your bastion host, you can either buy a pre-built server that satisfies your given requirements or you can build your own system. In most cases, a pre-built system will satisfy your needs. However, if you are very performance-conscious, you can buy the hardware components and build your own system.

Building your own system might prove economical and effective in the long run because parts from the wholesale market are quite inexpensive. You can also choose between different vendors for your components. For example, an Intel CPU might be more costly than an AMD CPU, or an AMD processor might provide greater clock speed than an Intel processor that costs the same amount. (These are just examples to illustrate a point, and should not be construed as advice to buy any specific make or brand.) You should also ensure that the vendor provides an appropriate warranty. In addition, when you build the system, you must document the appropriate components that you use. You must also document the setup details, such as the jumper settings or the wake-on LAN for the NIC.

Operating System Setup

After you set up the hardware, you can install the operating system that you have identified. Follow these steps to do so.

1. Start by partitioning the disk space on your hard drive and installing the operating system on the appropriate primary partition. Make sure you also set up the BIOS details before you install the OS. This is a necessary step; many of the old

UNIX boxes were hacked because of a bug in the BIOS software. Always read the manual provided by the motherboard manufacturer to understand the BIOS settings. Try to stick with a minimalist approach. In other words, try to install the minimum features of the OS. This will keep the installation and the final OS running on your bastion host simple.

2. Immediately after installing the OS, update the OS with all of the latest service packs and hot fixes. There might be other manual tweaking required for your operating system. In such cases, you should log on to the vendor site or any other newsgroups that might help you achieve the required setup. Configure all of the drivers on the OS. Make sure you also have the latest drivers for your systems—you don't want an attacker to compromise your system just because there was a bug in the display driver.

3. Configure all accounts and log settings that will help you trace the events on the host. Set up all of the alert mechanisms that are inherently built into the OS. Also, secure all of the sensitive folders and files. For example, you can set access permissions on folders in which you want to install additional applications and tools. You might want to set up permissions on system folders so that only an administrative account can access the folders. Protect all of the system logs to help you trace the attacker in the event of an attack. Remember to document all of the relevant setup details that you configure on the bastion host.

Configuring Services

After you configure the hardware, OS, and respective drivers, you are ready to install additional services on the bastion host. You must make sure that you have not enabled any services that are not required.

 NOTE

Keeping the system to the basic features simplifies the bastion host, which makes it easy to maintain and configure.

You need to identify the types of services that the bastion host should offer. As I mentioned earlier, a bastion host will typically offer the following services.

◆ WWW
◆ DNS
◆ FTP
◆ SMTP
◆ NNTP

You need to enable the appropriate services and install the respective server software on your bastion host. In most cases, you will only be installing a forwarding agent. For example, an SMTP service might be running on an internal mail server, and the bastion host might only be running a forwarding agent to forward all of the mail to the internal mail server.

Disabling all of the services that are not required will ensure hardening of your bastion host to a higher degree. You don't want to leave any loose ends for the attacker to use. You might have to edit some system configuration files to disable certain services. In such cases, you should keep a backup copy of all of the original files that are affected. This way, even if something goes wrong while you are configuring the services, you can revert to the initial state by copying the original files back to your system.

Sometimes you might have to tweak certain critical resources, such as system registries on Windows. However, an incorrect tweak might confuse the system and make it unusable. The worst that can happen is that you might not be able to properly boot the system. In such a case, you need to use the legendary patience that all administrators have to re-install the system from scratch, be prepared for the worst, and appropriately configure the bastion host. At a time like this, the documentation that you create when you configure the system will come in handy. You should document all of the misconfigurations that you made and the consequences of such misconfigurations. This will help you and other administrators avoid such misconfigurations in future.

After you have made all of the tweaks, you must create a repair disk, which will help you boot the system in emergencies. Update all of the backup copies of system files that you might have maintained and reboot the system to update the current changes.

You should disable all network-related services that you don't use. For example, if you don't use services such as Network DDE, fax services, or Net Logon, there is no need to keep them. Also, disable all of the daemon services that the bastion host does not use. Disable all of the ports that are not necessary for the operation of the installed services. This will ensure that the bastion host is not open for network scan attacks.

Finally, if you are setting up the bastion host as a dual-homed host, you must turn off routing and disable all of the applications that provide routing capabilities. In this scenario, you must also disable IP forwarding by any services on the host.

Security Measures

After you have made all of the configurations for the bastion host, you must implement additional security measures on the system.

1. Install system monitoring and audit tools that will help you monitor and analyze the bastion host.
2. Implement anti-virus tools that will help you defend any virus attacks on the system.

3. Install any external hardware locks.

4. Safeguard system resources using ACLs.

5. Secure system resources using cryptographic encryption. For example, set up audits based on checksum to ensure the integrity of your system files.

6. If you are using a packet-filtering system, make sure you configure the system using an easy-to-understand filtering rule. If you are using a proxy service instead, make sure that all of the applications are configured correctly for the proxy service to work.

7. Do not install any network-monitoring tool that might force the NIC in your bastion host into promiscuous mode.

Connecting and Running

Now that you have hardened the bastion host to a desired level, you can test its performance on your real network. You must monitor all of the network activities using the monitoring tool that is installed on the host. Initially, keep checking the event logs, system logs, and service-related logs frequently. You should understand all of the entries in such logs and fix any problems that might arise.

Next, you should document the number of users on the network and simulate the maximum network load on the bastion host. Document the performance dynamics of the bastion host using a system-monitoring tool and fix any bottlenecks. Document the resource usage, such as memory, CPU, and swap space of the bastion host. Reboot the bastion host multiple times while connected to the network and see if everything works. Allow the users to start using the network only after you are completely satisfied with the bastion host.

The preceding sections explained the general configuration of a bastion host. They also explained the process of identifying the bastion host requirements. In the following section, I will discuss the process of setting up a Windows-based bastion host.

Windows Bastion Host

As I mentioned earlier, the first step in building any bastion host is to identify the appropriate hardware components. For this example, assume that you have already decided to use Windows NT. You must now look for compatible hardware. Typically, an Intel-based machine is the first choice for the hardware.

After you have the appropriate hardware in place, you are ready to install the Windows NT operating system. You need to decide which version of Windows NT you want to install. There are two versions of the Windows NT system available on the market—Windows NT 4 Server and Windows NT 4 Workstation.

Generally, it is a good idea to choose the Windows NT Server software because it provides network-oriented features and services. A Windows NT Workstation is used as a client system that hooks up to a server on the network. Also, a Windows NT Workstation does not provide as many features as the Windows NT Server software.

Make sure that you have the latest release of the software for the OS you have selected. Obtain all of the service packs, hot-fixes, and security patches from the Microsoft Web site. It is a good idea to obtain the resource kit that is available for the Windows NT Server operating system. The kit contains administrative tools and extensive documentation that allows you to set up the Windows NT OS on your system.

Before you install the OS, you must format and partition the hard disk. Ensure that all of the partitions are using the NTFS file system, which is more reliable, robust, and secure than the FAT file system. When you are installing the operating system, choose only those services and features that are necessary for the bastion host to work. After the installation, upgrade the system with all of the service packs. You can manually tweak the configuration of your Windows NT server by using the guides and documentation available on the Microsoft site. Also, the Microsoft site contains all the known bugs that might cause security holes in your operating system. It is important to fix these known bugs either by applying hot-fixes or by manually editing the configuration files.

Installing the Services

After you install the operating system, you need to set up all of the services on the bastion host. Make sure you are installing only necessary services. Remove all of the services and subsystems that are not required. You must install and configure the services using the service interface provided by the Control Panel of the operating system. You can also install certain services using the Network interface of the Control Panel. Certain other types of services can be installed through applications that provide specific functionality for the operating system.

Windows NT manages the services using a kernel-level process that runs within the core of the operating system. It provides a user-level interface that you can use to administer the services. It also exposes the user-level APIs that you can use to query, start, and stop the services within the application. Typically, when you set up a service, you are asked to configure the startup of the service. You can configure the service to start up manually or as soon as the Windows system boots up. You can configure certain services to start at boot time and others to start only manually. This decision should be based on the type of service you are considering. Sometimes it is a good idea to start certain services only manually; this will allow you finer control when deciding which services should be running at a particular point in time.

A service can be implemented by executing an executable or by installing a process, which can be a device driver, a subsystem within the OS, or an application such as Web server. When you install the process, it might set up certain services that are not be visible within the SCM (*Service Control Manager*) of the Control Panel. (You will learn more about the SCM in "The Service Control Manager" section later in this chapter.) These services will be running with the kernel as a device driver or as some other process at the user level.

Either way, it is hard to control all of the services that execute within the Windows NT operating system. Even configuring the service parameters is comparatively harder than with UNIX boxes.

 NOTE

Technically, a UNIX box provides greater configurability and control on every service that executes with the OS.

Windows NT provides some level of configurability for certain services that are not visible within the SCM. To actually configure the parameters of such invisible services within the service interface, you need to create registry keys. One such registry entry is HKEY_LOCAL_MACHINE\System\CurrentControlSet\Services.

When you open the registry editor using the `regedit` tool, you will see a list of services with their configuration details. Typically, you will see all of the services within a registry entry. You will also see certain services that are not displayed within the SCM. For example, the SCM might display certain services such as Removable Storage, Telephony, Telnet, Event Log, DNS Client, Network DDE, or Indexing Service. The registry entry might also have services and device drivers listed, such as printer, scanner, display driver, or CD-ROM driver. Although these are not technically considered services, they are services for the OS. The OS considers these device drivers as services too, and expects their parameters to be configured. There are different parameters that can be used to configure such services within the registry.

 NOTE

By definition, services are those process that use the Win32 API to interact with the operating system to provide system-level processes; this does not require any user intervention.

Most of the services act as servers that satisfy clients' requirements, whether it is an HTTP client or a user process trying to obtain a handle to the print services. A Win32 service is based on the following three components.

◆ Service application
◆ Service accounts
◆ SCM

The following sections provide a detailed explanation of these three service components.

Service Applications

A service application provides a user-level interface to run and configure the service. Technically, any executable that runs as a Win32 service is called a service application. If you want to configure such services, you should use the SCM within the Control Panel. You can use the SCM to start, stop, or pause these services.

A service application does not need to have a GUI interface. Instead, it can be run through the console. Either way, when you install a service, it must register to the OS by invoking the Win32 CreateService API. The Win32 OS implements this API within the ADVAPI32.DLL file. Typically, when you say that the service is registered to the OS, it means that a registry key within the Win32 registry is created. As discussed earlier, this registry key will be created under the HKEY_LOCAL_MACHINE\SYSTEM\CurrentControlSet\Services location.

After the service is registered to the OS, it can be started using the StartService API within the Win32 API framework. Depending on how the service is registered, it can be started automatically without a reboot; otherwise, a reboot needs to be performed.

The parameters of the service configuration are stored within the registry key, as listed in Table 7.1.

Table 7.1 Service and Driver Registry Parameters

Value Name	Value Setting	Description
DependOnGroup	Group name	A dependency list. Drivers or services will not load unless a driver or service from the specified group loads.
DependOnService	Service name	A dependency list. Services will not load until after the specified service loads. This parameter does not apply to device drivers.
Description	Description of service	A service description of up to 1024 bytes.
DisplayName	Name of service	The name shown within the services Control Panel.
ErrorControl	IGNORE (0x00)	The I/O manager ignores failures and continues operation without any warning or display.
	NORMAL (0x01)	A warning message will be displayed for failures.

Value Name	Value Setting	Description
	SEVERE (0x02)	On failure, reboot using the LastKnownGood configuration. If the LastKnownGood configuration is not available, reboot anyway.
	CRITICAL (0x03)	On failure, reboot using the LastKnownGood configuration. If the LastKnownGood configuration is not available, then do not reboot. This produces a blue screen crash with stack dump on the screen.
Group	Group name	A name of a group.
ImagePath	Path to service or driver executable file	A place where the executable for the service is located. If this option is not specified, the I/O Manager looks for drivers in \winnt\system32\drivers, and the SCM looks for services in \winnt\system32.
ObjectName	Usually LocalSystem	Specifies the account name, which can be an account name under which the service runs. If the ObjectName is not specified, LocalSystem is used. This parameter does not apply to device drivers.
Start	SERVICE_BOOT_START (0x00)	NT Loader (NTLDR) or OSLOADER preloads the driver so that the driver is in memory during the boot. SERVICE_BOOT_START drivers initialize just before the SERVICE_SYSTEM_START drivers.
	SERVICE_SYSTEM_START (0x01)	The driver loads and initializes after SERVICE_BOOT_START drivers have initialized.
	SERVICE_AUTO_START (0x02)	The SCM starts the driver or service.

(continued on next page)

Table 7.1 Service and Driver Registry Parameters (continued from previous page)

Value Name	Value Setting	Description
	SERVICE_DEMAND_START (0x03)	The SCM must start the driver or service on demand.
	SERVICE_DISABLED (0x04)	The driver or service does not load or initialize.
Tag	Tag number	A specified location in a group initialization order. This parameter does not apply to services.
	SERVICE_KERNEL_ DRIVER (0x01)	Device driver.
	SERVICE_FILE_SYSTEM_ DRIVER (0x02)	Kernel-mode file-system driver.
	SERVICE_RECOGNIZER_ DRIVER (0x04)	File-system recognizer driver.
	SERVICE_WIN32_OWN_ PROCESS (0x10)	A service that runs in a process that hosts only one service.
	SERVICE_WIN32_SHARE_ PROCESS (0x20)	A service that runs in a process that hosts multiple services.
	SERVICE_INTERACTIVE_ PROCESS (0x100)	A service that can display Windows on the console and receive user input.

Service Accounts

A service account is the system account within which the services execute. It is a regular user account with specific properties that allow it to act as a part of the operating system.

There are different types of accounts, such as:

◆ Local account
◆ System account
◆ Domain account

Typically, a service runs within the security context of the system account. Different accounts provide different capabilities for the service. The system account is considered more powerful than other accounts in terms of security context because it owns all of the defined privileges within the OS and can access most of the files and registry keys. A service needs to run within the system services account only if it requires access to any of the network-related resources. For this reason, most of the services that are registered within the registry will be configured to run as system service accounts.

The Service Control Manager

SCM is the final component required to properly execute a service within the Win32 OS. It provides a management console to administer the services. It is a Windows NT Server process that manages all of the services in the Windows NT registry. SCM has an executable called services.exe within the Win32 OS. This executable is invoked when the OS boots. If you open the Task Manager within the Windows NT OS, you will notice this process running.

It is the SCM's responsibility to load all of the registered services within the Windows registry. It invokes the SvcCtrlMain function to start all of the services, which are configured as automatic start. In other words, SCM starts all of the services that are registered to start at boot time. It is also responsible for starting all of the device drivers that are registered within the registry. If there is any failure at the startup of these services or device drivers, SCM will appropriately invoke the event handlers to log the failure.

SCM is also used to administer the service. In other words, the Win32 OS will use it to start, stop, or pause any service that is running on the OS. The OS also uses it to perform the cleanup in order to properly shut down a service at the time the OS shuts down.

The following sections describe which services should be enabled and disabled with the Windows NT OS.

Services to Enable

The services that are explained within this section are the bare minimum that must be enabled for smooth functioning of a bastion host. These services are enabled apart from the other functional services for DNS, proxy, FTP, SMTP, Telnet, and other servers.

- ◆ **EventLog**. This is the most required service. It logs all of the system events that occur within the OS. The event logger logs the error details and descriptions of what went wrong at the system boot. It also logs warnings and information-related messages.

- ◆ **Net Logon**. This service must be enabled to authenticate user accounts for remote machines. It should be enabled only if the bastion host wants to authenticate users on the network.

- ◆ **NT LM Security Support Provider**. This service must be enabled if any of the other services that are running on the Windows NT OS need to authenticate users through the service. Some of the services, such as FTP or Web servers, might need to authenticate a user before providing any functionality.

◆ **Protected Storage**. This service must be enabled to provide functionality for the NTFS file system. It supports storage protection through encryption.

◆ **Plug-and-Play**. This service is required to enable hot-swapping functionality within the bastion host. If you want to hot-swap hard disks, CD-ROMs, or any other secondary storage device at run time, you should enable the Plug-and-Play service. Sometimes Plug-and-Play is required even if you are not planning to use the hot-swap functionality.

◆ **Remote Procedure Call**. Servers use an RPC to remotely invoke operations across the network. This service must be enabled for proper functioning of many network servers.

◆ **Spooler**. This service provides spooling for many processes over the network. Spooling is a process in which multiple jobs sent to a network resource are properly queued for execution. For example, a printer needs spooling to work properly on the network.

Services to Disable

This section details the non-critical services that need to be disabled within the Windows NT OS.

◆ **Microsoft TCP/IP Printing**. The TCP/IP printing service should be disabled if printing from the bastion host is not essential. The printing service is not a very secure service. If you must use a printer on the bastion host, then use it only as a local printer, without sharing it on the network.

◆ **Microsoft DNS Server**. This service is only available on the Windows NT 4 Server OS. It can be disabled if you are not interested in providing a naming service through the host. Disabling this service will also affect FTP and SMTP services because they are dependent on the DNS.

◆ **NetBIOS Interface**. This service should be disabled if you are not using Net-BIOS over your network. Usually a bastion host will never use NetBIOS over a perimeter network because it is not very secure. In any case, there might be no reason to use this interface.

◆ **Remote Access Service**. A remote access service enables network access over telephony, which allows PPTP over phone lines. There is no need for such access for a bastion host, and the service should be disabled. This service should be enabled only in the rare cases of VPN for the bastion host.

◆ **Server**. This is a default service on both the Windows NT 4 Workstation and NT 4 Server operating systems. This service is enabled only if a NetBIOS inbound connection is required on the bastion host. Typically, all NetBIOS-related services are disabled on the bastion host.

- **Simple TCP/IP Services**. This service provides simple TCP/IP services such as daytime or echo, which are not much help on a bastion host. To keep the bastion host simple, this service should be disabled.

- **SNMP Service**. This service must never be enabled on a bastion host because it opens a greater possibility for attack. An SNMP service provides a lot of administrative control to the attacker, and thus is highly insecure.

In the preceding sections, you learned how to set up a Windows NT-based bastion host. This following section explains how to set up a UNIX-based bastion host.

UNIX Bastion Host

The configuration of a UNIX-based bastion host is similar to that of a Windows-based bastion host. The first step is to build the hardware configuration. When you are working with UNIX, building a hardware configuration is not easy compared to the Windows world. The right hardware configuration depends on what flavor, version, or brand of UNIX system you want to install. You must first select the appropriate version of the software, and then make a decision about what type of hardware you need. After you have identified the OS, you can search the Internet to obtain an HCL (*Hardware Compatibility List*), which makes it relatively easy to build the system.

Although every flavor of UNIX has a different set of guidelines to be configured as a bastion host, I will stick to general guidelines that are applicable to most of the UNIX flavors. If you need a complete and comprehensive guide on setting up a particular flavor of the UNIX OS, you must refer to the vendor-provided guides and manuals. Also, there are many newsgroups and information sites on the Internet that are dedicated to helping particular UNIX user groups.

The real task in configuring a UNIX bastion host is to decide the right version of the OS. Typically, most security experts choose the version they are trained in or use most. Choosing the right UNIX flavor is mostly a matter of preference of the administrators and security experts. Often you will use the version supported by the organization, perhaps due to an already existing UNIX platform within the organization or certain constraints such as economic feasibility of the implementation. Sometimes a particular UNIX flavor is chosen due to its wide support of tools and applications.

The following is a partial list of the different flavors of UNIX currently available.

- SCO UNIX
- IBM AIX
- AT&T UNIX (System V)
- SUN Solaris
- Siemens SINIX (SNI)
- Berkley BSD

◆ DEC Ultrix

◆ HP UX

◆ SGI IRIX

◆ Digital UNIX (also OpenVMS on VAX and AXP)

◆ NCR UNIX

◆ Novell UNIXWare

◆ NeXTSTEP

◆ Apple Mac OS X

◆ Linux (many brands within this group)

You can choose any of the listed UNIX operating systems for the bastion host installation. Linux is a good choice because it is freely available. Also, there are numerous dedicated sites for Linux. Among the many brands available within the Linux community, the following are quite well known.

◆ Slackware

◆ Red Hat

◆ Debian

◆ Mandrake

◆ SuSE

◆ Caldera

◆ Conectiva

◆ TurboLinux

The preceding list is not exhaustive. Regardless of the flavor of UNIX or Linux that you choose, you get very similar security features. After you have decided on the right OS, install it using the guidelines in the vendor manuals. Make sure that the version you install is the latest. Install all of the security patches and hot fixes that are available. When you are installing the OS, start with a clean installation in which you have to format and partition the hard disk from scratch.

After the installation, you can set up all of the environment variables through the .profile file for the root, as well as the appropriate home directories for all users on the bastion host. The number of user accounts on the bastion host needs to be limited because you do not want too many people logging onto the system. You should keep the installation of the subsystems and the daemon processes to a minimum. As I explained earlier, you should keep the bastion host as simple as possible.

Installing the Services

After you install the OS, install the services that are necessary for the bastion host to operate. To configure the services on the UNIX OS, you must first understand how they work.

The services under UNIX are typically configured using the configuration files for the appropriate service. These files are located under the /etc/rc/ directory. All services that start through the configuration files within the /etc/rc/ directory are started at boot time. These services will stop only while the UNIX OS is being shut down. The only way to stop them is to obtain the root privilege (su) and kill the process using the process id (pid).

Most of the services are started through the configuration files located under the /etc/rc/ directory. These configuration files are scripts that are assigned an executable permission. They are called the *startup scripts*, and they are typically written under a particular shell (for example, csh and bash).

Different UNIX variations use different locations for the startup scripts. Many use the /etc/ directory for the startup scripts, while others use other subdirectories under /etc/. Make sure you study the vendor guide and Web sites to understand how and where the startup scripts are configured. Also, you need to understand the shell programming concepts to understand the content within the script. The following services are some examples that can be started through the scripts in /etc/rc/ directory.

◆ DNS

◆ SMTP

◆ NFS

Under Linux, the directory structure will be /etc/rc.d/, which might contain files as follows.

◆ rc

◆ rc.local

◆ rc.sysinit

Take a look at some sample files from the Red Hat Linux 7.3 OS. Following the listings will provide you with an idea of what these files might contain.

◆ A sample rc file

```
#!/bin/bash
#
# rc          This file is responsible for starting/stopping
#             services when the runlevel changes. It is also
#             responsible for the very first setup of basic
#             things, such as setting the hostname.
#
# Original Author:
#             Miquel van Smoorenburg, <miquels@drinkel.nl.mugnet.org>
#
```

```
# Now find out what the current and what the previous runlevel are.
argv1="$1"
set `/sbin/runlevel`
runlevel=$2
previous=$1
export runlevel previous

# Source function library.
. /etc/init.d/functions

# See if we want to be in user confirmation mode
if [ "$previous" = "N" ]; then
    if grep -i confirm /proc/cmdline >/dev/null ¦¦ [ -f /var/run/confirm ] ; then
      rm -f /var/run/confirm
      CONFIRM=yes
      echo $"Entering interactive startup"
    else
      CONFIRM=
      echo $"Entering non-interactive startup"
    fi
fi

export CONFIRM

# Get first argument. Set new runlevel to this argument.
[ -n "$argv1" ] && runlevel="$argv1"

# Is there an rc directory for this new runlevel?
if [ -d /etc/rc$runlevel.d ]; then
                # First, run the KILL scripts.
                for i in /etc/rc$runlevel.d/K*; do
                    # Check if the script is there.
                    [ ! -f $i ] && continue

                    # Don't run [KS]??foo.{rpmsave,rpmorig} scripts
                    [ "${i%.rpmsave}" != "${i}" ] && continue
                    [ "${i%.rpmorig}" != "${i}" ] && continue
```

```
        [ "${i%.rpmnew}" != "${i}" ] && continue


        # Check if the subsystem is already up.
        subsys=${i#/etc/rc$runlevel.d/K??}
        [ ! -f /var/lock/subsys/$subsys ] && \
            [ ! -f /var/lock/subsys/${subsys}.init ] && continue


        # Bring the subsystem down.
        if egrep -q "(killproc ¦action )" $i ; then
                $i stop
        else
                action $"Stopping $subsys: " $i stop
        fi
done


# Now run the START scripts.
for i in /etc/rc$runlevel.d/S*; do
        # Check if the script is there.
        [ ! -f $i ] && continue


        # Don't run [KS]??foo.{rpmsave,rpmorig} scripts
        [ "${i%.rpmsave}" != "${i}" ] && continue
        [ "${i%.rpmorig}" != "${i}" ] && continue
        [ "${i%.rpmnew}" != "${i}" ] && continue


        # Check if the subsystem is already up.
        subsys=${i#/etc/rc$runlevel.d/S??}
        [ -f /var/lock/subsys/$subsys ] ¦¦ \
            [ -f /var/lock/subsys/${subsys}.init ] && continue


        # If we're in confirmation mode, get user confirmation
        [ -n "$CONFIRM" ]   &&
          {
            confirm $subsys
            case $? in
              0)
                 :
                 ;;
```

```
            2)
               CONFIRM=
            ;;
            *)
               continue
            ;;
         esac
      }


   # Bring the subsystem up.
   if egrep -q "(daemon ¦action )" $i ; then
         if [ "$subsys" = "halt" -o "$subsys" = "reboot" ]; then
                  unset LANG
                  unset LC_ALL
                  unset TEXTDOMAIN
                  unset TEXTDOMAINDIR
                  exec $i start
         else
             $i start
         fi
      else
         if [ "$subsys" = "halt" -o "$subsys" = "reboot" -o
"$subsys" = "single" -o "$subsys" = "local" ]; then
               if [ "$subsys" = "halt" -o "$subsys" = "reboot" ];
then
                  unset LANG
                  unset LC_ALL
                  unset TEXTDOMAIN
                  unset TEXTDOMAINDIR
                  exec $i start
               fi
               $i start
         else
             action $"Starting $subsys: " $i start
         fi
      fi
done
```

◆ A sample `rc.local` file

```
#!/bin/sh
#
# This script will be executed *after* all the other init scripts.
# You can put your own initialization stuff in here if you don't
# want to do the full Sys V style init stuff.


touch /var/lock/subsys/local
```

Some other variants of UNIX (and Linux) have a /etc/inittab file, which starts the `init` process at boot time. /etc/inittab is a file that plays a crucial role at boot time. This file has the following entry format for every line within it.

```
id:runlevel:action:process
```

In the preceding format:

◆ `id` stands for a unique identifier that represents the process.

◆ `runlevel` represents the process' run level.

◆ `action` represents how the process needs to be run.

◆ `process` represents the name of the process that needs to be run.

The following is a sample inittab file from the Red Hat Linux 7.3 OS.

```
#
# inittab       This file describes how the INIT process should set up
#                 the system in a certain run-level.
#
# Author:       Miquel van Smoorenburg, <miquels@drinkel.nl.mugnet.org>
#                 Modified for RHS Linux by Marc Ewing and Donnie Barnes
#
# Default runlevel. The runlevels used by RHS are:
#    0 - halt (Do NOT set initdefault to this)
#    1 - Single user mode
#    2 - Multiuser, without NFS (The same as 3, if you do not have networking)
#    3 - Full multiuser mode
#    4 - unused
#    5 - X11
#    6 - reboot (Do NOT set initdefault to this)
#
id:5:initdefault:
```

```
# System initialization.
si::sysinit:/etc/rc.d/rc.sysinit

l0:0:wait:/etc/rc.d/rc 0
l1:1:wait:/etc/rc.d/rc 1
l2:2:wait:/etc/rc.d/rc 2
l3:3:wait:/etc/rc.d/rc 3
l4:4:wait:/etc/rc.d/rc 4
l5:5:wait:/etc/rc.d/rc 5
l6:6:wait:/etc/rc.d/rc 6

# Things to run in every runlevel.
ud::once:/sbin/update

# Trap CTRL-ALT-DELETE
ca::ctrlaltdel:/sbin/shutdown -t3 -r now

# When our UPS tells us power has failed, assume we have a few minutes
# of power left.  Schedule a shutdown for 2 minutes from now.
# This does, of course, assume you have power  installed and your
# UPS connected and working correctly.
pf::powerfail:/sbin/shutdown -f -h +2 "Power Failure; System Shutting Down"

# If power was restored before the shutdown kicked in, cancel it.
pr:12345:powerokwait:/sbin/shutdown -c "Power Restored; Shutdown Cancelled"

# Run gettys in standard runlevels
1:2345:respawn:/sbin/mingetty tty1
2:2345:respawn:/sbin/mingetty tty2
3:2345:respawn:/sbin/mingetty tty3
4:2345:respawn:/sbin/mingetty tty4
5:2345:respawn:/sbin/mingetty tty5
6:2345:respawn:/sbin/mingetty tty6

# Run xdm in runlevel 5
# xdm is now a separate service
x:5:respawn:/etc/X11/prefdm -nodaemon
```

Another way to start a service under UNIX is to use the `inetd` server. This is a daemon server (a service by itself) that is used to start other services on demand. The `inetd` daemon is started at the boot time of the OS. This is somewhat similar to what you did with SCM under the Windows NT OS. You are also allowed to stop the services that are started through the `inetd` server on demand. The services that you start using the `inetd` server are as follows.

◆ FTP proxy

◆ FTP server

◆ Telnet

Typically, the `inetd` servers listen to the requests from other services that are declared under the /etc/inetd.conf file. Under Linux, the file is named /etc/xinetd.conf. This conforms to the `xinetd` server under Linux. The `inetd` server is an Internet services daemon, while the `xinetd` server is an extended Internet services daemon. Following is the content of a sample xinetd.conf file.

```
#
# Simple configuration file for xinetd
#
# Some defaults, and include /etc/xinetd.d/

defaults
{
        instances            = 60
    log_type             = SYSLOG authpriv
    log_on_success        = HOST PID
    log_on_failure        = HOST
        cps               = 25 30
}


includedir /etc/xinetd.d
```

Note that xinetd.conf includes the files under the /etc/xinetd.d/ directory. This directory contains all of the services that can be started with the `xinetd` server. Next, take a look at what services should be enabled or disabled within the UNIX OS.

Services to Enable

The services that are explained in this section are essential for the OS to work. They must be enabled apart from the other functional services enabled for DNS, proxy, FTP, SMTP, Telnet, and other servers.

◆ `syslogd`. This is a daemon that collects the system events and logs them in the appropriate place. It is a collecting mechanism for various logging messages generated by the kernel and applications running on the UNIX OS.

◆ `Inetd` (or `xinetd`). This is the Internet services daemon used to start other services on demand.

◆ `cron`. This is a process that is configured to execute certain services at scheduled times. This helps to run some general OS maintenance scripts.

◆ `init`. This is a kernel process that is used as a general-purpose spawner. The `init` process spawns a new process based on the inittab file.

◆ `swap`. This is also a kernel process that is used to add, delete, and monitor the system swap areas used by the memory manager.

Services to Disable

The following services are not required for proper functioning of a UNIX bastion host. Moreover, enabling these services will increase the complexity of the system and possibly make the bastion host vulnerable to attack.

◆ **Booting services**. Disable all of the booting services such as `bootd`, `dhcpd`, `bootpd`, and `tftpd`. A bastion host should never provide booting services for other hosts.

◆ **Remote command services and RPC services**. Disable all of the "r" services, such as `rlogind` or `rececd`, under the UNIX OS because they make the bastion host vulnerable to attack. Also, there is no need to enable any remote administration or remote logins for your bastion host. You must also disable RPC-related services such as `NIS`, `rexd`, or `walld`.

◆ **NFS**. Disable NFS and related services, such as `nfsd`, `mountd`, `locd`, or `keyserv`, because you will not need them on a bastion host.

◆ **Other services**. Disable all of the other services such as `routed`, `fingerd`, `uucpd`, or `lpd`.

  • You do not need routed service because the bastion host does not need to listen to any routing information broadcast over the network.

  • You do not need the `fingerd` service because your bastion host should not serve any information about the existing accounts of the bastion host to other hosts on the network.

  • You do not need uucpd if you are not planning to support UUCP over TCP.

  • You do not need `lpd` because sharing of printing services over the network is not a good idea for a bastion host.

There are many configurations to set up perimeter security using a bastion host. For example, you can set up a perimeter security with many bastion hosts on the DMZ, each serving a single public service such as FTP or SMTP. In the following section, I will discuss how to set up a perimeter security using a single bastion host that forwards all of the service requests to the appropriate internal servers. This security setup is based on the screened subnet architecture.

Bastion Host Design

In a bastion host configuration based on the screened subnet architecture, an interior and exterior router are used with a bastion host in the DMZ. All of the public servers (DNS, WWW, and SMTP) are within the internal network and not within the DMZ. The bastion host acts as an advanced proxy to forward the protocol-specific details to the public servers within the internal network.

In such an architecture, the bastion host is the primary contact for inbound traffic from the Internet. All incoming DNS queries, e-mail (SMTP) sessions, and FTP connections are routed through the bastion host. All outbound traffic is handled in the following manner.

◆ The traffic can be handled by setting up a proxy server on the bastion host so that internal clients can communicate with the bastion host indirectly.

◆ You can set up packet filtering on both the interior and exterior routers so that the internal clients can directly access the external servers.

To better understand the screened subnet architecture, consider an example of a network. The configuration details for the network are as follows.

◆ Domain details

- Domain: conceptuniv.com
- Net ID: Class C (209.130.78)
- Architecture: Screened subnet architecture
- Host IP address range: 209.130.78.0 to 209.130.78.255
- Broadcast address: 209.130.78.255
- Netmask: 255.255.255.0

◆ Perimeter

- IP address range: 209.130.78.0 to 209.130.78.10
- Network address: 209.130.78.0
- Netmask: 255.255.255.245
- Gateway to the Internet (router): 209.130.78.1
- Gateway to the internal network (router): 209.130.78.9
- Bastion host: 209.130.78.2

◆ Internal network

- IP address range: 209.130.78.11 to 209.130.78.138
- Network address: 209.130.78.11
- Netmask: 255.255.255.128
- Gateway to the perimeter subnet (router): 209.130.78.12
- Internal mail server: 209.130.78.20
- FTP server: 209.130.78.21
- Primary DNS server: 209.130.78.22

Figure 7.3 illustrates the layout diagram for the aforementioned network and provides a layout for the screened subnet architecture.

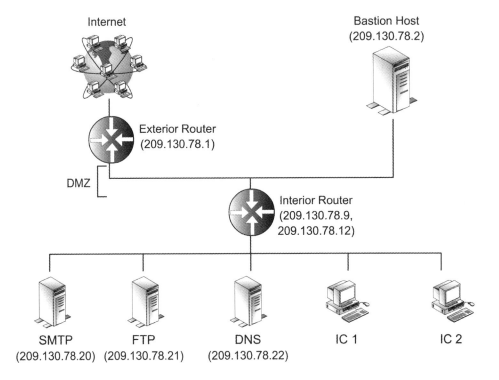

FIGURE 7.3 *The network layout diagram for the screened subnet architecture*

The perimeter layer is called the DMZ. Most times, an ISP provides the exterior router, so you might not have the privileges to fully configure it. This architecture is simple and can be set up with multiple layers. The architecture presented here is a two-router architecture. It uses an interior router that separates the internal network from the DMZ and an exterior router that acts as an Internet gateway, which separates the external network from the DMZ. Note that the bastion host sits within the DMZ, as shown in Figure 7.3.

The bastion host in this design is hosting a Web server to provide HTTP and HTTPS service to the Internet. It also hosts an HTTP proxy to provide HTTP access to the internal clients. The proxy service is cached to help reduce the bandwidth usage between the Internet gateway and the Internet. Using a caching proxy will also help the server be more efficient in rendering Web pages to internal clients.

This design publishes a DNS MX (*Mail Exchange*) record that is set up to redirect all of the inbound mail to the bastion host. The bastion host will direct all of the mail to the internal mail server (209.130.78.20). You must also configure all of the internal machines to direct all outbound mail to the internal mail server. The internal mail server will send the outbound mail to the bastion host, which in turn will direct the mail to the Internet.

This design hosts a DNS server as a secondary server on the bastion host. There is a primary DNS server that is hosted as an internal service of client 209.130.78.22. The FTP service is hosted on another internal client—209.130.78.21. You can choose to disable anonymous FTP connection.

Summary

In this chapter, you learned how to set up a bastion host. The chapter started by explaining the general setup of a bastion host, then it explained how to set up and configure a Windows NT-based bastion host. Finally, it described how to set up and configure a UNIX-based bastion host. The next chapter will discuss Internet services, such as WWW, electronic mail, file transfer protocol, and firewalls.

Check Your Understanding

Multiple Choice Questions

1. A bastion host is typically used to provide which of the following services?
   a. PPTP
   b. PostScript publishing
   c. FTP
   d. WWW

2. A bastion host can be used as _____.
   a. An internal bastion host
   b. A VPN

    c. A victim host

    d. A mail store

3. Screened subnet architecture is comprised of a _____ on the DMZ.

    a. Bastion host

    b. Hub

    c. Switch

    d. Bridge

4. A _____ acts as an intermediary for routing inbound and outbound mail through the bastion host.

    a. DNS MX record

    b. FTP

    c. WWW

    d. SMTP

Short Questions

1. Describe the role of a bastion host as a victim host.

2. Which services should be enabled on a Windows NT bastion host?

3. Which services should be enabled on a UNIX bastion host?

Answers

Multiple Choice Answers

1. c and d. A bastion host is typically used to provide FTP and WWW services.

2. a and c. A bastion host can be used as either an internal bastion host or a victim host.

3. a. Screened subnet architecture is comprised of a bastion host on the DMZ.

4. a. A DNS MX record acts as an intermediary for routing inbound and outbound mail through the bastion host.

Short Answers

1. A victim machine is like a sacrificial lamb that you offer to the attacker. If you are not sure about what type of security configuration is required for a particular service, you can set up such a service on a victim machine. The victim host will not

contain any sensitive information or any other data that can compromise the security of the internal network; it will only contain the bare minimum service configuration to run the appropriate service. Sometimes victim hosts are also set up to deliberately expose the system to attacks to gain time to facilitate tracking of such attacks on the network.

2. The following services should be enabled on a Windows NT bastion host.

   • EventLog

   • Net Logon

   • NT LM Security Support Provider

   • Protected Storage

   • Plug-and-Play

   • Remote Procedure Call

   • Spooler

3. The following services should be enabled on a UNIX bastion host.

   • syslogd

   • inetd (or xinetd)

   • cron

   • init

   • swap

Chapter 8

In the preceding chapters, you learned about firewall architecture and the steps to configure different types of firewalls. This chapter will elaborate on the relationship between Internet services and the firewall architecture that is configured on the internal network.

There are many Internet services that can be run on an internal network. When a user accesses any Internet service hosted by other servers on the Internet, or when the servers on your network host any such services, the most important task is to ensure the security of the client computers and the servers on the network.

These security issues have already been explained in the earlier chapters of the book. By now, you also know how to plan a firewall setup, build a firewall, and implement and configure perimeter security.

In this chapter, I will explain the important services that are used on the Internet and how you can specifically configure and secure the services over the network. The services that I will explain in this chapter are

- World Wide Web or HTTP
- E-mail or SMTP
- FTP

In the following sections, I will take a generic, non-vendor-specific approach to explain how to set up, configure, and secure the services over the Internet.

World Wide Web

The World Wide Web is a collection of Web servers on the Internet. The Internet and the Web are almost synonymous. Typically, the Internet is made up of many protocols, such as HTTP and SMTP. The Web is a collection of servers that only support the HTTP protocol.

The World Wide Web was a project started by the European Lab for Particle Physics (CERN). Tim Berners Lee was the individual behind the project. The objective was to create a distributed hypermedia system that used HTML as the authoring language. The Web slowly evolved from there. The Web and Internet are now interchangeable, although they have different meaning and roots.

Typically, you use a browser to surf the Web. A browser parses the markup scripts and languages that are used to author the Web page. In most cases, the scripts within the page that you view on the Web are safe. However, at times you might accidentally visit certain sites and Web pages that use scripts and code snippets that are intentionally written to hack into your system. When you come across harmful Web pages, you might be unaware of the type of attack or the kind of damage the page can cause your computer.

In this section, I will explain how the Web works and how you can secure your computer and network from harmful content and users on the Web. If you are planning to host a Web service on your network, you must secure the servers from external attacks. Therefore, this section will also explain how to secure a Web server on your network.

Web Servers

A Web server's function is to send Web pages to the requesting clients. Web pages are generally written using HTML, but you can also use many other types of scripting languages, including

- JavaScript
- VBScript
- Perl/CGI
- ASP (*Active Server Pages*)
- JSP (*JavaServer Pages*)
- Python
- DHTML (*Dynamic HTML*)
- XML (*Extensible Markup Language*)
- CFML (*ColdFusion Markup Language*)
- VRML (*Virtual Reality Markup Language*)

Every scripting language has its own strengths and weakness. The choice of the language is purely based on your requirements and the relative ease of authoring the page using the scripting language. For example, you can create a 3D view of a carbon molecule using VBScript. However, the same task is easier using VRML script because VRML is designed to script virtual reality, whereas VBScript is designed to write client-side Web applications. A client-side Web application needs a client-side UI, client-side validation, and client-side presentation logic.

Sometimes two scripts will fall into the same category to satisfy a given requirement. For example JSP and ASP fall into the same scripting category. The choice of the scripting language in this case depends on your level of comfort and the specific features of each language that are of interest to you.

A Web server can serve Web pages that have been authored using multiple scripting languages. Usually, the type of Web page is determined by the page's extension. For example, if the extension of a page is .html, the page is an HTML page. This information enables the browser to load the appropriate plug-in to view the page.

When you consider securing a Web server from other clients on the Internet, you might use a bastion host or employ perimeter security, such as a DMZ layer. (Bastion hosts and perimeter security were explained in detail in Chapters 5 and 7.) A Web server is mostly subject to denial of service attacks or buffer overflow attacks. The only way to secure your server from these attacks is to make sure that the server you are running is virus free and that you have upgraded all of the available security patches.

The firewall architecture makes a lot of difference in building a first line of defense for the Web server. Although you might have a very efficient firewall, the Web server can be subject to attack if there are any security holes in the server, such as when you have specified incorrect security permissions for the script files. Moreover, a Web server is a public server. Therefore, the server is visible to the public network, and the possibility of attack is relatively high.

To secure a Web server completely, you need to apply many techniques, which include a disciplined approach to configuring and maintaining the server. To configure your server, you need to make sure that you understand how the current Web servers work. Web server basics were explained in Chapter 1; to understand the complete workings of a Web server, you need to study the appropriate vendor guide for your server.

Most Web servers serve more than one type of file. Although they are meant to serve HTML pages on an HTTP protocol, current generation Web servers serve more than that. They also serve MIME (*Multimedia Internet Mail Extension*) types, which are listed in the following section.

MIME Types Supported by Web Servers

A partial list of MIME types served by the current generation of Web servers includes

- ◆ application/activemessage
- ◆ application/andrew-inset
- ◆ application/applefile
- ◆ application/atomicmail
- ◆ application/dca-rft
- ◆ application/dec-dx
- ◆ application/mac-binhex40 hqx
- ◆ application/mac-compactpro cpt
- ◆ application/macwriteii
- ◆ application/msword doc
- ◆ application/news-message-id
- ◆ application/news-transmission
- ◆ application/octet-stream bin dms lha lzh exe class

- ◆ application/oda oda
- ◆ application/pdf pdf
- ◆ application/postscript ai eps ps
- ◆ application/powerpoint ppt
- ◆ application/remote-printing
- ◆ application/rtf rtf
- ◆ application/slate
- ◆ application/smil smi smil sml
- ◆ application/wita
- ◆ application/wordperfect5.1
- ◆ application/x-bcpio bcpio
- ◆ application/x-cdlink vcd
- ◆ application/x-compress
- ◆ application/x-cpio cpio
- ◆ application/x-csh csh

- application/x-director dcr dir dxr
- application/x-dvi dvi
- application/x-gtar gtar
- application/x-gzip
- application/x-hdf hdf
- application/x-javascript js
- application/x-koan skp skd skt skm
- application/x-latex latex
- application/x-mif mif
- application/x-netcdf nc cdf
- application/x-sh sh
- application/x-shar shar
- application/x-stuffit sit
- application/x-sv4cpio sv4cpio
- application/x-sv4crc sv4crc
- application/x-tar tar
- application/x-tcl tcl
- application/x-tex tex
- application/x-texinfo texinfo texi
- application/x-troff t tr roff
- application/x-troff-man man
- application/x-troff-me me
- application/x-troff-ms ms
- application/x-ustar ustar
- application/x-wais-source src
- application/zip zip
- audio/basic au snd
- audio/midi midi kar
- audio/x-midi mid
- audio/mpeg mpga mp2 mp3
- audio/x-aiff aif aiff aifc
- audio/x-pn-realaudio ram
- audio/x-pn-realaudio-plugin rpm
- audio/x-realaudio ra
- audio/x-wav wav
- chemical/x-pdb pdb xyz
- image/gif gif
- image/ief ief
- image/jpeg jpeg jpg jpe
- image/png png
- image/tiff tiff tif
- image/x-cmu-raster ras
- image/x-portable-anymap pnm
- image/x-portable-bitmap pbm
- image/x-portable-graymap pgm
- image/x-portable-pixmap ppm
- image/x-rgb rgb
- image/x-xbitmap xbm
- image/x-xpixmap xpm
- image/x-xwindowdump xwd
- message/external-body
- message/news
- message/partial
- message/rfc822
- model/iges igs iges
- model/vrml wrl vrml
- model/mesh msh mesh silo
- multipart/alternative
- multipart/appledouble
- multipart/digest
- multipart/mixed
- multipart/parallel
- text/css css
- text/html html htm
- text/plain txt

- text/richtext rtx
- text/tab-separated-values tsv
- text/x-setext etx
- text/x-sgml sgml sgm
- text/xml xml dtd

- video/mpeg mpeg mpg mpe
- video/quicktime qt mov
- video/x-msvideo avi
- video/x-sgi-movie movie
- x-conference/x-cooltalk ice

The preceding list includes the content types that can be embedded within an HTML file. You might have noticed that this is a very exhaustive list. New additions will be made to the list over time. The MIME types can be used over protocols, such as HTTP or SMTP. Although MIME is a mail extension standard, it can still be used within Web servers.

A Web server needs to support streaming of all of these MIME types to Web clients whenever they request a page that contains these types. To do so, the Web server needs convert the MIME type to an appropriate byte stream. If the content type being served needs to be encrypted, then the Web server should also encrypt the content before sending it.

Compression also might be required at the time the data is sent. Eventually, a Web server needs to implement all of the functionalities to serve a page. Different Web servers use different algorithms to provide the stated functionality; the quality of implementation of these functions makes a lot of difference in the security of the Web server.

Securing Server Extensions

Apart from the MIME types, a Web server should also support extensions, which are similar to plug-ins for Web servers. An extension extends the functionality of a Web server. For example, you can extend the Web server's capability to serve JSP, ASP, or CGI programs. In other words, if you have a basic server that support only HTML pages, you can extend its functionality to provide server-side scripting capabilities. JSP or ASP programs are called *dynamic server-side programs*. These programs are executed at the server side before being served to the client.

Typically, you use JSP programs to create HTML pages dynamically on the server side if you want to serve information that is based on queries executed on a server-side database. You also have to use dynamic server-side programming if you are serving information based on the client's request parameters.

If a JSP program needs to work in tandem with the Web server, then you must install the JSP engine as a Web server extension. Depending on the type of server that you are using, there might be specific server-side APIs exposed so an extension can be written. For example, a vendor who writes a JSP engine as a Web server extension should use the appropriate server-side extension APIs to install the JSP engine. NSAPI (*Netscape Server API*) and ISAPI (*Internet Server API*) are two such APIs written for Netscape and

Microsoft IIS servers, respectively. A vendor who writes a JSP engine for IIS servers must use ISAPI to install the JSP engine on the server.

There are typically three ways to provide extra functionality from a Web server.

◆ **Built-in functionality**. When a vendor writes a functional module within the server, it is considered built in. The functional module runs in the same address space as the server.

◆ **Server extensions**. When a vendor uses the server API to plug in a functional module to the server, it is a server extension. A server extension also runs within the same address space as the server.

◆ **External process**. When a vendor writes a functional module to execute as a separate process and uses interprocess communication techniques to communicate with the server, it is an external process module. The external modules run in a separate address space from the server.

Before writing a server-side program, the server vendor should consider the security concerns of the organization. He or she should take extra care to ensure that the quality of the module is similar to the quality of the server. It is not just a Web server, but also an application server. Therefore, if the server and the module are secure but the application that the server runs is not, you still compromise the security of the Web server. Applications should conform to ACLs on the server to ensure security. Typically, servers that support application capabilities are not revealed to the public; they are placed behind the internal network (on a three-layered security), where a bastion host on the DMZ acts as a forwarding agent for the requests.

In other cases, where you have just a screening router architecture, you need to ensure that the program loaded to execute on the Web server has the necessary precautions in place to access the internal resources, because a hacker can use such programs to obtain sensitive information. Such attacks are called *Web application attacks*, and they occur when the hacker manipulates the input parameters for server-side programs to obtain information.

To prevent Web application attacks, you can take the following precautions.

◆ Preferably, use the screened-server architecture with a bastion host as a forwarding agent and run the server behind the internal network. Alternatively, you can isolate the server from internal resources by placing it in the DMZ.

◆ Use authentication schemas to allow only those users that are authentic.

◆ Assign extensive authorization or access control for applications.

◆ Run the program on the Web server in a least privilege mode.

In the case of a server extension module and the external process modules, you have to take extra precautions. The vendor who provides these functional modules might not be the same as your Web server vendor. There might be many integration issues between the functional modules and the Web server. The weakest link could be the link between the Web server and the functional module. Read on to learn how to examine the security constraints for server extensions and external process modules.

Server Extension Modules

Since server extension modules run within the same native address space as the server, they will share global resources allocated on the address space. This is an important security concern. If the server extension is not written with high-quality conformance, the extension will compromise the security architecture. Therefore, although such extension modules have the advantage of speed and scalability, it is risky to use them. If any code in the server extension crashes, the server will crash with it.

External Process Modules

In case of external process modules, the process link that connects the Web server and the external module is not secure. This link is open for exploitation because there is no encryption or other shielding technique you can apply for the process-to-process connection. In such cases, you should ensure that the Web server and the external module are running on a single computer, such as a bastion host. You need to fortify the computer that is running these services from external attacks. If you execute the external module on a system other than the Web server, the module can use RPC or similar mechanisms to communicate with the server. In this case, the process' security needs are complex. Therefore, you should not run the external module on a separate machine from the Web server.

Securing Web Clients

In addition to securing the Web server on your network, you need to secure the Web clients. The internal hosts on the network might want to access Web sites, so you need to ensure that the access to the external network is secured. In addition to applying the security policy explained throughout the book, you also need to take some extra precautions. The following list explains the precautions that a Web client must take while accessing external pages.

- ◆ Always use the latest version of browsers.
- ◆ Use the latest security updates for the browser.
- ◆ Disable cookies if possible. If this is not feasible, try to clear the cookie cache as often as possible.
- ◆ Disable ActiveX if possible. If this is not feasible, configure the browser to prompt you whenever an ActiveX control is about to execute.
- ◆ Avoid installing too many plug-ins on the browser. It will be very difficult to secure the client if it is downloading and executing different types of programs every time.
- ◆ Disable Java code downloads, if possible. If this is not feasible, configure the browser to prompt you whenever Java code needs to execute.
- ◆ Disable all software channels and push technology. Do not configure the browser to automatically obtain information that is sent from other URLs.

♦ Disable user data persistence.

♦ Disable anonymous logons. Configure the browser to always prompt for the user name and password.

♦ Delete the cache pages frequently.

♦ Block all of the Web sites that are determined to be harmful. This should preferably be independent of the default denial security policy your organization uses.

♦ Configure multiple security zones on the browser and appropriately set up the security policy for each zone from within the browser.

HTTP Filtering Rules

You use firewall rules to determine which data packets should be allowed to pass through the firewall and which packets should be stopped. Table 8.1 provides the general filtering rules for the HTTP protocol.

Table 8.1 Filtering Rules for the HTTP Protocol

Rule	Direction	Source IP	Destination IP	Protocol	Source Port	Destination Port	ACK	Action
HTTP-Outgoing	Out	Internal clients	Trusted	TCP/IP	>1023	80	No	Permit
HTTP-Outgoing	In	Trusted sites	Internal clients	TCP/IP	80	>1023	Yes	Permit
HTTP-Incoming	In	Trusted sites	Web server IP	TCP/IP	>1023	80	No	Permit
HTTP-Incoming	Out	Web server IP	Trusted	TCP/IP	80	>1023	Yes	Permit

Electronic Mail

E-mail is a primary means of communication in the world today. Businesses need e-mail for their minute-to-minute transactions. It is considered the quickest and the cheapest means of communication, next to paging.

Since e-mail is the most crucial form of communication media available on the Internet, it needs higher security standards. Most business transactions use e-mail systems to deliver sensitive information across the Web. Even if the organization's network is secured with a firewall, the e-mail messages that leave the organization are not secure. Another issue pertaining to e-mail messages is that the host that receives the e-mail is also subjected to security risks because the e-mail message might contain viruses or malicious code that can attack the system or network. Therefore, in addition to securing outgoing mail, you should also secure the receiving host. If your organization is hosting a mail server on the network, you should secure the mail server from external threats.

In the following sections, I will explain how to secure the multiple components involved in an e-mail system. First, take a moment to examine the components of a mail system.

Mail System Components

A mail system includes the following components.

◆ **MTA** (*Mail Transport Agent*). An MTA interacts with the external host that wants to send an e-mail message to a receiver. Examples of MTAs are `send-mail`, `qmail`, `exim`, and `postfix`.

◆ **MDA** (*Mail Delivery Agent*). An MDA receives e-mail messages from MTA and saves them to the user's mailbox. It also verifies the disk quota of the mailbox and performs additional actions such as processing the message rules, sending notifications, and forwarding e-mail. Examples of MDAs are `maildrop` and `procmail`.

◆ **MUA** (*Mail User Agent*). An MUA interacts with the receiving host to hand over the e-mail messages. It is typically used for composing and reading mail. Examples of MUAs are `mozilla`, `mutt`, and `pine`.

In a typical e-mail system on the Internet, composing and delivering mail to users requires the following steps.

1. A user composes and sends mail from an external host using an MUA.

2. The MUA on the external host hands the mail to the MTA on the network, which in turn passes the mail to other MTAs until it reaches the receiver's mail server.

3. The mail server on the receiving end has an MDA that verifies and filters the mail before storing it in the receiver's mail store.

4. When the receiver wants to read the mail, he or she uses an MUA to obtain it from the mail store.

An MUA uses two major protocols.

◆ **POP** (*Post Office Protocol*). MUAs use POP to communicate and access mail from user mail stores. Generally, the POP protocol uses a clear-text password to authenticate the MUA to the mail store. In such cases, POP is vulnerable to snoop attacks on the network. To secure the POP connection, you should either use SSL or TLS as the messaging channel. SSL/TLS is not readily supported over POP; however, there is currently a new implementation of POP client/server technologies (called *secure POP*) that allow POP over SSL/TLS. Also, POP extension protocols such as APOP (*Authentication POP*) or KPOP (*Kerberos POP*) provide higher security than the usual POP.

◆ **IMAP (*Internet Mail Access Protocol*)**. MUAs use the IMAP protocol to obtain mail from the mail store. IMAP is more flexible than POP, which allows only a single mailbox for storing messages for a particular user. IMAP provides multiple mailboxes for a single user. Like POP, IMAP does not readily support SSL/TLS for secure messaging. Instead, newer implementations of IMAP are evolving to support the secure messaging protocols.

All components of the mail system are vulnerable to hacker attacks. An easy way to secure the mail system is to secure the MTA and MUA on the network, and then ensure that your ISP has secured the MDA, mail store, and intermediary MTA. This only leaves the communication channel vulnerable. To secure mail on the communication channel, you can encrypt the mail using PGP or other similar techniques.

E-Mail Attachments

An e-mail message can carry different types of attachments, which are also called MIME types. Table 8.2 provides an extensive list of all of the content types that an e-mail can carry.

Table 8.2 MIME Types Used in E-Mail

Top-Level Media Type	Subtypes
Text	plain, richtext, enriched, tab-separated-values, html, sgml, vnd.latex-z, vnd.fmi.flexstor (uri-list, vnd.abc, rfc822-headers, vnd.in3d.3dml, prs.lines.tag, vnd.in3d.spot), css, xml, xml-external-parsed-entity (rtf) , directory, calendar (vnd.wap.wml, vnd.wap.wmlscript, vnd.motorola.reflex, vnd.fly), vnd.wap.sl, vnd.wap.si, t140, vnd.ms-mediapackage (Vnd.IPTC.NewsML, vnd.IPTC.NITF, vnd.curl), vnd.DMClientScript, parityfec
Multipart	mixed, alternative, digest, parallel, appledouble, header-set, form-data (related), report, voice-message, signed, encrypted, byteranges
Message	rfc822, partial, external-body, news, http (delivery-status), disposition-notification, s-http

continued on next page

Table 8.2 MIME Types Used in E-Mail (continued from previous page)

Top-Level Media Type	Subtypes
Application	octet-stream, postscript, oda, atomicmail, Andrew-inset, slate, wita, dec-dx, dca-rft, activemessage, rtf, applefile, mac-binhex40, news-message-id, news-transmission, wordper-fect5.1, pdf, zip, macwriteii, msword, remote-printing, mathe-matica, cybercash, commonground, iges, riscos, eshop, x400-bp, sgml, cals-1840, pgp-encrypted, pgp-signature, pgp-keys, vnd.framemaker, vnd.mif (vnd.ms-excel), vnd.ms-powerpoint, vnd.ms-project, vnd.ms-works, vnd.ms-tnef, vnd.svd, vnd.music-niff, vnd.ms-artgalry, vnd.truedoc, vnd.koan, vnd.street-stream, vnd.fdf, set-payment-initiation, set-payment, set-registration-initiation, set-registration, vnd.seemail, vnd.businessobjects, vnd.meridian-slingshot, vnd.xara, sgml-open-catalog, vnd.rapid, vnd.enliven, vnd.japannet-registration-wakeup, vnd.japannet-verification-wakeup, vnd.japannet-payment-wakeup, vnd.japannet-directory-service, vnd.intertrust.digibox, vnd.intertrust.nncp, prs.alvestrand.titrax-sheet (vnd.noblenet-web), vnd.noblenet-sealer (vnd.noblenet-directory, prs.nprend, vnd.webturbo, hyperstudio, vnd.shana.informed.formtemplate, vnd.shana.informed.formdata, vnd.shana.informed.package, vnd.shana.informed.interchange, vnd.$commerce_battelle, vnd.osa.netdeploy, vnd.ibm.MiniPay, vnd.japannet-jpnstore-wakeup, vnd.japannet-setstore-wakeup, vnd.japannet-verification, vnd.japannet-registration, vnd.hp-HPGL, vnd.hp-PCL, vnd.hp-PCLXL, vnd.musician, vnd.FloGraphIt, vnd.intercon.formnet), vemmi (vnd.ms-asf, vnd.ecdis-update, vnd.powerbuilder6, vnd.powerbuilder6-s, vnd.lotus-wordpro, vnd.lotus-approach, vnd.lotus-1-2-3, vnd.lotus-organizer, vnd.lotus-screencam, vnd.lotus-freelance, vnd.fujitsu.oasys, vnd.fujitsu.oasys2, vnd.swiftview-ics, vnd.dna, prs.cww, vnd.wt.stf, vnd.dxr, vnd.mitsubishi.misty-guard.trustweb, vnd.ibm.modcap, vnd.acucobol, vnd.fujitsu.oasys3), marc (vnd.fujitsu.oasysprs, vnd.fujitsu.oasysgp, vnd.visio, vnd.netfpx, vnd.audiograph, vnd.epson.salt, vnd.3M.Post-it-Notes, vnd.novadigm.EDX, vnd.novadigm.EXT, vnd.novadigm.EDM, vnd.claymore, vnd.comsocaller), pkcs7-mime, pkcs7-signature, pkcs10 (vnd.yellowriver-custom-menu, vnd.ecowin.chart, vnd.ecowin.series, vnd.ecowin.fil

Top-Level Media Type	Subtypes
	erequest, vnd.ecowin.fileupdate, vnd.ecowin.seriesrequest, vnd.ecowin.seriesupdate, EDIFACT, EDI-X12, EDI-Consent, vnd.wrq-hp3000-labelled, vnd.minisoft-hp3000-save, vnd.ffsns, vnd.hp-hps, vnd.fujixerox.docuworks), xml, xml-external-parsed-entity, xml-dtd (vnd.anser-web-funds-transfer-initiation), vnd.anser-web-certificate-issue-initiation (vnd.is-xpr, vnd.intu.qbo, vnd.publishare-delta-tree, vnd.cybank), batch-SMTP (vnd.uplanet.alert, vnd.uplanet.cacheop, vnd.uplanet.list, vnd.uplanet.listcmd, vnd.uplanet.channel, vnd.uplanet.bearer-choice, vnd.uplanet.signal, vnd.uplanet.alert-wbxml, vnd.uplanet.cacheop-wbxml, vnd.uplanet.list-wbxml, vnd.uplanet.listcmd-wbxml, vnd.uplanet.channel-wbxml, vnd.uplanet.bearer-choice-wbxml, vnd.epson.quickanime, vnd.commonspace, vnd.fut-misnet, vnd.xfdl, vnd.intu.qfx, vnd.epson.ssf, vnd.epson.msf, vnd.powerbuilder7, vnd.powerbuilder7-s, vnd.lotus-notes), pkixcmp (vnd.wap.wmlc, vnd.wap.wmlscriptc, vnd.motorola.flexsuite, vnd.wap.wbxml, vnd.motorola.flexsuite.wem, vnd.motorola.flexsuite.kmr, vnd.motorola.flexsuite.adsi, vnd.motorola.flexsuite.fis, vnd.motorola.flexsuite.gotap, vnd.motorola.flexsuite.ttc, vnd.ufdl, vnd.accpac.simply.imp, vnd.accpac.simply.aso, vnd.vcx), ipp, ocsp-request, ocsp-response (vnd.previewsystems.box, vnd.mediastation.cdkey, vnd.pg.format, vnd.pg.osasli, vnd.hp-hpid), pkix-cert, pkix-crl (vnd.Mobius.TXF, vnd.Mobius.PLC, vnd.Mobius.DIS, vnd.Mobius.DAF, vnd.Mobius.MSL, vnd.cups-raster, vnd.cups-postscript, vnd.cups-raw), index, index.cmd, index.response, index.obj, index.vnd (vnd.triscape.mxs, vnd.powerbuilder75, vnd.powerbuilder75-s, vnd.dpgraph, http, sdp), vnd.eudora.data, vnd.fujixerox.docuworks.binder, vnd.vectorworks, vnd.grafeq, vnd.bmi, vnd.ericsson.quickcall, vnd.hzn-3d-crossword, vnd.wap.slc, vnd.wap.sic, vnd.groove-injector, vnd.fujixerox.ddd, vnd.groove-account, vnd.groove-identity-message, vnd.groove-tool-message, vnd.groove-tool-template, vnd.groove-vcard, vnd.ctc-posml, vnd.canon-lips, vnd.canon-cpdl, vnd.trueapp, vnd.s3sms, iotp, vnd.mcd

continued on next page

Table 8.2 MIME Types Used in E-Mail (continued from previous page)

Top-Level Media Type	Subtypes
	(vnd.httphone, vnd.informix-visionary, vnd.msign, vnd.ms-lrm), vnd.contact.cmsg, vnd.epson.esf, whoispp-query, whoispp-response, vnd.mozilla.xul+xml, parityfec, vnd.palm, vnd.fsc.weblaunch, vnd.tve-trigger, dvcs, sieve, vnd.vividence.scriptfile, vnd.hhe.lesson-player, beep+xml, font-tdpfr, vnd.mseq, vnd.aether.imp, vnd.Mobius.MQY, vnd.Mobius.MBK, vnd.vidsoft.vidconference, vnd.ibm.afplinedata, vnd.irepository.package+xml, vnd.sss-ntf, vnd.sss-dtf, vnd.sss-cod, vnd.pvi.ptid1, isup, qsig (timestamp-query), timestamp-reply, vnd.pwg-xhtml-print+xml
Image	jpeg, gif, ief, g3fax, tiff (cgm, naplps), vnd.dwg, vnd.svf, vnd.dxf, png, vnd.fpx, vnd.net-fpx (vnd.xiff, prs.btif, vnd.fast-bidsheet, vnd.wap.wbmp, prs.pti, vnd.cns.inf2, vnd.mix), vnd.fujixerox.edmics-rlc, vnd.fujixerox.edmics-mmr, vnd.fst
Audio	basic, 32kadpcm, vnd.qcelp (vnd.digital-winds, vnd.lucent.voice, vnd.octel.sbc, vnd.rhetorex.32kadpcm, vnd.vmx.cvsd, vnd.nortel.vbk, vnd.cns.anp1, vnd.cns.inf1), L16, vnd.everad.plj, telephone-event, tone (prs.sid, vnd.nuera.ecelp4800, vnd.nuera.ecelp7470), mpeg, parityfec, MP4A-LATM, vnd.nuera.ecelp9600, G.722.1, mpa-robust, vnd.cisco.nse, DAT12, L20, L24
Video	mpeg, quicktime, vnd.vivo, vnd.motorola.video, vnd.motorola.videop, vnd.fvt, pointer, parityfec, vnd.mpegurl, MP4V-ES, vnd.nokia.interleaved-multimedia
Model	iges, vrml, mesh (vnd.dwf, vnd.gtw, vnd.flatland.3dml), vnd.vtu, vnd.mts, vnd.gdl, vnd.gs-gdl, vnd.parasolid.transmit.text, vnd.parasolid.transmit.binary

Securing E-Mail Messages

To safeguard mail and its attachments, you can use the following two technologies.

◆ **Secure MIME Version 3 (S/MIME v3)**. S/MIME v3 is an encryption mechanism that you can use with an MUA to encrypt outgoing mail. S/MIME uses digital certificates to authenticate the mail sender.

◆ **OpenPGP**. OpenPGP is a mail encryption technology that is based on PGP. Like S/MIME, it uses the public key/private key technology to secure e-mail messages. However, unlike S/MIME, OpenPGP uses a web-of-trust model to authenticate the sender.

Table 8.3 provides a comparison between S/MIME and OpenPGP.

Table 8.3 S/MIME versus OpenPGP

Features	OpenPGP	S/MIME v3
Message format	Binary, based on previous PGP	Binary, based on CMS
Signature algorithm	ElGamal with DSS	Diffie-Hellman (X9.42) with DSS
Hash algorithm	SHA-1	SHA-1
Symmetric encryption algorithm	TripleDES (DES EDE3 Eccentric CFB)	TripleDES (DES EDE3 CBC)
Certificate format	Binary, based on previous PGP	Binary, based on X.509v3
MIME encapsulation of signed data	Multipart/signed with ASCII armor	Choice of multipart/signed or CMS format
MIME encapsulation of encrypted data	Multipart/encrypted	Application/pkcs7-mime

An MTA uses SMTP to send mail and to exchange mail between different hosts on the Internet. Your network probably hosts an SMTP server to send mail across the Internet.

In order to secure SMTP servers, you must run the server on a separate bastion host on the DMZ. I discussed many such security configurations in Chapter 5. If you want to secure the messaging channel that connects the SMTP server to the Internet, you can use SSL or the TLS security channels. SSL is a socket layer that secures the messaging channel. TLS is also a security standard that safeguards the Transport layer.

Some general recommendations for securing the e-mail system follow.

◆ Implement the SMTP server on a bastion host.

◆ Use proxy servers to forward mail to the bastion host.

◆ Use an anti-virus program that checks all of the incoming mail.

◆ Use a secure MIME technology, such as S/MIME or OpenPGP, to encrypt and decrypt your mail.

♦ Use SSL/TLS to safeguard the messaging channels between the MUA and the mail store. You can also use SSL/TLS throughout the mail delivery path to safeguard the end-to-end message path.

Filtering Rules for SMTP and POP

Table 8.4 provides the general filtering rules for SMTP and POP protocols. These rules determine which types of packets should be allowed to pass through the firewall.

Table 8.4 Filtering Rules for SMTP and POP Protocols

Rule	Direction	Source IP	Destination IP	Protocol	Source Port	Destination Port	ACK	Action
SMTP-Outgoing	Out	Internal clients	Any	TCP/IP	>1023	25	No	Permit
SMTP-Outgoing	In	Any	Internal clients	TCP/IP	25	>1023	Yes	Permit
POP-Outgoing	Out	Internal clients	Any	TCP/IP	>1023	109, 110	No	Permit
POP-Outgoing	In	Any	Internal clients	TCP/IP	109, 110	>1023	Yes	Permit
SMTP-Incoming	In	Any	Mail server	TCP/IP	>1023	25	No	Permit
SMTP-Incoming	Out	Mail server	Any	TCP/IP	25	>1023	Yes	Permit
POP-Incoming	In	Any	Mail server	TCP/IP	>1023	109, 110	No	Permit
POP-Incoming	Out	Mail server	Any	TCP/IP	109, 110	>1023	Yes	Permit

File Transfer Protocol

FTP is a mechanism for transferring large files across the Internet. Although you can use an e-mail program to transfer files from one place to another, it is not an efficient mode for transporting large amounts of files at any given time. FTP is widely used over the Internet to transfer any type of files, some of which include

- Text (ASCII)
- Graphics
- PDF, PostScript
- Video
- Audio
- Binary (executables, libraries)

An FTP system uses an FTP client that requests a file and an FTP server that serves the requested file to the client. An FTP client can connect to the FTP server and search through the data on the server. This process is similar to a person searching for files on a local operating system. On an FTP system, the client uses FTP commands to perform the file transfer or wade through the FTP server. Before you learn how to secure an FTP system, you should examine the ways in which an FTP client can access the FTP server.

Accessing FTP Servers

Typically an FTP client can access an FTP server in the following ways.

- **Anonymous FTP access**. This type of access does not require the FTP client to authenticate itself before accessing the files on the FTP server. This is the least secure way of allowing file access on the server. Anonymous access is provided only if your FTP server is open to public users on the Internet. Typically, if you have any information that you want to share with all Internet users, such as an executable product download, you can provide anonymous access to the server.
- **Authenticated FTP access**. This type of access requires the FTP client to first authenticate itself before accessing the files on the FTP server. Such access secures the FTP server from public use. Only users with accounts on the FTP server can access the files.

To safeguard an FTP server, you should run it on a bastion host on a DMZ. Having a proxy system on the firewall will also ensure application-level security for the FTP server.

FTP is a TCP-based protocol. To retrieve mail from the FTP daemon, which is the FTP server, the FTP client needs to set up a session. An FTP session uses two TCP channels to operate smoothly, as follows.

- **Command channel**. The command channel is a TCP connection established between the FTP server and the FTP client to transport commands and status codes between the two hosts. Generally, the command channel uses port 21 on the FTP server and any port above 1023 on the client to set up a session.
- **Data channel**. The data channel is a TCP connection that is established between the FTP server and the FTP client to carry data files between the hosts. There are two different types of data channels—the normal mode and the PASV mode.

- **Normal mode**. The normal mode uses port 20 on the server. In normal mode, the client opens the connection for the command channel and sends the client port number to the server so that it can open a connection to the client. If you have firewall on your network that prevents an external FTP server from opening connections on the internal client, then the connection for the data channel will fail. To overcome this limitation, you can use PASV mode (passive mode) connections.

- **PASV mode**. In a PASV mode connection, the client opens a command channel connection to the server, and then sends a PASV command to the server. The server then creates a port greater than port 1023 on the server side and send the port number back to the client. Using the server port number, the client can create a data channel connection.

Securing an FTP Server

Assigning access control rules for the files and directories on the FTP server will ensure greater safety for your files. This way, only privileged user accounts can access sensitive data on the FTP server, while non-privileged user accounts can access only general files.

Following are some recommendations for securing the FTP system.

◆ Run the FTP servers on a separate bastion host on the DMZ.

◆ Use a proxy system to forward requests to the FTP server.

◆ Use PASV mode for the server and clients.

◆ Discourage the use of anonymous FTP access.

◆ Assign permission to directories and files to enable access control.

◆ Log all access to files so it is easy to trace the users.

◆ Use secureFTP or other similar protocols to secure the data and the command channels. A secureFTP protocol uses SSL to encrypt data and the command channel so it is safe from hackers.

◆ If PASV mode clients are not set, use packet filtering to allow only outgoing connections from ports above 1023. This will disable any incoming requests to open a connection on the internal client.

Summary

This chapter explained the Web, e-mail, and FTP services available on the Internet. You learned how to safeguard Web servers and application servers from the Internet. You also learned how to safeguard different mail system components, such as MTA, MDA, and MUA, from attackers. The section on e-mail explained the steps to secure different mail protocols, such as POP, IMAP, and SMTP, and the steps to secure MIME content over the mail system. Finally, in the FTP section, you learned about different FTP operation modes, such as normal mode and PASV mode, and ways to secure the FTP system from attackers.

The next chapter describes the preventive measures that can help you counter a security breach on the network. It also details the legal measures available for you to combat illegal intrusion into an organizational network.

Check Your Understanding

Multiple Choice Questions

1. The Web service uses which of the following protocols to serve Web pages?
    a. HTTP
    b. FTP
    c. SMTP
    d. POP

2. Which of the following protocols does the mail server use to serve mails to the Internet?
    a. SMTP
    b. HTTPS
    c. POP
    d. FTP

3. Which of the following components belong to a mail system?
    a. MUA
    b. IMAP
    c. MDA
    d. S/MIME

4. Which of the following protocols is used to secure a communication channel?
    a. POP
    b. SSL
    c. S/MIME
    d. TLS

5. Which of the following technologies is used to secure mail extensions?
    a. OpenPGP
    b. S/MIME

    c. VPN

    d. IMAP

Short Questions

1. What precautions do you need to take against a Web application attack?
2. Explain the terms MUA, MTA and MDA.
3. What are the differences between normal mode FTP and passive mode FTP?

Answers

Multiple Choice Answers

1. a. The HTTP protocol is used to serve Web pages.
2. a. The mail server uses the SMTP protocol to serve mail to the Internet.
3. a and c. The MUA and MDA components belong to a mail system.
4. b and d. The SSL and TLS protocols are used to secure communication channels.
5. a and b. The OpenPGP and S/MIME technologies are used to secure mail extensions.

Short Answers

1. You should take the following precautions against a Web application attack.
   - Preferably, use screened-server architecture with a bastion host as a forwarding agent and run the server behind the internal network. Otherwise, you can isolate the server from internal resources by placing it in the DMZ.
   - Assign extensive authorization or access control for the programs.
   - Run the program on the Web server in a least-privilege mode.

2. Following are explanations of the terms MUA, MTA, and MDA.
   - **MTA**. The MTA interacts with the external host that intends to send an e-mail message to a receiver.
   - **MDA**. The MDA receives e-mail messages from the MTA and saves them to the user's mailbox. It also verifies the disk quota of the mailbox and performs additional actions, such as processing message rules, sending notifications, and forwarding e-mail messages.
   - **MUA**. The MUA is an agent that interacts with the receiving host to hand over the received mail. It is typically used in composing and reading mail.

3. Following are the differences between the normal mode and the PASV mode.

    *   The normal mode uses port 20 on the server while the PASV mode uses a port above 1023. (The client always uses a port above 1023 on the client side.)

    *   In normal mode, the client opens the connection for the command channel while it sends the client port number to the server, so the server can open a connection to the client. If you have firewall on your network that prevents an external FTP server from opening connections on the internal client, then the connection for the data channel will fail. However, you can overcome this limitation by using PASV mode. In a PASV mode connection, the client opens a connection to the server as usual (a command channel). Next, the client sends a PASV command to the server, which creates a port on the server side (above port 1023) and sends the port number back to the client. By using the port number, the client can create the second connection (a data channel).

Chapter 9

Computer systems and networks are always vulnerable to attack, no matter how secure they are. Security of a network is a matter of perspective. A network is secure only until a new hacking technique is invented or a new security bug appears from the setup. You must plan preventive measures for any security incidents long before you put the network into production mode. Although you cannot prevent an overall security breach, you can reach a level of security compliance with such measures.

Entities such as businesses, people, governments, and other organizations must always be ready with an incident response system to counter any attacks. All of these entities should understand the degree of damage that can occur in the worst security attacks. In addition, they should know what immediate measures to take in such an event.

 NOTE

You should conduct a vulnerability assessment after all of the security systems are in place. This assessment should document all of the system's strengths. Most important, it must be targeted toward predicting the possible attacks on the system and the degree of damage if such attacks occur. This will help you be aware of the losses in case an incident occurs.

The world has started to rely on electronic systems and information produced by them. Commerce, trade, business, and many other sensitive transactions are being conducted over the Internet. Any breach in security could inflict huge monetary losses and possibly emotional and psychological damage. To cope with these damages, you need to make sure you have the proper remedies.

This chapter explains the preventive measures that you must take whenever a security breach occurs on your network. It also explains how to help prevent a security breach and the immediate steps that you need to take if a breach occurs.

Remedial Measures

To begin with, you should plan how to respond to a security incident. The following steps constitute a typical response to an attack.

1. Evaluate the damage that has been inflicted by an attack. When you evaluate the damage, you need to determine whether the attack is still in progress or whether it has already been made. You also need to analyze the type of attack and the

number of systems that were affected. You need to document everything, starting from the time when you became aware of the attack. The most important thing to do when you find out that an attack has occurred is to shut down the network. If you are unable to shut down the network because of some sensitive processes that are running internally, then disconnect the Internet connection from the network and disconnect database servers and any application servers that might contain sensitive information if at all possible.

2. Try to trace the attacker by using the appropriate tools. At the same time, you should inform all of the users on the network about the attack and let the chain of command know too. The controlling authorities of the organization should be informed immediately about such attacks, regardless of the time of the day when the attack occurs.

3. Back up all logs for proof of the incident in case any legal measures are required.

4. Call for an immediate meeting with all of the key players from management and the user group, as well as the respective representatives from the technology team. You should update this group about the type of attack and whatever reports were created after you evaluated the incident. In the meeting, you should discuss the recovery plans and preventive measures that need to be taken to avoid such attacks in the future.

5. Fix the loophole in the system. To do this, you need to carefully monitor all of the network logs and analyze what went wrong. Monitoring the network will also give you traces of the attacker, which will make it easier for you to effectively trace him or her.

6. Document the discussion in the meeting and the reasons for the decisions that are made. You need to get permission from the proper authorities to immediately edit the security policy within the organization to prevent such attacks. You also need to also get appropriate financial backing to implement any new infrastructure necessary to fix the problem. You should call in outside consultants, security experts, and legal advisors, depending upon the amount of damage to your system.

7. Inform all service providers and vendors from whom you bought the appropriate resources to set up the network. This will help you obtain security fixes and patches for any loopholes within the system. If you have any contracts with external incident response teams such as CERT-CC, you need to let them know about the incident and call for immediate help.

While you are fixing the system, you need to make changes to policy files within the system. You also need to apply any patches that you obtain from the vendors. If the damage to your system is severe, then you probably need to rebuild the system from scratch with additional hardware and software reinforcement. You should take all of the recommended safety measures when you reinstall the system and make sure to document each step that you take.

In most cases, you have to make a backup of the network logs even before you start fixing the problem. It is always a good idea to make a backup of the systems on which there was a security breach. This helps you study the system later, to completely understand the modalities of the attack in depth. The backup that you make will also be used as evidence in any legal proceedings. Usually backups can be made on tapes or CD-ROMs. Once you have conducted all of the evaluation and backup measures and documented every action, you should be ready to restore the system to normal.

After you restore the system, increase the level of monitoring on the network. Initially this will help you be on the highest guard against any further attacks. Next you need to study the backup that you made of the damaged system. You must do a thorough and detailed study of the following components.

- Network logs
- Policy files
- Access control lists
- System databases
- Routing table
- System cache
- Filtering rules
- Proxy services
- Reports from network monitoring tools
- Reports on system usage based on user accounts
- Auditing logs

You should also pursue the intruder based on the evidence that you have. If you can trace the intruder using route-tracing utilities while the attack is in progress, your chances of identifying him or her are comparatively higher than if you trace the intruder after the attack is made.

Tracking down the attacker after the attack is very time-consuming and frustrating because it is a complex process to trace the route back to an attacker. Even if you are able to trace the route, you cannot expect the attacker to be still there, waiting to be intercepted. From then on, it becomes a legal pursuit for the police to physically trace the attacker. You should mention all of the suspects regardless of whether they belong to the same organization or are outsiders.

Legal Measures

Many legal statutes and laws have been passed to discourage hacking. Most of the laws are international, although some of them are specific to a given country. The computer crimes laws help govern the attacks on information systems.

You should immediately report all Internet-related crimes to law enforcement agencies. You should report attacks on your system to the following agencies.

◆ Federal Bureau of Investigation (FBI)

◆ United States Secret Service

◆ United States Customs Service

◆ United States Postal Inspection Service

These agencies get involved based on the severity of damage and the type of attack on your network. You can find out to which federal investigative law enforcement agency you should report a breach at the United States Department of Justice reporting site, at http://www.usdoj.gov/criminal/cybercrime/reporting.htm.

The Computer Fraud and Abuse Act, which was amended in October 1996, details the types of computer fraud and the maximum permissible punishment for committing these crimes. You can view the details of this act on the U.S. Department of Justice Web site at http://www.usdoj.gov/criminal/cybercrime.

Summary

This chapter provided guidelines for the measures that you need to take in the case of a security breach on your network. It also explained the immediate remedial measures that you need to conduct. Finally, it explained the legal aspects of a cybercrime and the possible actions you need to take.

With this chapter, you have completed your education on the topic of firewalls. In the next two chapters, you will learn how to implement application-level and router-level firewalls on different platforms.

Check Your Understanding

Short Questions

1. Explain the sequence of steps you might follow to handle a network attack, assuming that the attack was still occurring.

2. Which US-based organizations handle Internet-related crimes?

Answers

Short Answers

1. If you detect a network attack that is still occurring, follow these steps.

   a. Evaluate the type of attack and the number of systems affected.

   b. Try to trace the attacker.

   c. Shut down the systems and inform users about the attack.

   d. Back up all log files.

   e. Fix the security loophole.

   f. Generate a long-term solution to the problem and initiate legal proceedings.

2. The US-based organizations that handle Internet-related crimes are

   a. Federal Bureau of Investigation

   b. United States Secret Service

   c. United States Customs Service

   d. United States Postal Inspection Service

Chapter 10

Implementing
Windows- and Linux-
Based Firewalls

In the previous chapters, you learned about different aspects of firewalls. This chapter focuses on firewall implementations on Windows and Linux platforms using Microsoft ISA Server (*Microsoft Internet Security and Acceleration Server 2000*) and IP Chains, respectively. ISA Server integrates with Microsoft Windows 2000 Server, and IP Chains can be used on Linux-based computers. Both of these products more or less solve the basic requirement of securing networks. However, they have different implementations.

Implementing Firewalls Using Microsoft ISA Server 2000

Microsoft ISA Server provides fast, secure, and easy-to-manage Internet connectivity for Web-based enterprises. With the increasing use of the Internet, you must effectively administer a network and provide secure access to the Internet. Microsoft ISA Server helps you accomplish these tasks. You can deploy ISA Server 2000 as a firewall server, a cache server, or both. I will explain the features and steps to install and configure ISA Server 2000, as well as the use of ISA Server 2000 as a firewall server and cache server, later in this section.

Features of ISA Server

In a typical setup, you install ISA Server between the internal and external networks, as shown in Figure 10.1. The internal network is a trusted network, such as an organization's LAN, and an external network refers to untrusted networks that are not part of the organization, such as the Internet. ISA Server protects the internal network from public networks and helps increase the productivity of application services through features such as Web caching.

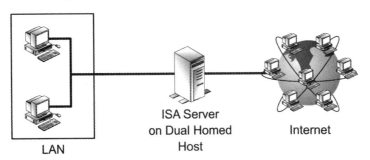

FIGURE 10.1 *Typical location of ISA Server in a network*

ISA Server works at Communication layers to provide security to your network. It allows rule-based packet filtering for IP packets and keeps a log of the packets that are dropped. The server filters incoming packets and compares them with rules defined for the network before allowing them to access your internal network.

You can also determine how your network clients access the Internet. You can restrict access to specific hosts on the Internet. You can even define customized rules based on your organization's needs. On a broad level, ISA Server includes the following features.

- ◆ Internet security through a firewall

- ◆ Internet acceleration through Web caching

- ◆ Windows 2000 integration for unified management

- ◆ A platform for customization and extension

I will discuss these features in the following sections.

Internet Security through a Firewall

You can implement ISA Server as a firewall server. In the firewall server mode, you need to configure firewall rules and policies that are used by ISA Server to secure your network. ISA Server, when configured as a firewall, has the following features.

- ◆ Multi-layered firewall

- ◆ Intrusion detection

Multi-layered firewalls are covered in the following section; intrusion detection is covered later in this chapter, in the "Intrusion Detection" section.

Multi-Layered Firewalls

The presence of a multi-layered firewall is an advanced feature of ISA Server. A multi-layered firewall is the first and the most important step for a defense in-depth strategy. ISA Server works at the Network, Transport, and Application layers to provide a secure firewall solution. You can filter network traffic at any or all of the three layers. The filtering options available are

- ◆ IP packet filtering

- ◆ Circuit-level filtering

- ◆ Application-level filtering

IP Packet Filtering

Packet filtering operates at the Network or IP layer. These layers scrutinize packets before they proceed to other layers. When packets are received at the network, their header contains information such as the packet's source, destination, or protocol. ISA Server uses this information to filter IP traffic on an allow or deny basis. Allow filters are exception-based, which means that by default they will deny all traffic except the packets that are explicitly allowed to pass. Deny or block filters allow all traffic to pass through except the traffic that is specifically denied.

Filters in ISA Server can be based on the following criteria.

◆ **Inbound/outbound packets**. This criterion specifies whether the packets are entering or leaving the system.

◆ **IP protocol used**. This criterion defines the protocols on which packet filtering is based.

◆ **IP address**. This criterion specifies the source and destination IP addresses. A single computer or a group of computers can be mentioned here.

◆ **Port number**. This criterion defines the port numbers for TCP or UDP packet filters. You need to specify ports for each protocol separately.

When you configure packet filtering on ISA Server, you can use customized IP packet filters instead of predefined ones. Figure 10.2 shows the Filter Settings screen of the New IP Packet Filter wizard, which you can use to configure custom packet filters.

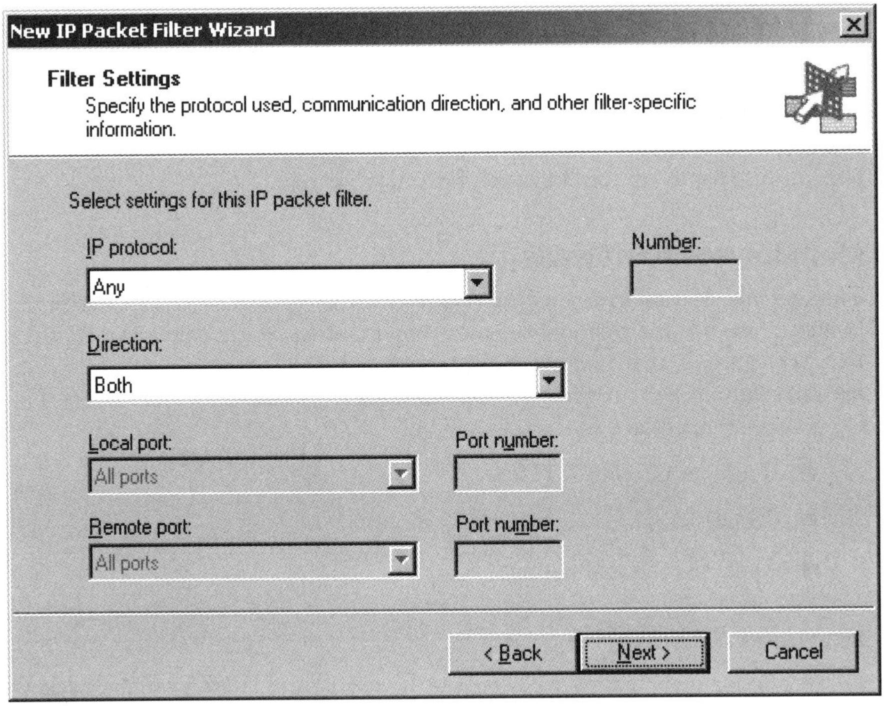

FIGURE 10.2 *Configuring packet filtering in ISA Server 2000*

Advantages and Disadvantages of Packet Filtering

Packet filtering provides the following advantages.

◆ It is easy to implement.

◆ It is not CPU-intensive.

◆ It drops all packets by default, making the network secure.

◆ It operates fast because it is based on the lower layers of the network communication hierarchy.

Following are some disadvantages of packet filtering.

◆ It does not check the data content of a packet. In addition, it cannot accept or reject packets based on the users or groups that have requested them, which poses a limitation to its functionality.

◆ It cannot modify data packets.

◆ Packet filters are static; you have to manually configure them to allow or deny any new IP traffic that is not included in an existing filter.

Circuit-Level Filtering

Circuit-level filtering allows filtering of IP traffic based on the session state. This type of filtering cannot read data packets. Instead, it ensures that the computers that communicate with each other have established a valid session. A session starts when the server authenticates the request from the client.

You can successfully implement circuit-level filtering to prevent DoS attacks because most DoS attacks exploit networks by establishing unwanted sessions on a host. To prevent this, you can specify limits to the number of simultaneous sessions that can be opened.

Advantages and Disadvantages of Circuit-Level Filtering

Circuit-level filtering provides the following advantages.

◆ Like packet filtering, circuit-level filtering works on an allow-deny basis, which imparts security to the network.

◆ Circuit-level filtering can check common DoS attacks if it is implemented effectively.

Circuit-level filtering has the following disadvantages.

◆ It requires Winsock for implementation. Therefore, applications that are filtered by circuit-level firewalls need additional programming to work.

◆ It does not inspect data transported by the packet.

Application-Level Filtering

The Application layer is the top layer in the network communication hierarchy. Application-level filters work in this layer. In packet and circuit-level filtering, only the data packet's header is inspected; the content of the packet is not. However, at times, access control based on the content of a packet is required. ISA Server uses application-level filters to perform this function.

ISA Server can implement user authentication for filtering Application-layer protocols. Application filters are more sophisticated and secure than packet or circuit filters. The built-in application filters in ISA Server include support for common Application-layer protocols, referred to as *protocol definitions*, such as HTTP, FTP, and RPC. ISA Server supports many pre-configured protocol definitions, such as AOL, Archie, DNS, FTP, and HTTP, which you can use to create protocol rules to filter traffic based on content.

FTP Access Filter

In ISA Server, you can use FTP access filters to control FTP communication that can occur through the firewall. The major advantage of application filters is that they can provide only one-way transfer of data through FTP. ISA Server provides three main protocol definitions for FTP access filters.

♦ **FTP client**. This definition allows Internet-based FTP server access to an internal user.

♦ **FTP server**. This definition allows an external user to access a protected internal FTP server.

♦ **FTP client read-only**. This definition allows read-only commands, such as ls and get, to be executed. All write commands, such as put, are barred.

SMTP Filter

ISA uses SMTP filters to construct rules for SMTP communication. All SMTP requests are compared to these rules, and only valid requests are allowed to pass. You can filter SMTP requests for following factors.

♦ Sender's e-mail address

♦ E-mail content

♦ Attachments

Web Filter

A Web filter monitors HTTP requests sent to the Internet. These requests pass through the proxy servers. All requests are compared to the rules before they are forwarded or rejected.

SOCKS Filter

The SOCKS filter can be used by non-Windows applications to communicate with Windows applications.

H.323 Protocol Filter

The H.323 protocol filter is required to handle H.323 packets. These packets are used for communication purposes, such as teleconferencing by Microsoft NetMeeting. H.323 filter works with an H.323 gatekeeper that provides options for allowing incoming or outgoing calls, audio, video, and other applications.

Streaming Media Filter

The streaming media filter is used for streaming media applications. It provides the feature for splitting the Windows media stream, which can save a lot of bandwidth. Many standard formats are supported, including MMS (*Microsoft Windows Media*), RTSP (*Real Time Streaming Protocol*), and PNM (*Progressive Networks Management*) protocol.

RPC Filter

RPC filters are used to filter Remote Procedure Calls. The filters enable the RPC services to be published so that external clients can access them.

Using ISA Server as a Proxy Server

You can use ISA Server as a proxy server. To better understand the idea of a proxy server, consider a gatekeeper. A gatekeeper's job is to let only authorized persons enter the premises. ISA Server goes a step further by allowing authorized data to enter the protected network, as well as checking to make sure that only authorized data leaves the network.

Internet Acceleration through Web Caching

Along with security, speed is a major factor for the success of Web applications. Sites that are visited more frequently should be cached on the server so that data for any further requests for the site can be retrieved from the cache.

You can implement ISA Server as a cache server. Web sites frequently visited by users in the organization are cached. Whenever a client requests a Web site that has previously been cached, the request is served by the local cache. This feature works very well for static pages that are rarely modified, and it helps speed up data access because file transfer is faster on the organization's LAN than on the Internet.

Caching in ISA Server can be one of the following types.

◆ **Forward caching**. Forward caching provides the Web content requested by the internal users from the cache, if available.

◆ **Reverse caching**. Reverse caching improves the access speed of the external user accessing the organization's Web server.

◆ **Distributed caching**. Distributed caching is implemented by spreading the cached objects across the server array. This is done for forward as well as reverse caching. It further improves the performance through load balancing and imparts fault tolerance to the network.

◆ **Hierarchical caching**. Hierarchical caching uses chained ISA Server arrays to establish hierarchies of cache. A client can access the cache nearest to it.

A network administrator can schedule caching of a Web site. For example, in Figure 10.3, the New Scheduled Content Download Job wizard is used to specify that the content from www.niit.com should be cached in the ISA cache.

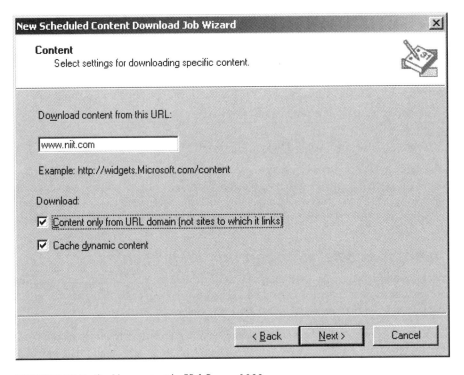

FIGURE 10.3 *Caching content in ISA Server 2000*

Windows 2000 Integration for Unified Management

Windows 2000 includes many unified management features. ISA integrates with Windows 2000 and enables you to use the Windows management features from the ISA console. You can use ISA Server to perform the following management tasks.

◆ **Access control and authentication**. ISA Server allows you to define policies for access control. These policies can be based on factors such as data, source, user, group, and so on.

◆ **Active Directory integration**. ISA Server integrates with the Windows 2000 Active Directory. This feature is available in the Enterprise Edition of ISA Server. The Active Directory stores information about user or ISA configuration files.

◆ **Allocation of bandwidth**. You can specify various rules regarding distribution of bandwidth. You can set priorities based on user, group, Web content, and so on.

◆ **Alerts and documentation**. You can maintain a log, which can be helpful from a security point of view.

◆ **Secure NAT**. ISA Server makes the NAT provided by Windows 2000 more secure and extends its functionality.

Platform for Customization and Extension

Security policies and data exchanged by an organization are specific to each organization. Therefore, each organization might have its own customized requirements. ISA Server addresses this need. The ISA Software Development Kit (SDK) enables you to customize the product according to the organization's needs.

ISA provides a very flexible platform for adding customized user interfaces, which you can develop using COM (*Component Object Model*). COM objects are developed in programming languages, such as C++, or scripting languages, such as JScript.

ISA Installation Considerations

Before you install ISA Server, you need to consider security and array policies. Unless you have defined a security policy for your organization, you cannot implement ISA Server effectively because a security policy will determine how you need to configure it. Take a look back at Chapter 6, which covered security policies in more depth, for a review of this topic.

After you specify security policies, you need to specify array policies, which are implemented only if the servers are designed into arrays. Array policies hold true for a particular array and can provide further restrictions. For example, if your network needs remote administration, then you should install ISA Server Management tools.

Editions of ISA Server

ISA Server 2000 comes in two editions. Which version you should use mainly depends upon your organization's requirements. The editions are

◆ **Standard edition.** The Standard edition provides most of the features of ISA Server except for a few advanced features, such as distributed caching and array formation. This edition is typically used for small networks and is less expensive than the Enterprise edition.

◆ **Enterprise edition.** This is the advanced version of ISA Server. It is used by those enterprises that have elaborate networks. The main problem areas in such networks are traffic monitoring and security management. These problems can be solved by a high-end firewall, which is provided by the Enterprise edition of ISA Server. The Enterprise edition includes all of the features of the Standard edition and removes limitations, such as the limit on the number of processors used by the server.

Installing ISA Server 2000

To install ISA Server 2000, follow these steps.

1. Insert the ISA Server CD in the CD-ROM drive. The Microsoft ISA Server Setup screen will appear (see Figure 10.4).

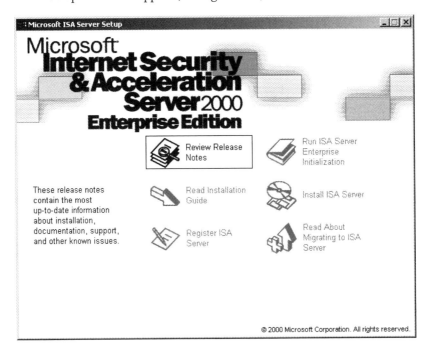

FIGURE 10.4 *The Microsoft ISA Server Setup screen*

2. If you want to use ISA Server as an array member, you need to install the ISA Server schema in the Active Directory. However, this step, which you perform by clicking on Run ISA Server Enterprise Initialization, is irreversible; you should performed this step only when you want to install ISA Server as an array member. To continue without installing the ISA Server schema in the Active Directory, click on Install ISA Server.

3. The Microsoft ISA Server (Enterprise Edition) Setup screen will appear. Click on Custom Installation to perform a custom installation of ISA Server.

 NOTE

A custom installation enables you to select the components of ISA Server that you want to install.

---

4. The Microsoft ISA Server (Enterprise Edition) - Custom Installation screen will appear (see Figure 10.5). On this screen, select the components that you want to install and click on Continue.

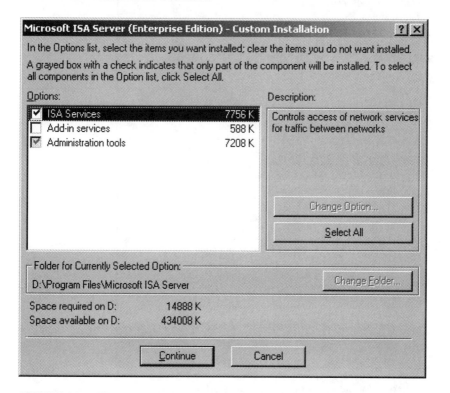

FIGURE 10.5 *The Microsoft ISA Server (Enterprise Edition) - Custom Installation screen*

TIP

As you select components, you can view their descriptions in the Description box.

5. If you have installed the ISA Server schema in the Active Directory, the Microsoft Internet Security and Acceleration Server Setup dialog box will appear. In this dialog box, you can specify whether you want to install ISA Server as an array member. If you have not installed the ISA Server schema in the Active Directory, this dialog box will not appear. Click on Yes or No, depending upon whether you want to install ISA Server as an array member.

6. The Microsoft ISA Server Setup dialog box will appear, as shown in Figure 10.6. In this dialog box, you need to select the ISA Server mode. ISA Server can either run in the Firewall, Cache, or Integrated mode.

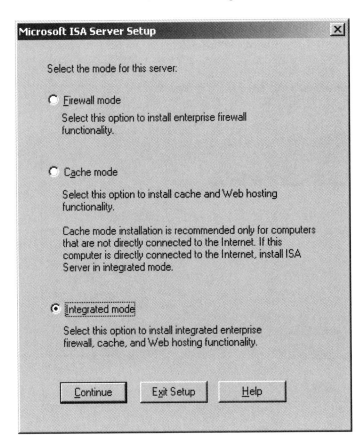

FIGURE 10.6 *The Microsoft ISA Server Setup screen*

- **Firewall mode**. This mode will install only the firewall feature of the server, which is the most commonly used feature.

- **Cache mode**. This mode will install only the cache and Web acceleration functionality of the ISA Server, along with the Web-hosting feature. Cache mode cannot provide you with firewall security, and the computer can become prone to hacking. Therefore, either the Firewall or the Integrated mode is recommended.

- **Integrated mode**. This mode will install all three functions of ISA Server, namely firewall security, caching, and Web hosting. This is the most frequently used mode of ISA Server.

Select the mode that you want to use for ISA Server and click on Continue.

7. The IIS service will be stopped and a dialog box will appear, stating that you can uninstall IIS after you complete the installation of ISA Server, since IIS is no longer required. Click on OK to proceed to the next step.

8. The Microsoft Internet Security and Acceleration Server Setup dialog box will appear, as shown in Figure 10.7. In this dialog box, you can allocate space on NTFS (*New Technology File System*) partitions for the ISA Server cache. Specify the size of cache on each drive and click on OK.

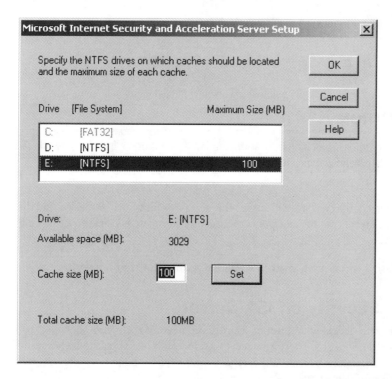

FIGURE 10.7 *The Microsoft Internet Security and Acceleration Server Setup dialog box*

9. The IP address ranges dialog box will appear, as shown in Figure 10.8. In this dialog box, you need to specify the range of IP addresses that spans the internal network of your organization. Specify the range of IP addresses and click on OK.

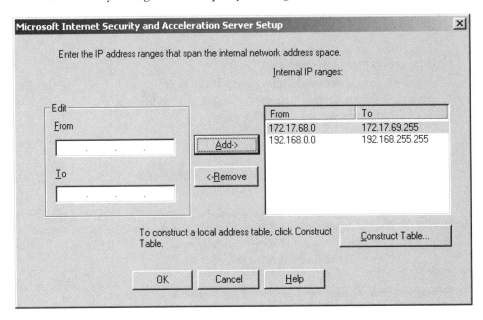

FIGURE 10.8 *The IP address ranges dialog box*

 CAUTION

You should carefully specify the IP addresses of internal hosts in your network. Any error in this step can compromise the security of your network.

10. The installation wizard will install the necessary files for ISA Server and display a message when the installation is successfully completed. Click on OK to close the wizard.

After you install ISA Server, you can configure security for your network.

Configuring Security on ISA Server

It is important to decide what level of security you need to configure on your ISA Server. Security should not degrade performance; this tradeoff, if it occurs, can be harmful for the organization. Therefore, you should carefully draft security policies to provide maximum security with minimum performance degradation.

Security Policies

These policies are rules or guidelines decided by the administrator to implement the network's security structure. They are very important because the safety of company's sensitive data depends on them.

First, you should determine the kind of attacks from which you are protecting your network. Without answering this question, it would be difficult to differentiate between a friendly transaction and a non-friendly transaction. Next, you should define methods or rules to help the ISA Server keep malicious users from entering the secured area. The entry points of the internal network should be carefully guarded to prevent virus attacks.

After you draft a security policy that includes the role of ISA Server for the organization, you can configure security rules by using the ISA management console.

Security Rules

There are different sets of rules for inbound and outbound traffic, due to the difference in the function and structure of these packets. Some of the rules, such as packet filtering, are shared between the two traffic types. Before you configure the rules for inbound and outbound traffic, I will list a set of global rules that are applied to all data packets.

Global Rules

The global rules that are applied to all data packets include

◆ **Packet filtering**. The server rejects all of the packets by default. This is in contrast to the initial version of Microsoft Proxy Server that was configured by default to accept packets. In ISA Server, the packets are accepted only if there exists a specific rule regarding their acceptance.

◆ **Bandwidth allocation**. This is a part of Windows 2000 Quality of Service (QoS) functionality. You can set rules describing the bandwidth a particular user or a group of users or services is allotted. The rules define the priority for using bandwidth. This feature is useful in scenarios in which bandwidth is limited and expensive.

◆ **Routing of packets**. As the name suggests, these rules deal with the route a packet takes in the network.

◆ **Redirecting of packets to another server**. The packets can be redirected to another server. This feature is useful when there are multiple servers that offer different services.

Specific Rules for Inbound Data Packets

In addition to the global rules described in the preceding section, there are specific rules for inbound data packets. These rules pertain to Web publishing and are important because the request from an external client is transferred to internal Web servers on the protected network. The rules are checked before the request is allowed to enter the network.

Specific Rules for Outbound Data Packets

There are two specific rules for outbound data packets.

- ◆ **Content administration**. ISA Server analyzes the outgoing request. The packets are dropped if rules are set prohibiting the internal clients from accessing certain Web resources. All of the dropped packets are logged in the ISA Server. This helps the administrator keep track of users trying to access barred sites on the Internet.

- ◆ **Protocol-related rules**. ISA Server enables administrators to define protocol rules. They can enable or disable protocols per organization requirements. All outgoing traffic is checked for the validity of the protocol before it is allowed to leave the network.

Managing Protocol Rules

ISA Server includes an MMC (*Microsoft Management Console*)-based administration tool. After you install IIS server, you can invoke the administration tool by clicking on Start, Programs, Microsoft ISA Server, ISA Management. Figure 10.9 displays the ISA Management window.

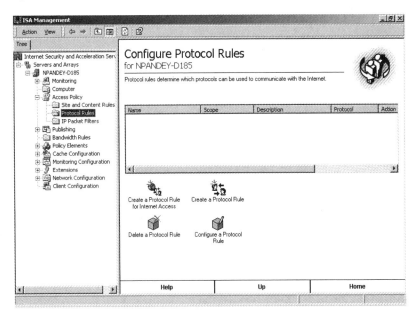

FIGURE 10.9 *The ISA Management window*

You can use the ISA Management window for the complete administration of ISA Server 2000. In this section, I will show you how to use this window for managing protocol rules. To create a protocol rule, follow these steps.

1. Navigate to the Protocol Rules section of the ISA Management console (refer to Figure 10.9).

2. Click on Create a Protocol Rule. The New Protocol Rule wizard will appear (see Figure 10.10).

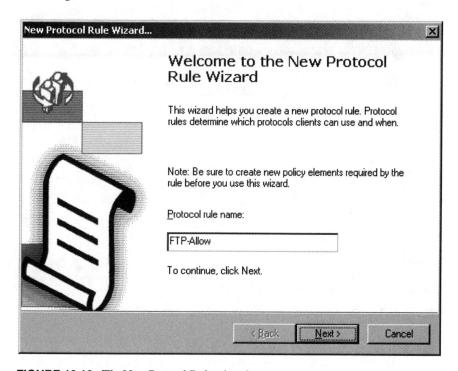

FIGURE 10.10 *The New Protocol Rule wizard*

3. Specify the name of the protocol rule and click on Next. The Rule Action screen will appear.

4. Specify how you want ISA Server to respond to client requests for the rule that you are creating. To allow client requests, select Allow; otherwise, select Deny. Click on Next to continue. The Protocols screen will appear.

5. You need to specify which protocols will be affected by the Rule Action that you specified on the previous screen. Therefore, if you selected the Allow option on the Rule Action screen, you need to specify which protocols are allowed. To select a specific protocol that you want to allow or disallow, choose the Selected

Protocols option in the Apply This Rule To list. The Protocols list will appear. Figure 10.11 displays the Protocols screen with the Protocols list visible.

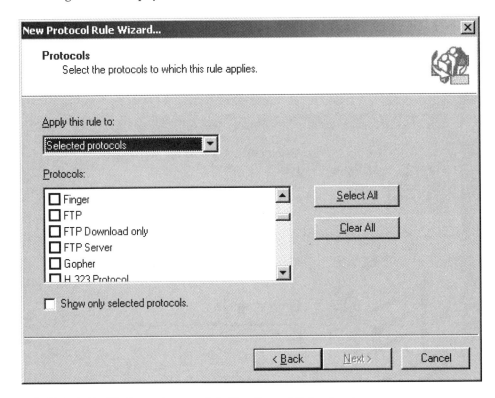

FIGURE 10.11 *The Protocols screen of the New Protocol Rule wizard*

6. Select the protocol that you want to enable or disable. For example, if you want to enable the FTP protocol, select the Allow option in Step 4 and check the FTP option in the Protocols list. Click on Next to continue.

7. The Schedule screen will appear. ISA Server allows you to specify the schedule based on which the rule should be used. For example, if the rule is associated with a nighttime schedule, the FTP protocol will be enabled only during the night. By default, you can select the Always schedule to apply the rule at all times. Select a schedule or retain the default and click on Next. The Client Type screen will appear (see Figure 10.12).

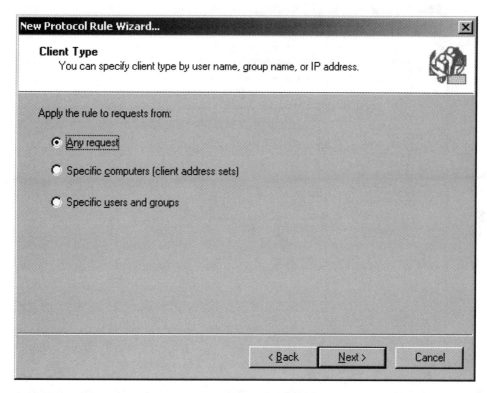

FIGURE 10.12 *The Client Type screen of the New Protocol Rule wizard*

8. You can specify the user name, group name, or IP addresses of the clients to whom the rule will apply. By default, the rule applies to all requests received by ISA Server. To apply the rule to all requests, retain the default option and click on Next.

9. The Completing the New Protocol Rule wizard screen will appear. Click on Finish.

The rule that you created enables clients to use the FTP service on the network. This rule appears in the ISA Management window, as shown in Figure 10.13.

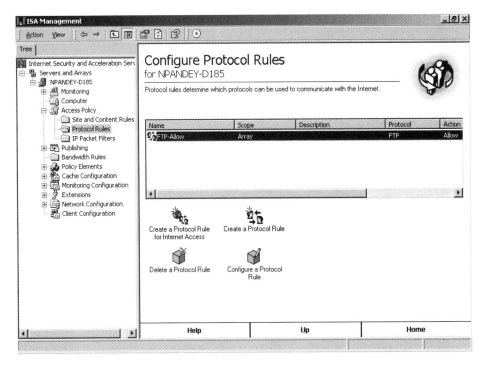

FIGURE 10.13 *Protocol rules displayed in the ISA Management window*

I will now discuss another important aspect of network security—intrusion detection.

Intrusion Detection

When the security policy of a company is being developed, the method to counter intrusions is a crucial point that is decided. Intrusions can be very harmful, depending on their nature. A good intrusion detection system provides not only a mechanism for detecting intrusions, but also various options for alerting the concerned person. ISA Server provides some very good features for detecting and reporting intrusions.

In this section, I will discuss the types of attacks detected by ISA Server and then explain how you can configure ISA Server to detect intrusions.

Types of Attacks Detected by ISA Server

For intrusion detection, ISA Server uses the software mechanism developed by Internet Security Systems. More information about this mechanism is available at http://www.iss.net. ISA Server also provides tools that continually check the firewall system for vulnerabilities. ISA Server checks all incoming packets for intrusions in two layers of communication. These checks are performed at both the packet level and the application level. The attacks that ISA Server can detect include

- **Land attack**. In this attack, the attacker creates fake IP packets. The source and destination IP address fields are specified as those of the computer to be attacked. This makes the computer infer that it is sending packets to itself, which creates a loop in which the victim machine keeps sending the packet and acknowledgments to itself, gradually leading to a system crash.

- **Ping of death**. This attack is aimed at the victim computer's buffer overflow. It is achieved by flooding the victim computer with ping requests using ICMP. These packets lead to buffer overrun, which in turn causes the computer to crash.

- **Out-of-band**. This attack falls in the category of DoS attacks. The network on which the victim computer is connected crashes.

- **Port scan**. To hack a computer, a hacker needs to know which ports are enabled. The hacker can scan all ports to check the number of ports functioning. ISA Server allows you to configure the maximum number of ports that can be opened. If the attacker attempts to access more ports than are allowed, ISA Server treats it as an intrusion.

- **UDP bomb**. In this attack, the attacker creates a UDP packet with invalid fields in the header section. When this packet is sent to the victim system, it can cause the machine to crash.

- **IP half scan**. This attack is aimed at getting information about the ports that are open for communication. The attacker who probes for an open port sends a request to the server but does not acknowledge the packet with which the sever replies after receiving the request. This leads to an incomplete communication, but the hacker can detect the open ports. To counter this threat, ISA Server maintains a list of unsuccessful connections. When the number reaches a certain limit, the server assumes an attack.

Configuring Intrusion Detection

You can use the ISA Management console to detect intrusions. Use the following steps to configure ISA Server for intrusion detection.

1. Open the ISA Management window and navigate to the IP Packet Filters section. Figure 10.14 shows the location of this section.

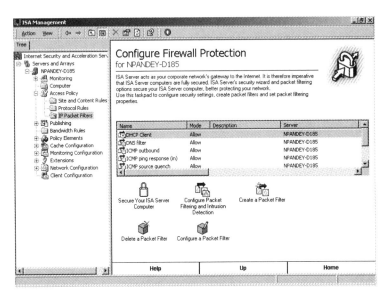

FIGURE 10.14 *Configuring intrusion detection in ISA Server*

2. Click on Configure Packet Filtering and Intrusion Detection. The IP Packet Filters Properties dialog box will appear.

3. On the General tab of the dialog box, check the Enable Intrusion Detection option, as shown in Figure 10.15.

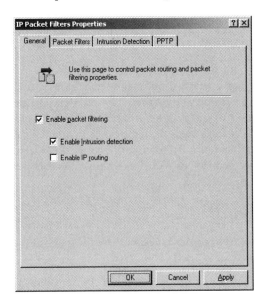

FIGURE 10.15 *Enabling intrusion detection*

4. Click on the Intrusion Detection tab. The list of attacks that ISA Server can detect will appear, as shown in Figure 10.16.

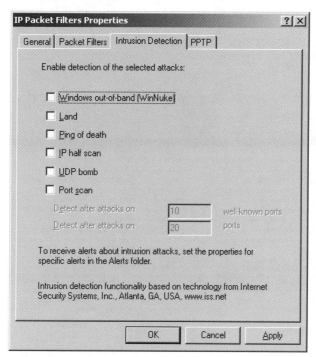

FIGURE 10.16 *Selecting the types of attack to detect*

5. Select all of the attacks that you want to monitor and click on OK.

Sending Alert Messages on Intrusion

When an attack is detected, the firewall should generate an alert to warn the concerned person about the attack. This is as important as detecting an intrusion. Following is a list of available alert types in ISA Server.

◆ **Send an e-mail message**. ISA Server can send an alert through an e-mail message to the concerned person, usually the administrator. The message can also be sent to more than one person, if required.

◆ **Stop the firewall service**. You can configure ISA Server to stop its services when a certain type of intrusion is detected.

◆ **Log the intrusion**. You can configure ISA Server to log the details of intrusions.

◆ **Run a program**. You can configure ISA Server to run a pre-defined program in case of an intrusion.

To configure ISA Server to send alerts upon detecting intrusions, follow these steps.

1. Navigate to the Alerts section of the ISA Management console. A list of alerts available in ISA Server will appear, as shown in Figure 10.17.

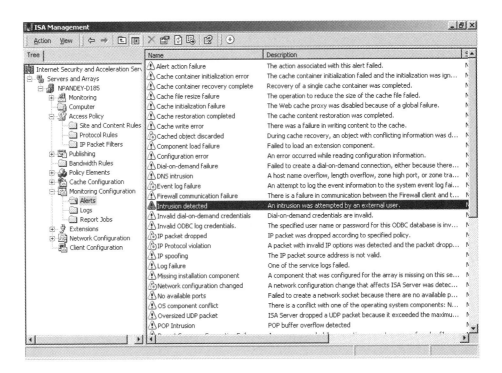

FIGURE 10.17 *Alerts available in ISA Server*

2. Double-click on the Intrusion Detected alert. The Intrusion Detected Properties dialog box will appear.

3. Click on the Actions tab in the dialog box. The available alerts will be displayed, as shown in Figure 10.18.

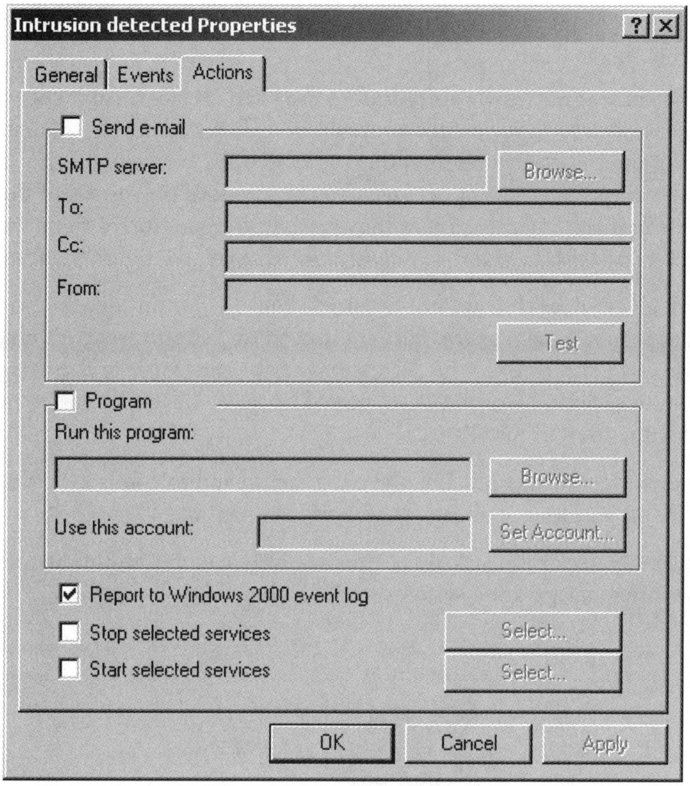

FIGURE 10.18 *The Intrusion Detected Properties dialog box*

4. Select an alert option from the list of available options. For example, to send an e-mail alert, check the Send E-Mail option and specify the name of the SMTP server and e-mail addresses in the To, CC, and From fields.

5. Click on Apply and then OK to close the Intrusion Detected Properties dialog box.

After you perform the preceding steps, ISA Server will send an e-mail alert whenever it detects an intrusion into the network.

Implementing Firewalls in Linux

Linux is gradually becoming a common choice for servers, primarily because of the strict security policies it follows. Firewall implementation is a very crucial part of Linux server setup. In this section, I will describe considerations related to the installation of a firewall on a Linux platform.

Before you install a firewall on Linux, you should perform a system check, which should include the following steps.

◆ **Review the current network configuration**. You can use commands such as `ipconfig` and `route` to review the configuration. The `ipconfig` command displays the current network configuration, and the `route` command displays the routing table of the current network. You should save the output of the `ipconfig` command in a file so that the original configuration of the network is available if you wish to revert to old settings after you configure the firewall.

◆ **Shut down all services that are not required**. You should shut down services that are not required, such as ftp, talk, and finger, to decrease security vulnerabilities. This will also counter the decrease in performance due to the firewall installation, to an extent. Ideally, there should be no visible effect on the performance after the firewall installation.

◆ **Test all network connections**. Use the `ping` command to confirm that the network is accessible from the outside as well as from within.

Figure 10.19 depicts the use of a Linux server to effectively connect an internal network running clients on different operating systems to the Internet.

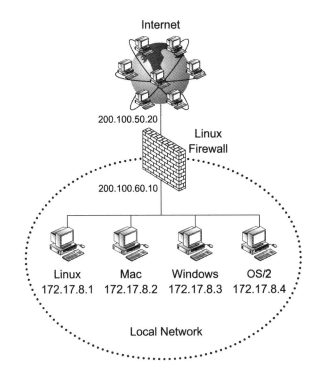

FIGURE 10.19 *Firewall implementation in Linux*

Types of Firewalls in Linux

There are three types of firewalls in Linux.

◆ Service-level firewalls

◆ Proxy-based firewalls

◆ Packet-filtering firewalls

Service-Level Firewalls

Service-level firewalls include filtering in the user space. They require no kernel support. The most important part of a service-level firewall is the TCP wrappers, which wrap services and provide the following functionality in the firewall.

◆ Access control

◆ List restrictions

◆ Logging requests

TCP wrappers use two files to implement access control. These files are located at

◆ **/etc/hosts.allow**. This file specifies the allow list.

◆ **/etc/hosts.deny**. This file specifies the deny list.

You use these two files to impose restrictions on all services. A connection can be accepted or dropped according to the configuration mentioned in these files. Policies are set for individual daemons, and the client's IP address is used to configure these policies.

Proxy-Based Firewalls

There are two types of proxy-based firewalls.

◆ **Application proxy**. These firewalls provide the option of authenticating users. They are a link between the internal and external hosts. Therefore, they make it easy for a network administrator to log and review all communication across the network.

◆ **SOCKS proxy**. Linux uses the SOCKS V version as the SOCKS proxy firewall.

Packet-Filtering Firewalls

Packet filtering is the most basic operation in the Linux firewall technology. This type of firewall is built in the kernel. The incoming packets are intercepted and filtered using various criteria, such as IP addresses or subnets, specific TCP or UDP port numbers, or a combination of both.

To enable packet firewalls, the Linux kernel should be compiled with the following compile-time options switched on.

◆ `CONFIG-FIREWALL`

◆ `CONFIG_IP_FIREWALL`

◆ `CONFIG_SYN_COOKIES`

The basic functions of an IP packet filter include

◆ **Packet filtering**. This involves comparing the information in the packet header to the set of rules defined for this purpose. It helps in deciding whether to pass or block each IP packet. Packets are normally filtered based on their source/destination IP address, the protocol used, and the port number.

◆ **Packet redirection**. This involves redirecting the packets to a different location. It is required when you use a proxy server. All requests, such as HTTP, SMTP, and FTP, are redirected to the proxy port.

◆ **Packet accounting**. This involves recording the number of bytes input and output and calculating the traffic over the network. It can determine the bandwidth used.

The incoming and outgoing traffic is checked using chains, which are a set or collection of rules. The chain scans the header of the message, and the firewall determines what should be done. There are three basic types of chains.

◆ **Input chain**. These chains check the incoming data packets.

◆ **Output chain**. These chains check the outgoing data packets.

◆ **Forward chain**. These chains check packets meant for another computer.

When a packet is filtered, one of the following actions can take place.

◆ The packet is accepted.

◆ The packet is refused and the source is informed about it.

◆ The packet is refused and the source is not informed.

IPchains and IPtables are two firewall subsystems available with Linux. The next two sections discuss these subsystems in detail.

IPchains

IPchains is used to set up, maintain, and inspect the IP firewall rules in the Linux kernel. IPchains has four different chains.

◆ IP input chain

◆ IP output chain

◆ IP forwarding chain

◆ User-defined chain

Packets are analyzed and compared to different rules in the chain. If the packet matches the rule, the action mentioned in the rule is executed. The action can be redirected to a user-defined chain or one of the following.

◆ **ACCEPT**. This action lets the packet pass through the firewall.

◆ **DENY**. This action rejects and drops the packet. The packet source is not notified.

◆ **REJECT**. This action is similar to DENY. The difference is that in the REJECT action, the packet source is notified about the dropped packet.

◆ **MASQ**. This action is used in forward chains. The kernel should be compiled using CONFIG_IP_MASQUERADE defined for this option. The packets are masqueraded before being forwarded, which makes the sender invisible to the external host. All packets are sent using the IP address of the masquerader.

◆ **REDIRECT**. This action is used only in the case of input and user-defined chains. To use this option, the Linux kernel should be compiled with CONFIG_IP_TRANSPARENT_PROXY. When you use this option, the packets are redirected to a local port.

◆ **RETURN**. In this action, the fate of the packet depends on the type of chain used to compare the packet. A built-in chain executes and compares the data with its rules. In a user-defined chain, the packet is returned to the original caller of the chain.

You can use the IPchains program with options for handling the chains. For example, chains can be created or deleted. Similarly, you can also append, remove, or modify rules residing in the chain. Table 10.1 lists various options that are available for the IPchains program.

Table 10.1 Options Available in the IPchains Program

Option	Significance
-N	Creates a new chain.
-X	Deletes an empty chain.
-P	Modifies the policy of a built-in chain.
-L	Lists the rules of a chain. Lists all chains if no specific chain is selected.

continued on next page

Table 10.1 Options Available in the IPchains Program (continued from previous page)

Option	Significance
-A	Appends the rule to the end of the chain.
-I	Inserts the rule in a specific position inside a chain.
-R	Replaces the rule in the specified chain.
-D	Deletes one or more rules from a chain.
-F	Flushes a chain—in other words, deletes all rules in a chain.
-Z	Zeroes byte and packet counters of all rules in a chain.

IPtables

A chain is a set of rules. As I mentioned previously, a chain can be built-in or user-defined. An IPtable is comprised of a set of IPchains. The primary function of IPtables is to create and manage tables of filter rules for IP packets.

In IPtables, the firewall rules are compared with packets. The result of this comparison can be one of the following.

◆ ACCEPT

◆ DROP

◆ QUEUE

◆ RETURN

There are three types of IPtables in Linux—filter, nat, and mangle.

◆ **filter**. This is the default table. It contains three built-in chains—INPUT, OUTPUT, and FORWARD.

◆ **nat**. Packets are compared to this table when a new connection is encountered. It has three built-in chains.

  • **PREROUTING**. This chain is used to alter the incoming packets.

  • **POSTROUTING**. This chain is used to alter the packets that are scheduled to go out.

  • **OUTPUT**. This chain is used to alter the outgoing packets.

◆ **mangle**. The basic purpose of this table is to perform specialized packet alteration. It contains two built-in chains.

- **PREROUTING**. This chain alters incoming packets before they are routed.

- **OUTPUT**. This chain alters locally generated packets before they are routed.

Table 10.2 lists various options that are available for the IPtables program.

Table 10.2 Options Available for the IPtables Program

Option	Significance
-A	Appends one or more rules to the end of the selected chain.
-I	Inserts one or more rules in the selected chain.
-R	Replaces a rule in the selected chain. The command does not work if the source and/or destination names resolve to multiple addresses.
-D	Deletes one or more rules from the selected chain.
-L	Lists all rules in the selected chain. All chains are listed if no chain is specified.

Folllowing are examples of usage of IPtables.

```
iptables -[RI] chain rulenum rule-specification [options]

iptables -D chain rulenum [options]
```

Summary

The concept of firewalls remains the same, even though their implementation might differ on different platforms. In this chapter, you learned about the implementation of firewalls in Windows and Linux.

You can implement firewalls on Windows by using ISA Server 2000, which provides a number of features such as packet filtering, content caching, and extensibility. You can use these features to configure security policies, protocol rules, intrusion detection, and so on.

You can implement firewalls in Linux by using IPchains and IPtables. Linux provides three types of firewalls—service-level firewalls, proxy-based firewalls, and packet-filtering firewalls.

This chapter described the implementation of application-based firewalls using ISA Server 2000 as an example. In the next chapter, you will learn about the implementation of router-based firewalls using Cisco routers.

Check Your Understanding

Multiple Choice Questions

1. What features does Microsoft ISA Server 2000 provide?
   a. Firewall security
   b. Web hosting
   c. Web acceleration through cache
   d. All of the above

2. ISA Server performs packet filtering in which layer?
   a. Physical layer
   b. Data Link layer
   c. Network layer
   d. Application layer

3. What types of filtering does ISA Server perform?
   a. IP packet filtering
   b. Circuit-level filtering
   c. Application-level filtering
   d. All of the above

4. Which of the following attacks is prevented using the ISA server's dynamic port-opening feature?
   a. Ping of death attack
   b. Out-of-band attack
   c. IP half-scan attack
   d. UDP bomb attack

5. Which firewall type requires kernel support in Linux?
   a. Proxy-level
   b. Packet filtering
   c. Service level
   d. All of the above

Short Questions

1. What are the global rules used for incoming and outgoing data packets in ISA Server 2000?

2. Name some common application filters available in Microsoft ISA Server 2000.

3. What are the various alert types provided by ISA Server in case of intrusion detection?

4. What are the three levels of firewalls present in Linux?

Answers

Multiple Choice Answers

1. d. Microsoft ISA Server 2000 provides all of these functions if you select Integrated mode during installation.

2. c. ISA server performs packet filtering in the Network layer.

3. d. ISA server incorporates all the three types of filtering.

4. c. The dynamic port-opening property of ISA Server 2000 opens a port only when required. This reduces the chance of attack through ports.

5. b. Packet filtering requires the kernel to be installed with extra configurations, such as `CONFIG_FIREWALL` or `CONFIG_IP_FIREWALL`.

Short Answers

1. There are some common rules that are applied to both incoming and outgoing traffic.

   - **Packet filtering**. ISA Server by default rejects all packets. Specific rules have to be mentioned in order to accept valid packets.

   - **Bandwidth allocation**. This is part of Windows 2000 QoS functionality. The administrator can decide the bandwidth that should be allocated to a user or user group.

   - **Routing rules**. These rules decide the route a packet takes in the network.

2. ISA server provides some built-in applications filters, including

   - **FTP access filter**. This filter is used to control the kind of FTP communication that can occur through the firewall. You can use this filter to provide only one-way transfer of data through FTP. ISA Server provides three main protocol definitions for this filter—FTP client, FTP server, and FTP client read-only.

   - **SMTP filter**. These filters are used by ISA Server to check all SMTP requests and allow only valid requests to pass. You can filter SMTP requests for factors such as the sender's email address, e-mail content, and attachments.

   - **Web filter**. These filters monitor the HTTP requests that are sent to the Internet. All requests are compared to the rules before they are forwarded or rejected.

For example, you can use the `HTTP REDIRECTOR FILTER` to redirect requests over the Internet.

- **Other filters**. A few other filtering mechanisms are also available for applications, such as streaming media and conferencing.

3. In the event of intrusion detection, you can configure ISA server to alert the concerned person in following ways.

- Via an e-mail message containing alert.
- By logging the activity so it can be checked later.
- By running a custom script or program.
- By shutting down the firewall service.

4. The three types of firewalls in Linux are

- **Service-level firewalls**. These do not require kernel support and use TCP wrappers to provide access control.
- **Proxy-based firewalls**. These are further divided in two categories—application proxy and SOCKS proxy. They provide user authentication options and are therefore considered very secure.
- **Packet-filtering firewalls**. These require built-in kernel support. They provide packet filtering, packet redirection, and packet accounting.

Chapter 11

**Implementing
Router-Based
Firewalls**

As you learned earlier, the basic function of a firewall is to restrict access to a network. In most cases, this restriction is based on a set of rules that define access to the network. These rules, which can be called *firewall rules*, are implemented on an allow-deny basis for both incoming and outgoing traffic. In other words:

◆ You can allow incoming traffic into your network if the traffic is marked as allowed in your firewall rules.

◆ You can deny incoming traffic into your network if the traffic is marked as denied in your firewall rules.

◆ You can allow outgoing traffic from your network if the traffic is marked as allowed in your firewall rules.

◆ You can deny outgoing traffic from your network if the traffic is marked as denied in your firewall rules.

In the previous chapter, you learned how to implement firewalls with Microsoft ISA Server 2000 and Linux. In this chapter, you'll learn how to implement firewalls using routers. To begin, refresh your knowledge about routers.

An Introduction to Routers

Routers enable traffic to flow from one network to another. To better understand this, you must understand how packets travel in a point-to-point network. In such a network, multiple connections exist between individual machines, and all of the machines are capable of accepting and sending data packets to any other machine. A packet might have to visit some machines in between while going from the source to the destination. The path that a packet takes from the source machine to a destination machine is called a *route*. In point-to-point networks, it is very common to have multiple routes of different lengths. Routing algorithms determine the routes that exist between two or more machines and hence play an important role in point-to-point networks.

Routers are devices that route packets between machines based on the routing protocols they support. They break data from a network into packets and then transmit them to another network. During the packet conversion process, they add a packet header to the data packet. In large networks with multiple routers, data packets often travel more than one router. Once the packet header is added, routers will look at just the packet header and not the entire data packet before forwarding it to the next router or machine. However, the goal is still to deliver the packets to the right machine on the destination network.

NOTE

There is a difference between a routing protocol and a routable protocol. A *routing protocol* calculates routes to a network (for example, BGP, OSPF, or RIP). On the other hand, a *routable* protocol is one that can be routed (for example, IP).

A basic router can allow traffic to pass from one network to another. To do so, it maintains routing tables that define the routes that exist between two networks. If no routes exist to connect two networks, then traffic cannot flow between them. The decision on where to deliver the packet is based on the addresses contained in the packet header and the routing tables maintained by the router. Therefore, the router needs to update its routing table whenever there is a change in the network. Any machine or router that is added to or removed from the network will affect the way packets are forwarded. All routers allow updating of their respective routing tables to change the way packets are forwarded between networks. Both manual and dynamic updates of the routing tables are possible using different protocols.

There are many reasons why you might consider using a dedicated and special purpose router instead of a machine that has routing capabilities. These reasons range from performance benefits to improved security. Some of the tangible advantages of a dedicated special purpose router are

◆ Better performance

◆ Scalability because a dedicated router can support many interface slots

◆ Low total cost of ownership because there is less administrative overhead

◆ Increased security because the router is dedicated and has no extra functionality

Now take a look at the router hardware and software.

◆ **Router hardware**. A router does not need any hard disks, floppy disks, or CD-ROM drives, but it does have a CPU and memory. A router's performance depends on CPU speed and memory size. Router memory can be RAM, ROM (EEPROM or PROM), NVRAM, or Flash. Router bootstrap software is stored in ROM and RAM (NVRAM) and is used to store the router's startup configuration files. A router has several interfaces, called *ports*, which provide physical connections to the router itself. Most routers provide interfaces for Ethernet, fast Ethernet, token ring, and ISDN. In addition to these ports, most routers also have a console and an auxiliary port. The console ports are used to configure brand new routers that are placed in a network. Auxiliary ports are used to connect modems, and should be disabled in most cases.

◆ **Router software**. A router has an operating system, referred as a *router OS*, which varies from vendor to vendor. For example, Cisco routers use Cisco's IOS (*Internetwork Operating System*). Because Cisco routers are the most common in today's network, I'll base this chapter on Cisco routers. The router OS is responsible for configuration changes and interpreting ACLs for the router.

Using a router as a firewall has two major advantages. First, it is platform neutral, so attackers can't exploit certain OS vulnerabilities. Second, since all of the incoming network traffic must pass through the router anyway, it's an ideal location for blocking unwanted content and users from accessing a site.

However, router-based firewalls have drawbacks, too. Applying rigorous filtering policies can degrade a router's performance significantly. Furthermore, many routers aren't immune to spoofing attacks.

An application-proxy firewall, or application gateway, is another type of firewall. Instead of running on a router, it operates on a computer. It replaces the connection between external users and a local network, accepts the original IP packets, and substitutes them with corresponding data. In other words, it serves as a conduit and interpreter between external users and the local network.

Using Routers as Firewalls

A router can be configured as a basic packet-filtering firewall, which can allow or disallow traffic based on source destination address, protocols, and ports. This allows the network administrator to define what traffic is received and sent by the router. Packet filtering is useful when private networks are connected to public networks such as the Internet.

Packet filters can be applied separately for inbound and outbound (bi-directional) traffic or for unidirectional traffic. Most modern routers allow bi-directional filtering. Packet-filtering firewalls operate at the Network layer of the OSI or TCP reference model, so they cannot check the content of the packet they are filtering. For example, a packet-filtering firewall that allows only port 80 to be accessed cannot monitor HTTP requests such as GET and POST.

Packet filters are extremely important if your router is a gateway between trusted and untrusted networks. Figure 11.1 depicts the layout of a router acting as a gateway between a corporate LAN and the Internet.

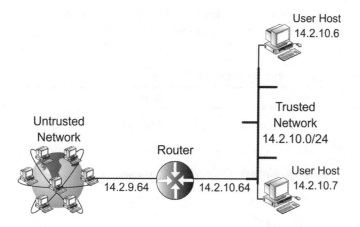

FIGURE 11.1 *The layout of a router acting as a gateway*

In Figure 11.1, you can see that only the router exists as a barrier between the Internet (untrusted network) and the local network (trusted network). The router allows hosts from the trusted network to connect to the untrusted network, but it does not allow any traffic from the untrusted network to reach the trusted network. This type of setup is typically used in small organizations that do not have a dedicated firewall. Here, the router acts as a gateway between the local network and the Internet.

 NOTE

The term *gateway* here refers to an IP gateway—not a gateway that contains a stack of multiple protocols.

In such a setup, the router must screen traffic coming from the Internet to public servers (servers that are part of the Internet, such as HTTP and SMTP) that are part of the local network. For example, the public server is a Web server on a public IP and is also connected to the Internet. Because most Web servers, by default, run on port 80, the router should block all of the traffic coming from any source to any other port, such as port 21.

You should always block unwanted ports and protocols that are not absolutely essential. Some services have inherent weaknesses that can be easily exploited and should be disabled if they are not being used.

 NOTE

All TCP/IP services run on specific ports; by blocking a port on which a service is running, you can effectively block the service.

Table 11.1 lists the ports that the router should block. Traffic originating from these services should not be allowed across the router unless there is a reason to use them.

Table 11.1 Ports That Should Be Blocked

Port	Transport	Service
1	TCP and UDP	tcpmux
7	TCP and UDP	echo
9	TCP and UDP	discard
11	TCP and UDP	systat
13	TCP and UDP	daytime
15	TCP and UDP	netstat
19	TCP and UDP	chargen
37	TCP and UDP	time
43	TCP	whois
67	UDP	bootp
69	UDP	tftp
93	TCP	supdup
111	TCP and UDP	sunrpc
135	TCP and UDP	loc-srv
137	TCP and UDP	netbios-ns
138	TCP and UDP	netbios-ssn
139	TCP and UDP	xdmcp
177	UDP	xdmcp
445	TCP	netbios (ds)
512	TCP	rexee
515	TCP	lpr
517	UDP	talk
518	UDP	ntalk

Port	Transport	Service
540	TCP	uucp
1900, 5000	TCP and UDP	Microsoft UPnP SSDP
2049	UDP	nfs
6000-6063	TCP	X Window System
6667	TCP	irc
12345	TCP	NetBus
12346	TCP	NetBus
31337	TCP and UDP	Back Orifice

Next, I'll discuss some features of routers that enable them to work as firewalls, which include

♦ Rejecting protocols

♦ IP filtering

♦ Using IP packet filtering to prevent IP spoofing

The following sections describe these features in detail.

Rejecting Protocols

Packet filtering also allows you to block protocols that you do not use but which are enabled on your router. These protocols should not be allowed to pass the router and in some cases should be disabled at the router itself. For example, if you are only using a Web server, you can block the UDP protocol so that no one from the Internet can establish a UDP connection to your system. You can also consider disabling IPX/SPX from the router itself. IPX/SPX is Novell's proprietary protocol that is mostly used in LANs.

Router-based firewalls are a simple and cost-effective solution for implementing security on networks. They are platform neutral and easy to implement compared to Application-layer firewalls. You can use the firewall features of a router even if your network has a dedicated firewall, since all incoming traffic passes through the router before any other device on the network. Enabling packet filtering on your external router will add an extra layer of security to your network because your router will filter traffic before it reaches the dedicated firewall. However, a firewall router alone is not the most secure defense strategy because routers can be tricked in many ways. Most routers are susceptible to IP spoofing and DoS attacks. I will discuss how you can use a router to restrict the IP spoofing attacks later in this chapter, in the "Setting an Inbound Access List on the External Interface" section.

TIP

The Internet uses TCP/IP as the communication protocol, which is robust compared to UDP, a stateless protocol. Certain critical services such as DNS use UDP. It is a good idea to restrict the UDP and ICMP protocols because they are susceptible to DoS attacks.

IP Filtering

A router can allow or disallow specific inbound or outbound IP traffic on a network. This feature is referred to as *IP packet filtering*. A typical use of IP packet filtering is in a router that routes traffic between an intranet and the Internet. Most IP packet filters have separate filters for monitoring inbound and outbound traffic and at least two interfaces. For the sake of convenience, I'll consider an IP filter with two interfaces—an external interface that is connected to the external network and an internal interface that is connected to the internal network.

You can apply inbound and outbound filters to each interface separately. IP packet filters cannot filter higher-level Application-layer protocols such as HTTP and FTP. They can, however, allow or disallow traffic to these services by restricting ports. Input and output filters on IP routers are generally configured as an exception, which means that the filters will either allow all traffic except what is specified or deny all traffic except what is specified. Most traffic filters filter TCP and UDP traffic based on ports, and some routers have a limited capability for allowing or denying ICMP traffic. Take a look at some common filtering scenarios.

◆ **Allow only Web traffic**. In this case, you configure your packet filter to deny all services except HTTP services. The best way to implement such a filter would be to block all ports except the HTTP port (80).

◆ **Allow only FTP and SMTP traffic or a combination of Web, FTP, and HTTP traffic**. In such cases, you should open only the respective TCP ports for these services and disable all UDP ports.

Using IP Packet Filtering to Prevent IP Spoofing

As you learned earlier, IP spoofing is a method in which someone (usually an attacker) forges his IP address, which enables the person to hide his identity. In most cases, the spoofed IP address falls in the range of the reserved private IP addresses.

> **TIP**
>
> It is a good practice to disable all incoming traffic on the external interface and drop all packets that have a source IP address that falls in the range of private IP addresses.

It is important to note that a filter that prevents spoofed private addresses has to be applied on the external interface because this interface is connected to the Internet, and there will not be a host with a private IP address on the Internet. You must prevent the following ranges of IP addresses from entering through the external interface.

◆ 172.16.0.0 with subnet mask 255.240.0.0

◆ 10.0.0.0 with subnet mask 255.0.0.0

◆ 192.168.0.0 with subnet mask 255.255.0.0

Now that you have an overview of routers and their role as firewalls, I will discuss how Cisco routers can be used as firewalls.

Using Cisco Routers as Firewalls

Commercial firewalls provide a high level of security but are very expensive. Because most organizations already have perimeter routers, it is cost-effective to use the router itself as a firewall. You can use packet filtering and ACLs on routers to form a basic firewall solution. Cisco routers running IOS 11.2 have modest firewall capabilities that are somewhere in between a basic packet-filtering firewall and a dedicated firewall such as Cisco PIX or Checkpoint.

The Cisco IOS firewall feature set per Cisco IOS release 12.0(1) XA consists of the following features.

◆ CBAC (*Context-Based Access Control*)

◆ Java blocking

◆ Detection and prevention of DoS attacks

◆ Provision of real-time alerts and audit trails

The Cisco IOS firewall feature set allows you to configure your Cisco router as:

◆ An Internet firewall

◆ An intranet firewall between different LAN/WAN groups

◆ A tunneling firewall that provides secure connections

◆ An extranet firewall

◆ A firewall between a main network and a DMZ

 NOTE

Currently, the Cisco IOS Release 12.0(1) XA supports only the Cisco 1720 router.

In Figure 11.2, the area between the two screening routers is the DMZ. The proxy Web server is part of the DMZ. In the event that it is compromised, the second screening router that is between the internal network and the DMZ will still protect the internal network.

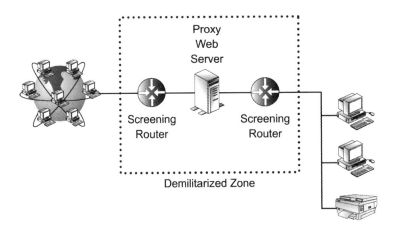

FIGURE 11.2 *A sample DMZ*

In the subsequent sections, I'll focus on CBAC, how it operates, and its benefits and limitations.

Context-Based Access Control

CBAC is the core of the Cisco IOS firewall feature set. Although it's not a complete firewall solution, it does have its uses in perimeter security. It operates at the Network, Transport, and Application layers. It can maintain state information for TCP and UDP connections and use this information to make access decisions. It also inspects outgoing IP traffic in real time.

The Cisco IOS firewall feature set is supported on the following platforms.

- Cisco 800 series
- Cisco uBR900 series
- Cisco 1600 series
- Cisco 1700 series
- Cisco 2500 series
- Cisco 2600 series
- Cisco 3600 series
- Cisco 7100 series
- Cisco 7200 series

CBAC Functions

CBAC provides the following functions to protect a network.

- Application-level traffic filtering
- Stateful traffic inspection
- Dynamic addition of rules to ACLs
- Alerts and audit trails
- Intrusion detection

 NOTE

CBAC features are applicable only to IP networks that recognize TCP, UDP, and Application-layer protocols such as RPC, Microsoft NetShow, and Real Audio.

Following is a list of the Application-layer protocols that CBAC supports.

- CU-SeeMe (only the White Pine version)
- FTP
- H.323 (such as NetMeeting and ProShare)
- HTTP (Java blocking)
- Java
- Microsoft NetShow

- UNIX R-commands (such as `rlogin`, `rexec`, and `rsh`)
- RealAudio
- RPC (Sun RPC, not DCE RPC)
- Microsoft RPC
- SMTP
- SQL Net
- StreamWorks
- TFTP
- VDOLive

NOTE

For protocols that are not supported, CBAC will still allow the protocol to pass through if the ACLs on the router-firewall permit the traffic. Only the CBAC-specific filtering options, such as stateful inspection, can be applied for such traffic.

Next, take a look at the functions of CBAC in detail.

Application-Level Traffic Filtering

Traditional traffic-filtering routers examine packets only at the Network and Transport layers. CBAC has the ability to examine packets at both of these layers, as well as examining the Application-layer protocol information. It can do this for traffic that originates from either side of the router. This allows you to permit limited TCP and UDP traffic through a router only when the connection request comes from a trusted network.

Because CBAC examines the Application-layer protocol information by maintaining connection state information for individual connections, it supports protocols that involve multiple channels, such as RPC, FTP, and most multimedia protocols.

You can configure CBAC to filter or reject Java content based on server address. If you want to protect users from downloading destructive Java applets, you can create a CBAC inspection rule that filters Java applets at the router-firewall and allows only those applets to pass that originate from a trusted network.

Stateful Inspection of Traffic

CBAC uses timeout and threshold values to discover and manage session state information for all TCP and UDP traffic, which it inspects at the router-firewall. Once CBAC gets the state information, it uses the information to create temporary openings in the router-firewall's ACL to allow outgoing and incoming return traffic and additional connections for trusted sessions.

NOTE

All sessions that originate from the internal network are deemed trusted.

Because CBAC inspects traffic at the Application layer and maintains session information for TCP and UDP sessions, it can detect and restrict certain DoS attacks, such as SYN flooding. In a SYN flood attack, an attacker sends too many TCP SYN requests to a target host using spoofed addresses and then does not complete the connections. The host is left with many half-open connections and keeps waiting for an acknowledgment from the attacker's system, which never comes. This can be very taxing on the host machine, which stops servicing valid requests, resulting in a denial of service.

CBAC has the ability to track TCP sequence numbers. If a packet has a TCP sequence number that is not within an expected range, CBAC drops it. You can also configure CBAC to terminate half-open connections, prevent IP fragmentation attacks, and issue alert messages when it detects very high rates of new connections.

To control UDP connections, CBAC uses UDP idle timeout settings and estimates session information because UDP is a connectionless protocol.

NOTE

Configuring CBAC to drop half-open connections takes up processor and memory resources, which can lead to performance loss.

Dynamically Adding Rules to Access Control Lists

CBAC can dynamically update rules in ACLs to temporarily allow traffic to pass through after stateful inspection. Once the connection is terminated, it again updates the ACL rules to inspect all traffic to untrusted networks. CBAC requires at least one ACL to operate—either an ACL on the external interface that checks for inbound traffic to the trusted network or one on the internal interface that checks for outbound traffic to the untrusted network.

Alerts and Audit Trails

CBAC supports event logging and can send alert messages using SYSLOG. The messages are based on the events at the router-firewall. It is a good security practice to enable such auditing and keep monitoring audit logs to see what kind of traffic the router-firewall is blocking, filtering, and allowing. SYSLOG provides enhanced audit trails that record network transactions by recording time stamps, source address, destination address, ports used, and the total number of bytes transmitted. You can use CBAC inspection rules to configure alerts and audit trails for each protocol. For example, you can audit HTTP and FTP traffic by specifying what to audit in your CBAC rules that cover HTTP and FTP inspection.

Intrusion Detection

The Cisco IOS firewall's intrusion detection is an in-line IDS sensor that monitors packets on router interfaces and acts upon the traffic based on the IDS rules. Although it is not an enterprise-level IDS, it is handy when deployed with perimeter security in mind. The IOS firewall can identify 59 of the most common attacks using misuse detection techniques. You can configure the IDS to respond to various threats. The following responses can be configured in the IDS.

◆ Send an alarm to a SYSLOG server

◆ Drop the packet

◆ Reset the TCP connection

 NOTE

The Cisco IOS firewall's IIDS is not an enterprise-level IDS system. Instead, Cisco has a separate enterprise-level IDS called *Cisco Secure Intrusion Detection*. The IOS firewall IDS is compatible with this IDS.

Advantages of CBAC

The stateful packet-filtering feature is more comprehensive than traditional ACL-based filtering methods. You can use it to provide security for intranet or extranet setups and between an organization and the Internet. Some advantages of CBAC follow.

◆ It modifies temporary ACL rules dynamically. Since the duration when traffic is allowed to flow is temporary, it reduces the duration of any vulnerability.

◆ It provides protection against DoS attacks by protecting against common attacks using session state information and thresholds.

◆ It provides real-time alerts and audit trails, which can be used to track the source of an attack or attempted attack.

◆ It provides VPN support.

- ◆ It is available on a variety of Cisco routers and can meet the demands of large high-speed networks.

- ◆ It provides protection against malicious Java applets.

Limitations of CBAC

CBAC also has some limitations, which are listed here.

- ◆ It supports only IP traffic. It inspects only TCP and UDP traffic; it does not inspect ICMP traffic.

- ◆ It does not check packets with a source or destination address to the router-firewall itself.

- ◆ It ignores ICMP unreachable messages.

- ◆ It does not inspect IPSec packets if the router firewall is not an IPSec endpoint.

- ◆ Session state information is specific to a single router; therefore, you cannot have a separate CBAC router-firewall for redundancy.

- ◆ It impacts system performance. You must ensure that the router has enough memory and processing power.

How CBAC Works

CBAC modifies ACLs dynamically to create temporary holes in the firewall. This allows specific outbound traffic from your network to pass. These holes also allow incoming return traffic to enter through the firewall. Once the session is terminated or times out, CBAC modifies the ACLs back to their original state. Figure 11.3 depicts how CBAC works.

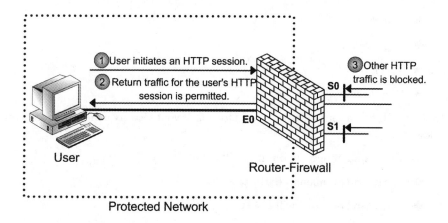

FIGURE 11.3 *How CBAC works*

In the setup shown in Figure 11.3, inbound ACLs at the S0 and S1 interfaces block HTTP traffic, and the E0 interface does not have an outbound ACL. When the user connection request passes through the router-firewall, CBAC creates a temporary opening in the inbound ACL at S0, which allows incoming return HTTP traffic for the user's HTTP session.

Configuring CBAC

Before you configure CBAC on your router, you must have a clear security policy in place. The router itself should be secured because an incorrectly configured CBAC router-firewall can compromise the firewall. Only people who have a clear understanding of how CBAC works should do the configuration.

CBAC can specify the kinds of traffic that can be permitted to flow inside and outside. In addition, you can configure CBAC to inspect traffic based on Application-layer protocols that are supported by CBAC. The following Application-layer protocols are supported by CBAC.

- ◆ CU-SeeMe
- ◆ FTP
- ◆ H.323
- ◆ Microsoft NetShow
- ◆ UNIX R commands (`rlogin`, `rexec`, `rsh`)
- ◆ RealAudio
- ◆ SMTP
- ◆ RPC
- ◆ SQL*Net
- ◆ StreamWorks
- ◆ TFTP
- ◆ VDOLive

To set up CBAC in your router, you need to look at your security policy and decide on the following items.

- ◆ What kind of outbound traffic will CBAC allow?
- ◆ What kind of inbound traffic will CBAC allow?
- ◆ What kind of traffic will CBAC inspect?

Next I will discuss typical CBAC configurations to answer the preceding three questions.

Outbound Traffic Allowed by CBAC

As an example, I will assume that all outbound IP traffic from your internal network is allowed. If you specify in the outbound ACL that all IP traffic should be denied, then no IP traffic will be allowed outside. It is important to note that CBAC can dynamically modify access lists to allow outbound traffic if it is the return traffic to a session which originated from the internal network. Following is an example that specifies outbound traffic.

```
Extended IP Access List 111
access-list 111 permit ip [source-network] [source-mask] any
access-list 111 deny ip any any
```

In the preceding example, the first line permits all IP traffic from the IP addresses that are in the [source-network] [source-mask] range to any external address. The second line denies all IP traffic from reaching the outside network. The order of the commands here is very important because the CBAC process accesses lists line by line. To better understand this, consider that you permit outbound traffic from limited addresses from your internal network to the external network in the first line and explicitly deny all outbound traffic in the second line. In this scenario, how will any kind of traffic reach the external network? It is important to remember that CBAC will permit return traffic to the outside network by dynamically modifying access lists to allow temporary openings in the router-firewall.

Inbound Traffic Allowed by CBAC

Your security policy must outline certain inbound traffic from the external network that is deemed harmful or malicious for your internal network. The simple rule is to prevent all such traffic from entering your network. You can do this by setting up an inbound CBAC access list at the external interface. An efficient way of doing this is by permitting only traffic that is deemed legitimate. The following extended access list shows an example of providing only SMTP services to the external network. It also allows limited ICMP traffic to the internal network from any external host.

```
Extended IP Access List 101
permit icmp any 66.34.55.0 0.0.0.255  echo-reply
permit icmp any 66.34.55.0 0.0.0.255 unreachable
permit icmp any 66.34.55.0 0.0.0.255 administratively-prohibited
permit icmp any 66.34.55.0 0.0.0.255 echo
permit icmp any 66.34.55.0 0.0.0.255 time-exceeded
permit tcp any host 66.34.55.150 1 eq smtp
```

In the preceding configuration, only limited ICMP traffic is allowed into your internal network. Anyone from the external network can send limited ICMP message packets and use your SMTP server, which is a specific host with address 66.34.55.150.

Traffic Inspected by CBAC

CBAC can inspect traffic only for the Application-layer protocols it supports. The following sample configuration inspects FTP, SMTP, and HTTP traffic.

```
Big(config)# ip inspect name sample ftp
Big(config)# ip inspect name sample smtp
Big(config)# ip inspect name sample http
```

Configuration Steps

Following are the steps for configuring CBAC.

1. Check whether the router supports CBAC. If it doesn't, install a version of IOS that supports CBAC.

2. Determine a comprehensive list of services on the untrusted network that will be used by trusted network users (for example, HTTP, FTP, and RealAudio).

3. Select external and internal interfaces.

4. Configure IP ACLs at each interface. Configure inbound and outbound access lists on the external interface.

5. Set CBAC global timeouts and thresholds. Global timeout values determine the duration of the opening at the router-firewall in response to a request from the trusted network. Timeout values should be low.

6. Define inspection rules.

7. Apply inspection rules per the desired services list.

8. Configure the logging and audit trail.

9. Test and verify CBAC.

These steps are described in the following sections.

Checking for CBAC Support on the Router

The easiest way to check whether a router supports CBAC is to issue a CBAC command to the router. If the command fails, then the router does not support CBAC. Following are two examples; the first one shows a router `Fire` without CBAC, and the second one shows a router `Big` with CBAC.

```
Example 1
Fire# show ip inspect all
         ^
%Invalid input detected at '^' marker.

Fire#
```

```
Example 2
Big# show ip inspect all
Session audit trail is enabled
Session alert is enabled
Big#
```

Determining Required Services

After you decide which services on the public network should be used from your protected network, you should deny all other services. Even if some protocols, such as FTP and SMTP, are marked as allowed by CBAC, some features might still be restricted. For example, CBAC watches the FTP authentication exchange and disables the use of non-standard ports for FTP data. If you are using Web traffic filtering, the Java blocking feature of CBAC might not be very reliable because CBAC does not filter encapsulated Java content that is in a .zip or .jar format. CBAC only supports standard SMTP commands, which are listed here.

- ◆ DATA
- ◆ EHLO
- ◆ EXPN
- ◆ HELO
- ◆ HELP
- ◆ MAIL
- ◆ NOOP
- ◆ QUIT
- ◆ RCPT
- ◆ RSET
- ◆ SAML
- ◆ SEND
- ◆ SOML
- ◆ VRFY

Choosing an Interface

You must choose an interface on which you want to configure CBAC. It is a good practice to configure CBAC access lists on the external interface. However, there might be cases in which you need to configure a CBAC access list on the internal router (for example, in a DMZ topology or if more than one external connection is terminating at the router).

Figure 11.4 shows a CBAC configured at an external interface.

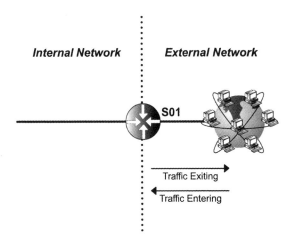

FIGURE 11.4 *CBAC configured at an external interface*

In the topology shown in Figure 11.4, the CBAC access lists are configured on the external interface S01. Traffic from the specified protocols is not allowed to enter the internal network; only traffic that is part of a session initiated from the internal network is allowed to pass. Note that the access lists will filter incoming traffic. All external traffic is in response to a request initiated from a host in the internal network.

Figure 11.5 shows CBAC configured at an internal interface.

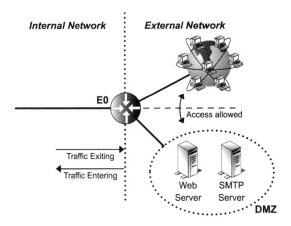

FIGURE 11.5 *CBAC configured at an internal interface*

If you decide to host services that can be accessed from an external network, you can set up a DMZ to isolate your internal network from the servers that would be hosting specified services for the external network. In such a topology, you need to apply CBAC access lists on the internal interface. In Figure 11.5, access lists are configured on the internal interface E0. Here, the external traffic is allowed to access services in the DMZ, and specified protocol traffic to the internal network is restricted. In this setup, as in other setups, the access lists will filter incoming traffic. All external traffic is in response to a request initiated from any host in the internal network.

Setting Up Access Lists

For CBAC to work, you must configure access lists. You must take care when setting up the access lists because they can make your router-firewall vulnerable if they are configured incorrectly.

Following are some recommendations for a basic CBAC configuration.

◆ Don't filter traffic coming from a trusted network to the external network. This simplifies management but assumes that no attacks will be launched from the internal network.

◆ Prevent all traffic originating with an IP address that exists in your internal network to prevent spoofed IP packets from entering your network. This has to be configured only at the external interface because you know that no incoming packets with an IP address that matches an internal IP address can come from the external interface. You might also consider adding the entire range of private IP addresses in this list. However, this might lead to disruption of VPN connections if the interface allows them.

◆ Deny all broadcast messages with IP 255.255.255.255. This will prevent broadcast storms.

Setting an Outbound Access List on the External Interface

Outbound access lists at the external interface can be either standard or extended. You must permit all traffic that needs to be inspected by CBAC in the outbound access list. All traffic that is not permitted will be dropped and not be inspected by CBAC.

CBAC lists allow you to use keywords to specify the protocols. Table 11.2 shows a list of application protocols supported by CBAC and their associated keywords.

Table 11.2 Application Protocols Supported by CBAC and Associated Keywords

Application Protocol	Protocol Keyword
CU-SeeMe	cuseeme
FTP	ftp
H.323	h323
Microsoft NetShow	netshow
UNIX R commands (rlogin, rexec, rsh)	rcmd
RealAudio	realaudio
SMTP	smtp
RPC	rpc
SQL*Net	sqlnet
StreamWorks	streamworks
TFTP	tftp
VDOLive	vdolive

Consider a scenario in which you want to allow users in your internal network to access HTTP, FTP, and DNS services available anywhere on the Internet. For SMTP and POP 3 services, your internal hosts can only connect to a specified mail server on the Internet with IP address 66.34.55.150. For this scenario, you must use the following configuration.

```
Big (config)# ! Outbound access list
Big (config)# no access-list 101
Big (config)# ipaccess-list extended 101
Big (config-ext-acl)# permit icmp 66.34.55.0 0.0.0.255 any
Big (config-ext-acl)# permit udp 66.34.55.0 0.0.0.255 any eq domain
Big (config-ext-acl)# permit tcp 66.34.55.0 0.0.0.255 any eq www
Big (config-ext-acl)# permit tcp 66.34.55.0 0.0.0.255 any eq ftp
Big (config-ext-acl)# permit tcp 66.34.55.0 0.0.0.255 host 66.34.55.150 eq smtp
Big (config-ext-acl)# permit tcp 66.34.55.0 0.0.0.255 host 66.34.55.150 eq pop3
Big (config-ext-acl)# deny ip any any
Big (config-ext-acl)# exit
Big (config)# ! Apply the access list to the external interface
Big (config)# interface eth0/0
```

```
Big (config-if)# ipaccess-group 101 out
Big (config-if)# exit
Big (config)#
```

Setting an Inbound Access List on the External Interface

The inbound access list at the external interface has to be an extended access list. You should deny all traffic that you want CBAC to inspect. Only return traffic that is part of an existing session that originated from the internal network should be allowed to pass. CBAC will create temporary openings in the inbound access list by dynamically modifying it when required. The following sample access list blocks all TCP and UDP traffic, allows a few ICMP messages, and protects against IP spoofing by denying all incoming traffic from the external interface. Incoming traffic from the internal network will always come from the internal interface.

```
Big(config)# ! Protect against IP spoofing
Big(config-ext-acl)# deny ip 66.34.55.0 0.0.0.255 any
Big(config)# ! This is the inbound CBAC access list
Big(config)# no access-list 102
Big(config)# ipaccess-list extended 102
Big(config-ext-acl)# permit icmp any any echo-reply
Big(config-ext-acl)# permit icmp any any unreachable
Big(config-ext-acl)# permit icmp any any ttl-exceeded
Big(config-ext-acl)# deny ip any any log
Big(config-ext-acl)# exit
Big(config)# ! Apply the access list to the external interface
Big(config)# interface eth0/0
Big(config-if)# ipaccess-group 102 in
Big(config-if)# exit
Big(config)#
```

Setting CBAC Global Timeout and Threshold Parameters

The global timeout and threshold parameters play a crucial role in the CBAC session management process. You can use the default values or change them to suit your requirements. The global parameters can determine timeouts and thresholds, such as:

◆ The time to wait for a TCP session to reach an established state

◆ The time to manage a TCP session after no activity (idle timeout)

◆ UDP idle timeouts

◆ DNS name lookup inspection timeouts

◆ The maximum number of half-open sessions maintained

CBAC adds a rule to the inbound access list whenever there is a connection request from a host on the internal network. This rule permits return traffic to the external network and is removed when any one of the following conditions are met.

◆ The response fails to arrive within the timeout value

◆ The connection closes down (only for TCP connections)

◆ The connection is idle for more than the allotted time

Table 11.3 outlines the timeout and threshold values, the commands used to change them, and their default settings.

Table 11.3 Timeout and Threshold Values and Related Commands

Timeout or Threshold Value to Change	Command	Default Value
The time a UDP session will still be managed after zero activity (the UDP idle timeout)	`ip inspect udp idle-time seconds`	30 seconds
The time a DNS name lookup session will still be managed after no activity	`ip inspect dns-timeout seconds`	5 seconds
The number of existing half-open sessions that will cause the IOS to start deleting half-open sessions	`ip inspect max-incomplete high number`	500 existing half-open sessions
The number of existing half-open sessions that will cause the IOS to stop deleting half-open sessions	`ip inspect max-incomplete low number`	400 existing half-open sessions
The rate of new sessions that will cause the IOS to start deleting half-open sessions	`ip inspect one-minute high number`	500 half-open sessions per minute
The rate of new sessions that will cause the IOS to stop deleting half-open sessions	`ip inspect one-minute low number`	400 half-open sessions per minute

Timeout or Threshold Value to Change	Command	Default Value
The number of existing half-open TCP sessions with the same destination host address that will cause the IOS to start dropping half-open sessions to the same destination host address	`ip inspect tcp max-incomplete host` *`number`* `block-time` *`minutes`*	50 existing half-open TCP sessions; 0 minutes

Table 11.4 describes some suggested parameters to change. These settings can vary depending on the speed of the network.

Table 11.4 Parameters Settings

Timeout Name	Description	Default	Suggested
`Synwait-time`	The time that CBAC waits for a new TCP session to reach an established state	30 seconds	15 seconds
`Finwait-time`	The time that CBAC continues to manage a TCP session after a FIN exchange has closed it down	5 seconds	1 second
`TCP idle-time`	The time that CBAC continues to manage a TCP session with no activity	1 hour (1800 seconds)	30 minutes
`UDP idle-time`	The time that CBAC continues to manage a UDP session with no activity	30 seconds	15 seconds

The following example shows how to set global timeout parameters.

```
Big(config)# ip inspect tcpsynwait-time 15
Big(config)# ip inspect tcpfinwait-time 1
Big(config)# ip inspect tcpidle-time 1800
Big(config)# ip inspect udpidle-time 15
Big(config)# exit
Big#
```

HALF-OPEN SESSIONS

TCP uses a three-way handshake process to establish a connection. To better understand this, consider a scenario. For Host A to initiate a TCP session with Host B, the following activities take place.

◆ Host A sends a SYN packet to Host B.

◆ Host B sends an acknowledgement SYN-ACK packet.

◆ Host A responds back with an acknowledgement ACK packet.

Now a TCP session is established between Host A and Host B. This process is popularly known as the TCP three-way handshake. Figure 11.6 explains this process.

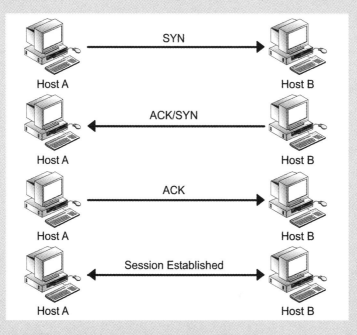

Now that you understand how a complete TCP session is established, it will be easy to understand a half-open session. Half-open means that the TCP three-way handshake process is not complete. In most half-open sessions, only the first process of the three-way handshake has been completed. If the CBAC router does not get a SYN-ACK or an ACK packet within the timeout values set, it disconnects the half-open session. Half-open sessions are exploited by DoS attacks, such as SYN floods and "Land" attacks. Such attacks send multiple SYN packets to a target host using a spoofed IP address. This results in the target host sending SYN-ACK requests to the spoofed IP address, which might not exist. The target system keeps waiting for the ACK packet, which never comes. During this time, genuine requests for TCP sessions are denied because the previous requests for TCP sessions are still queued, which causes the legitimate hosts to suffer.

FIGURE 11.6 *The TCP three-way handshake process*

Defining Inspection Rules

Inspection rules specify what CBAC will inspect at an interface. In other words, inspection rules specify what Application-layer protocols and generic TCP and UDP rules (if you want to filter them as well) CBAC will inspect. You must define at least one inspection rule for CBAC to inspect IP traffic for the supported Application-layer protocols. You can set options to log audit trails, control alert messages, and check for IP fragmentation in your inspection rules. The statements in your inspection rules should contain the following pieces of information.

- ◆ The name of the inspection rule

- ◆ The protocol that needs to be inspected (Application layer and Transport layer protocols, TCP or UDP)

- ◆ The global timeout values

- ◆ The control options for alerts and audit trails

NOTE

An Application-layer protocol inspection rule will always take precedence over a generic TCP or UDP inspection rule. Also, if you allow a protocol in your inbound or outbound access lists and you don't specify it in your inspection rule, CBAC will allow traffic to pass without inspection.

Configuring an Application-Layer Protocol Inspection

You can use the following global configuration commands to inspect Application-layer protocols supported by CBAC.

```
Myrouter(config)# ip inspect name inspection-name
protocol [alert {on¦off}] [audit-trail {on ¦ off}]
[timeout seconds]
```

This command will configure the CBAC inspection for an Application-layer protocol defined in Table 11.3 (other than RPC or Java). You must repeat this command for each specified protocol and use the same inspection-name to create a single inspection rule.

Take a look at the following command.

```
Myrouter(config)# ip inspect name inspection-name
rpc program-number number [wait-time minutes]
[alert {on ¦ off}] [audit-trail {on ¦ off}]
[timeout seconds]
```

This command is used to enable CBAC inspection for the RPC protocol. You can specify multiple RPC program numbers by repeating this command for each program number.

Configuring an IP Fragmentation Inspection

IP fragmentation inspection is disabled by default. You can use the `ip inspect name` command to enable CBAC to inspect IP packet fragmentation. However, this command can cause undesirable effects because it can discard genuine IP packets if they arrive in a fragmented state. The following is an outline of the command to configure IP fragmentation.

```
Myrouter(config)# ip inspect name inspection-name
fragment [max number timeout number]
```

Configuring a Generic TCP and UDP Inspection

If you configure CBAC to inspect TCP and UDP traffic without any Application-layer protocol inspection, the router-firewall will still inspect the traffic but it will not inspect it at an application level. Also, services such as FTP might not work correctly because the return packets will use a different port than the previous packet that was sent. However, if you configure an application protocol inspection, CBAC will give precedence to the Application-layer protocol over generic TCP or UDP. The following is the command outline for configuring a TCP inspection.

```
Myouter(config)# ip inspect name inspection-name tcp
[timeout seconds]
```

UDP inspection is similar and can be enabled by replacing `tcp` with `udp` in the preceding statement.

Applying Inspection Rules

You can apply the CBAC rule set on either the external or internal interface. In most cases, you need to apply it in the external interface. You can use the following command to apply the inspection rule to an interface.

```
Myrouter(config-if)# ip inspect inspection-name {in |out}
```

For example, if your external interface is `eth 0/0` and your inspection rule name is `inspout`, the following command will work.

```
Myouter(config)# interface eth0/0
Myouter(config-if)#ip inspect inspout out
Myouter(config-if)#end
```

Configuring Logging and Audit Trails

You can configure your router to send logs to a SYSLOG server in your network. Logging and audit trails provide crucial information that can help you maintain your CBAC firewall. You can use the following commands in the global configuration mode.

◆ To add the date and time to SYSLOG and audit trail messages, use the following command.

```
Myrouter(config)# service timestamps log datetime
```

◆ To specify the host name or IP address of the host where you want to send SYSLOG messages, use the following command.

```
Myrouter(config)# logging host
```

◆ To configure the SYSLOG facility in which error messages are sent, use the following command.

```
Myrouter(config)# logging facility facility-type
```

◆ To limit messages logged to the SYSLOG servers based on severity, use the following command. (The default level is 7.)

```
Myrouter(config)# logging trap level
```

◆ To turn on CBAC audit trail messages, use the following command.

```
Myrouter(config)# ip inspect audit-trail
```

Testing and Verifying the CBAC Configuration

You must test the CBAC configuration by testing all inspected protocols and checking whether hosts from the internal network can access permitted services from external networks. The following commands allow you to test the CBAC configuration.

◆ To view a particular configured inspection rule, use the following command.

```
Myrouter# show ip inspect name inspection-name
```

◆ To view the complete CBAC inspection configuration, use the following command.

```
Myrouter# show ip inspect config
```

◆ To view interface configuration with regard to applied inspection rules and access lists, use the following command.

```
Myrouter# show ip inspect interfaces
```

◆ To see the existing sessions being monitored by CBAC, use the following command.

```
Myrouter# show ip inspect session [detail]
```

◆ To view all CBAC configuration and session information, use the following command.

```
Myrouter# show ip inspect all
```

To define a set of inspection rules, use the `ip inspect name global configuration` command.

```
ip inspect name (global configuration)
```

The following is Cisco's command line reference with complete detail of the `ip inspect name global configuration` command. You can use the `no` form of this command to remove the inspection rule for a protocol or to remove the entire set of inspection rules.

```
ip inspect name inspection-name protocol [alert {on ¦ off}]
[audit-trail {on ¦ off}] [timeout seconds]
```

or

```
ip inspect name inspection-name http [java-list access-list]
[alert {on ¦ off}] [audit-trail {on ¦ off}]
[timeout seconds] (Java protocol only)
```

or

```
ip inspect name inspection-name rpc program-number number
[wait-time minutes] [alert {on ¦ off}] [audit-trail {on ¦ off}]
[timeout seconds] (RPC protocol only)
```

or

```
ip inspect name inspection-name fragment
        [max number timeout seconds]
no ip inspect name inspection-name protocol
        (removes the inspection rule for a protocol)
no ip inspect name inspection-name fragment
        (removes fragment inspection for a rule)
no ip inspect name
        (removes the entire set of inspection rules)
```

In the preceding command syntax:

◆ `inspection-name` is the name of the set of inspection rules. If you want to add a protocol to an existing set of rules, use the same `inspection-name` as the existing set of rules.

◆ `protocol` is a protocol keyword.

◆ `alert {on ¦ off}` sets alert generation to either on or off. If no option is selected, alerts are generated based on the setting of the `ip inspect alert-off` command.

◆ `audit-trail {on ¦ off}` enables or disables audit trails. If no option is selected, audit trail messages are generated based on the setting of the `ip inspect audit-trail` command.

◆ `http` specifies the HTTP protocol for Java applet blocking.

◆ `timeout` is used to override the global TCP or UDP idle timeouts for the specified protocol and specify the number of seconds for a different idle timeout. This timeout overrides the global TCP and UPD timeouts but will not override the global DNS timeout.

◆ `java-list access-list` specifies the access list (name or number) to determine trusted sites. The `java-list access-list` keyword is available only for the HTTP protocol and for Java applet blocking. Java blocking works only with standard access lists.

◆ `rpc program-number` specifies the program number to permit. This keyword is available only for the RPC protocol.

◆ `wait-time` specifies the number of minutes to keep an opening in the firewall to allow subsequent connections from the same source address and to the same destination address and port. The default `wait-time` is zero minutes. This keyword is available only for the RPC protocol.

◆ `fragment` specifies the fragment inspection for the named rule.

◆ `max number` specifies the maximum number of unassembled packets for which state information (structures) is allocated by the Cisco IOS software. Unassembled packets arrive at the router interface before the initial packet for a session. The acceptable range is 50 through 10,000. The default is 256 state entries. Memory is allocated for the state structures, and setting this value to a larger number might cause memory resources to be exhausted.

◆ `timeout seconds` specifies the number of seconds that a packet state structure remains active. When the timeout value expires, the router drops the unassembled packet, freeing that structure for use by another packet. The default timeout value is one second. If this number is set to a value greater than one second, the Cisco IOS software will automatically adjust it when the number of free state structures goes below certain thresholds. When the number of free states is less than 32, the timeout will be divided by two. When the number of free states is less than 16, the timeout will be set to one second.

To define a set of inspection rules, enter this command for each protocol that you want CBAC to inspect, using the same `inspection-name`. Some points that you should keep in mind while using this command follow.

◆ Give each set of inspection rules a unique `inspection-name`.

◆ Define either one or two sets of rules per interface. You can define one set to examine both inbound and outbound traffic, or you can define two sets—one for outbound traffic and one for inbound traffic.

◆ To define a single set of inspection rules, configure inspection for all of the desired Application-layer protocols and for TCP or UDP as desired. This combination of TCP, UDP, and Application-layer protocols joins together to form a single set of inspection rules with a unique name.

◆ In general, when you configure inspection for a protocol, return traffic entering the internal network will be permitted only if the packets are part of a valid and existing session for which state information is being maintained.

Summary

In this chapter, you learned that a router has the ability to provide basic firewall capabilities to your network. The Cisco IOS firewall feature set extends the ability of a traditional router to provide stateful inspection of Application-layer protocols. You learned that the CBAC feature is not a substitute for an enterprise-level firewall, but that it is a cost-effective solution that is ideal for small organizations that require a basic to medium level of network security. Finally, you learned how to configure CBAC.

This chapter completes all of the concepts you need to know about Internet security and firewalls. The three appendices cover the best practices, tips and tricks, and FAQs for firewall technologies.

Check Your Understanding

Multiple Choice Questions

1. Identify the routing protocol from the following list of protocols.
   a. PPTP
   b. BGP
   c. IP
   d. FTP

2. By default, most Web servers run on which port number?

    a. 21

    b. 81

    c. 80

    d. 144

3. How many attacks can a Cisco IOS firewall identify, using misuse detection techniques?

    a. 1202

    b. 57

    c. 59

    d. 29

Short Questions

1. Why might you consider using a dedicated and special purpose router instead of a machine that has routing capabilities?

2. What configurations are possible for Cisco routers using the Cisco IOS firewall feature set?

Answers

Multiple Choice Answers

1. b. BGP is a routing protocol.

2. c. By default, most Web servers run on port 80.

3. c. A Cisco IOS firewall can identify 59 of the most common attacks using misuse detection techniques.

Short Answers

1. There are many reasons why you might consider using a dedicated and special purpose router instead of a machine that has routing capabilities. These reasons range from performance benefits to improved security. Some advantages of a dedicated special purpose router are

    • Better performance

    • Scalability, because a dedicated router can support many interface slots

- Low total cost of ownership, because there is less administrative overhead

- Better security, because it is dedicated with no extra functionality

2. The Cisco IOS firewall feature set allows you to configure your Cisco router as:

- An Internet firewall

- An intranet firewall between different LAN/WAN groups

- A tunneling firewall that provides secure connections

- An extranet firewall

- A firewall between a main network and a DMZ

Appendix A

Best Practices, Tips, and Tricks

This appendix will cover the best practices and tips and tricks for network administrators who implement firewalls. Although this is not a complete list, you can use these points as a reference while implementing firewalls.

Best Practices

Securing data over the Internet is a major challenge for network administrators. Security is mainly implemented with the help of firewalls. Due to the importance of firewalls, they should be installed in a planned manner. There are some points that you should keep in mind to help you decide the type and level of security you want in the firewall.

◆ By default, you should deny all traffic entering or leaving the network. This feature is implemented in most firewalls; it helps keep a check on the accidental leakage of secret data from the network.

◆ You should analyze all packets and compare them to the rules that check their authentication. You should write the rules in accordance with the specific organizational requirements so that:

- Useful flow of traffic is not affected. Data required by the organization, or the safe data, should not be blocked from entering or leaving the network.

- There is not a considerable loss of performance. Speed of data transfer between the networks is very important, and bandwidth is expensive. Therefore, make sure that only necessary rules are designed and implemented so that network time is not wasted scanning data.

◆ Some rules for detecting potentially harmful packets are listed below. These packets should be denied access through your firewall. Incoming packets should be dropped if:

- They contain the IP address of an internal host in their source IP address fields.

- They do not contain the IP address of your internal network in their destination IP address fields.

Outgoing packets should be dropped if:

◆ They have your internal network's IP address in the destination field.

- They do not contain an IP address of an internal host in the source field.

◆ You must create a security policy for your organization. This policy should include

- The company's security requirements

- Required services

- Criteria for designing rules for packet filtering

◆ According to an organization's policies, you should turn off services that are not required. Many services open ports to enable communication and data transfer, which creates security vulnerabilities that a hacker can use to intrude upon the system. Most of the services requiring access to the Internet are risky. These services, which should be regularly checked and stopped if they are not required, include

- Mail services such as SMTP, POP, and IMAP

- Web services such as HTTP and SSL

- Login services such as rlogin, TELNET, and FTP

- DNS zone transfers

- ICMP-based ping requests

- Other services such as LDAP, NFS, and SOCKS

◆ You should divide the internal structure of the network to help the firewall provide controlled access to specific parts of the network.

◆ You should integrate the firewall into the operating system. This leads to a hardened system, which is more difficult to penetrate than the normal system.

◆ You should enable firewall logging because it is necessary for the administrator to know who is accessing the network. You should log all inbound connections. This information enables you to determine which connections failed and which succeeded. You can use this information to analyze the sources from which the incoming traffic originates.

◆ Log files are usually stored in a default location. A hacker can modify these files to mislead the administrator. Therefore, you should move these files to a safer place where access is restricted. If possible, back up log files regularly. They are important in tracing the cause of any breakdown.

◆ You should use additional software suites with firewalls for extra security. Such software includes

- Anti-virus software

- Authentication software

- Application-filtering software for e-mail content, attachments, URLs, and so on

- Fault-detecting software

◆ You should update the operating system on which the firewall is installed with the latest security patches. Patches are released periodically; you should keep track of them and install them when they become available.

◆ Just like security patches, you should also update anti-virus software regularly. You should install new definitions to protect the system from the latest viruses.

◆ You should install an alert mechanism. Alerts can be sounded after:

- An intrusion is detected

- Unsuccessful login

- Service failure

- An error is detected in the log files

- System crashes

◆ You should be notified of alerts using methods such as:

- An audible alert, such as a sound

- A mail alert, including the reason and the log file

- A message on a pager or a network broadcast

◆ You should do regular security audits to confirm that your firewall is working. These audits expose security vulnerabilities, which you should deal with immediately.

◆ In many circumstances, you should install personal firewalls on internal hosts. These circumstances include

- **Presence of remote hosts**. If a hacker compromises a remote host, a personal firewall can still prevent him or her from accessing and damaging the rest of the network.

- **Presence of wireless network**. Wireless networks are also very vulnerable to hacking attacks. The personal firewall should be implemented on individual hosts.

◆ Firewall software comes with a default admin or root password. You should change these passwords immediately after installation. There are certain guidelines to follow to create good passwords.

- Passwords should be at least eight characters long.

- Passwords should not be a dictionary word (to protect against brute force attacks).

- Administrators should not use their name, telephone number, license plate number, or any other publicly known value as a password.

- Passwords should use a combination of uppercase and lowercase letters, numbers, and special characters.

◆ Firewall configuration files are also targets for a hacker. Like log files, these are stored in a default directory. You should back up these files regularly so that you can retrieve them if the original files are tampered with or deleted.

◆ Record all of the changes made to the system. This information is helpful if you decide to roll back to a previous state.

Tips and Tricks

The following tips should help you organize the security structure for your organization and create a security policy that is customized to the specific needs of the organization.

◆ **Analyze and understand the risks involved**. This includes identifying

- Data to be protected

- Location of data

- Systems to be protected

- Points where these systems can be secured

- Cost of loss of data

◆ **Identify the likely types of attack on your system**. There are two main categories of threats.

- **External threats**. These threats represent attacks from outside of your network.

- **Internal threats**. These threats represent attacks from within your network.

◆ **Write a security policy for your company**. The security policy should clearly define the rules that the company should follow to minimize security risk. These rules can include

- Firewall structure to be implemented

- Regular backups of important data

- Rules and regulations for employees

- Disabling of applications that are not required or might be harmful from a security point of view

- Implementation of logging both incoming and outgoing traffic

◆ **Regularly update software**. To update software, you can

- Keep anti-virus definitions up to date.

- Install the latest security patches available.

- Get the latest version of firewall and other crucial security software. Newer versions are usually more secure.

◆ **Check the security periodically**. You should perform regular security audits on the network. There are certain advantages to this step.

- The faults in your system will be exposed so that you can fix them with security patches.

- A check is kept on the latest security threats and vulnerabilities.

Appendix B

Frequently Asked Questions

Q. What is a firewall?

A. A firewall is a system or group of systems that enforce an access control policy between the internal network and the outside world. Physically, it is a group of security hardware and/or software that acts as a choke point. A firewall can be considered a gatekeeper that either allows or denies incoming and outgoing traffic. It can be implemented at the IP layer or the Application layer. A firewall might also be used to create security pockets within the internal network.

Q. What are the different technologies used in implementing a firewall?

A. The different technologies used in implementing a firewall are

◆ Packet filtering (IP layer)

◆ Proxy systems (Application-level gateway)

◆ Circuit gateways

Q. What are the limitations of firewalls?

A. Although firewalls offer a very good level of overall security to a network, they do have a few limitations.

◆ A firewall can only prevent attacks that are made using the data that passes through the firewall. If a network has other data links with the outside world, the firewall has no control over them. Leakage of sensitive company data is the simplest example of such a security breach.

◆ A security-ignorant user can easily leak information out of the organization without the interference of a firewall. He or she can easily be persuaded by an external hacker to provide access to resources such as an organization's modems. This provides the hacker with an easy entry into the organization's network.

◆ Firewalls cannot provide reliable protection against viruses. There are many ways in which viruses can elude a firewall. They are easily transferred using encoded binary files. There are numerous viruses out there, and searching for all of them can drastically reduce the firewall's performance. You should install and use virus scanners on each host in the network rather than relying on the firewall to do the job. Desktop anti-virus software can also guard you from data-driven attacks. For example, you can configure anti-virus software to scan e-mail because it is easy to embed a virus in an e-mail message and have it executed on the system.

- Firewalls cannot protect against tunneling over most application protocols, trojan-infected programs, or poorly written software. Tunneling over HTTP, SMTP, and other protocols is simple, and almost every computer is susceptible to it. Even with a firewall, you need to implement software controls on internal networks and check host security on servers.

Q. What critical resources are needed to implement a firewall efficiently and effectively?

A. Understanding and analyzing the available resources is important if you want to get the best performance from a firewall. Some of these resources include

- **RAM**. This is a very important resource that is necessary to decrease the time required to access frequently used files. If you run out of RAM, the CPU will resort to swapping. This creates a major bottleneck in the performance of the system and can lead to problems such as denial of service or delays.

- **Processor**. A good processor is required for many applications. The need for a resource depends upon the service provided by the computer.

- **Socket**. Many applications, such as Web caches and IP routing, depend upon the performance of the socket in the host's operating system.

Q. What is packet filtering?

A. Packet filtering, as the name suggests, selectively allows IP packets in or out through the firewall according to the packet-filtering rules set by the administrator. Packet filtering is done in the IP layer and is generally implemented using a router. *Screening routers* filter packets. Each packet's header is checked for:

- Source IP information

- Destination IP information

- The type of the packet and the port to which it is directed

Depending upon the firewall packet-filtering rules, the packet is

- **Accepted by the firewall**. The packet is allowed to pass through.

- **Rejected by the firewall**. The sender of the packet is informed of the rejection.

- **Denied by the firewall**. The sender never gets to know the fate of the packet.

Apart from these rules, a packet-filtering system may use state tracking. Every outgoing packet is tracked, but only those packets that arrive as a response to a sent packet are allowed access.

Q. What are the advantages of packet filtering?

A. There are several basic advantages to packet filtering.

- Since packet filtering is done in the IP layer, it is much faster than any other firewall system and involves very little overhead.

- Packet filtering is the easiest of all firewall systems to implement in hardware.

- Since all of the inter-network traffic has to go through the packet-filtering system, a single choke point is created. Therefore, setting up and monitoring the system becomes very easy.

- Packet filtering is effective against IP spoofing, sniffing, port scanning, and some types of network sweeping threats.

Q. What are the limitations of packet filtering?

A. There are a few basic limitations of packet filtering.

- Since packet filtering is done in the IP layer, the filtering has no control or check over the contents of the packet. The filtering can base its decision only on the packet's header information, which makes it vulnerable to session hijacking or any other attack that operates in the higher layers.

- Access control can only be based on the source address, destination address, and type and target port of the packet. It cannot be based on users, user groups, and so on.

- Since a router is used to filter all incoming and outgoing packets, the performance of the router is drastically downgraded.

Q. What is meant by network scanning?

A. Network scanning is the technique of identifying all of the services, ports, and applications of a network that are open or available to the outside world. It is done mostly by potential intruders as an initial step in hacking a system. Network scanning can and should be used by network administrators as a tool to determine the services, ports, and applications of the network that are open but not required.

Q. How can a firewall prevent network scanning?

A. Network scanning can be limited to some extent by blocking all IP-directed broadcasts at the router.

Q. What is meant by footprinting?

A. The process of obtaining extensive internal information about a network is called *footprinting*. A footprinting attack targets information including the internal IP address range, details of different servers used within the network (such as DNS or mail servers), crucial contact details, or any other internal network information.

Q.   How can I prevent source IP address spoofing attacks?

A.   In a source IP address spoofing attack, the intruder sends IP packets to the target network from outside while pretending that the packets originated from the target network itself. The sent packets falsely contain the source IP address of an inside system of the target network.

You can prevent source spoofing attacks by trashing every arriving packet that has an inside source IP address.

Q.   How can I prevent source routing attacks?

A.   In a source routing attack, the attacker specifies the route that a packet should take to reach its destination. Due to this unexpected path, the packet might bypass the network's security check. You can prevent a source routing attack by simply trashing all packets that contain the source route option.

Q.   How can I prevent tiny fragment attacks?

A.   In a tiny fragment attack, the attacker uses the IP fragmentation feature to divide the packet into tiny fragments so that the TCP header information is forced into a separate packet fragment. If the filtering router examines only the first fragment of the packet and allows all others to pass, the packet might bypass user-defined filtering rules. You can prevent a tiny fragment attack by trashing all TCP protocol packets with IP `FragmentOffset` equal to 1.

Q.   What are data-driven attacks?

A.   A data-driven attack occurs when malicious code that is disguised as harmless passes through the security wall of a network into an internal host and is executed to launch an attack. The best way to prohibit direct connections from the outside and reduce the threat of data-driven attacks is to deploy proxy servers on a bastion host.

Q.   What is dynamic packet filtering?

A.   In dynamic packet filtering, a port is opened dynamically only when it is required. The port is closed as soon as the communication ends. This greatly increases the security of the network because at any given time only a minimum number of ports are open.

Q.   What are Application-layer firewalls?

A.   Application-layer firewalls are generally hosts that run proxy servers. They allow the network administrator to implement a much stricter security policy than is possible with packet filtering. Rather than relying on a generic packet-filtering tool that can only base its decision on IP header information, special purpose applications such as proxy servers are used for each service that is required. Moreover, Application layers can be configured to support only those specific features of an application that the network administrator considers acceptable, while disabling the rest. A proxy server can disable IP routing between two networks. Therefore, there is no direct traffic between the two networks. The proxy server usually performs detailed auditing and logging.

Q. What are the different components of an Application-layer firewall?

A. The various Application-layer firewall components are

◆ **Application gateway**. This consists of a proxy server on a multi-homed host.

◆ **Proxy server**. This is the most important component of the Application-layer firewall. It can be considered the engine that drives the whole system.

◆ **Dual-homed host**. This is the host system on which the proxy server executes. It is called dual-homed because it has two network interfaces with unique IP addresses—one for the trusted network and the other for the external network.

◆ **Proxy client**. This is the software that is present on each client machine on the internal network. Proxy client forwards the internal host application's data requests to the proxy server and the proxy server's data response to the internal host application.

Q. Why should I use a proxy server?

A. Proxy servers come with a number of features that make them the ideal choice for a firewall between a trusted and a non-trusted network. Some of these features include

◆ **User authentication**. You can configure proxy servers to grant different network access rights to different users on the network. From restricting access to particular ports or services to completely blocking external network access, proxy servers support a very flexible network policy.

◆ **Transparency**. By pretending to be the application service host when interacting with the external components and pretending to be the external system when interacting with the internal application host, a proxy server remains transparent to both of the end systems. Neither ever knows about the presence of a proxy server between them.

◆ **Application-specific services**. To gain access to the external network, each application-specific protocol needs to have a proxy service designed for that protocol and an application running on the proxy server. Since the proxy services are designed specifically for the particular application, they can scan, monitor, and manipulate the protocol-specific application data.

◆ **Dual-homed host**. Since the proxy server executes on a system with two network interfaces with unique IP addresses, the host's ability to directly forward traffic between the two networks, bypassing the proxy server, is disabled. All of the inter-network traffic is forced to go through the proxy server. This way, the proxy server host is the only internal system that can be directly accessed from the external network. This limits the set of systems open to attack to only the application gateway.

◆ **Single access node**. A proxy server host is the only connecting node between the external and internal networks. This allows the network administrator to assign IP addresses of his choice to the internal network hosts, while having a valid IP address assigned to the gateway interface.

Q. What are the disadvantages of a proxy server?

A. Although proxy servers are the most widely accepted implementation of firewalls, they have a few disadvantages as well, such as:

◆ **Inconvenience to users**. The "off by default" system blocks most of the services that a genuine user often requires. Most of the time, users have to request that the network administrator individually enable the services they require. This makes the system less user-friendly.

◆ **Need for a proxy client**. You must install a proxy client on each machine that requires connectivity. Moreover, a few modifications to the client machine network configuration are almost always required.

◆ **Cost**. The enhanced security and flexibility of a proxy server comes at a cost in terms of a gateway hardware platform, proxy server, and proxy client software suite, as well as the time and specialization required to configure the proxy server.

◆ **Low performance**. Since all of the inter-network traffic goes through a single system with overhead activities such as scanning and logging, the performance of the network is adversely affected.

Q. What are the advantages of a proxy server?

A. The advantages of a proxy server are

◆ **Caching**. A proxy server can cache the traffic that goes through it. Since the proxy server has a common cache pool for all of its clients, files downloaded for one client get cached for other clients as well. The efficiency of the overall system is thus greatly enhanced.

◆ **Flexible access control**. Since a proxy server operates at the application level, it has much more control over the traffic flowing through it than you can achieve using packet filtering. A proxy server can monitor and control application-specific content and headers, and thus it allows a much stricter security policy that can control access based on service-specific features.

◆ **Enhanced security**. Due to the dual-homed host architecture, the absence of a particular proxy service means that there is no way for the applications that require a proxy service to interact with the external network. This "off by default" system enhances the overall security of the network.

◆ **User authentication**. Proxy servers can treat each user differently. You can configure them to grant different access rights to different authenticated users on the network. From restricting access to particular ports or services to completely blocking external network access, proxy servers offer a great degree of flexibility in the network security policy. Since a Network-layer firewall has no knowledge of users, it can only base its decision on the source, destination address, port, and protocol of the IP packet.

◆ **Logging and auditing**. Since all of the inter-network traffic flows through the proxy server, this is the best place to record and log all of the activity and traffic flow between the two networks. Proxy servers offer a very comprehensive logging and auditing system. Since there is a separate proxy service running for every application enabled on the proxy server, each proxy service can audit information by logging all traffic activity, each connection, the duration of each connection, and other application-specific details. The audit log is not only a very helpful tool for discovering and countering intruder attacks; it also helps the network administrator monitor user activity.

Q. What is a bastion host?

A. A well-defended and secure application-level gateway is often referred to as a bastion host. It is a designated system that is specifically armored and protected to withstand network attacks.

Q. How can the security of a bastion host be enhanced?

A. The security of a bastion host can be enhanced in the following ways.

◆ A bastion host hardware platform should execute a secure and stable version of its operating system that is specifically designed to protect against operating system vulnerabilities and attacks.

◆ Each proxy service should run as a non-privileged user in a private and secured directory to minimize the access that a hacker can gain if he is ever able to enter the network.

◆ You should install only the services that are considered essential by the network administrator on the bastion host. With a minimum number of services running on the server, you greatly reduce the chances of a service being attacked. A service that is not installed can't be attacked.

◆ You should configure a bastion host for enhanced user authentication to allow access to its proxy services. You can enhance the user authentication mechanism using a two-tier authentication system. In this system, in addition to the normal authentication, users must enter their passwords for each proxy service they use.

◆ You should restrict each proxy service to support only a subset of the standard application's command set. A standard command that is not supported by a proxy service will not be available even to an authenticated user.

◆ Each user group or user should have access to only those proxy services that are essential to that user or group. Only those hosts that demand a service should get access to that specific proxy service, depending on privileges granted to them. This way, only the limited feature or command set of the essential proxy services is available to a subset of hosts, users, or user groups on the protected network.

◆ A proxy service should not perform any disk activity other than reading initial configuration files and logging. This will make it extremely difficult for an attacker to install trojans or other malicious code on the bastion host, which thereby enhances the security.

◆ Each proxy service should maintain its own detailed audit information by logging all traffic activity, each connection, whether or not each connection is successful, the duration of each connection, and any other possible application-specific details.

◆ Programming each proxy service should be as uncomplicated and precise as possible, with special consideration given to what is least expected. A successful hack attempt will occur where it is least expected. The uncomplicated nature of the code allows you to review the source code of the proxy and check it for bugs and security loopholes.

◆ The operation of each proxy should be independent of all other proxies running on the bastion host. Failure or security vulnerability of one proxy service should not affect others. This way, you can uninstall the problematic proxy service safely, without worrying about the other proxy services present on the server. When a new service needs to be installed, you can do it easily because the already present and running services remain unaffected.

Q. What is a DMZ?

A. DMZ stands for *De-Militarized Zone*. A part of a network that is neither part of the internal network nor the external network is called a DMZ. The DMZ network functions as a small, isolated network that is positioned between the external and private networks.

You can create a DMZ by defining an access control list on the access router, thereby minimizing the host exposure on the external network by allowing only recognized services on those hosts to be accessible.

Basically, the DMZ is configured in such a way that the direct transmission of inter-network traffic across the DMZ network is prohibited. Only a limited number of systems on the DMZ network are accessible by the internal and external networks.

You can implement a DMZ on a bastion host by simply adding a third network interface on it. This third network interface becomes the de-militarized zone.

Q. What is NAT ?

A. NAT stands for *Network Address Translation*. It is a means of providing Internet access to hosts on the internal network that do not have valid IP addresses. A firewall is the most logical place to install an NAT.

Q. How does NAT work?

A. A network address translator installed at the application gateway translates the IP addresses of the hosts on the internal network when they communicate with the Internet. The internal network hosts can have any IP address in the private addressing range. When an internal network host tries to send a packet to a host on the Internet, NAT modifies the source address of the packet. NAT uses a network address translation table to map the IP addresses of the internal hosts.

Q. What are the advantages of NAT?

A. There are several advantages to NAT.

◆ It is a step in overcoming the problem of a global IP address shortage.

◆ It makes it convenient for a network administrator to assign any IP address to the internal network hosts without worrying about whether the IP address is valid.

◆ It enhances the security of the network in the sense that the real IP addresses of the internal network hosts remain hidden.

Q. What are the disadvantages of NAT?

A. Although NAT is a very simple system with many advantages, it has a few disadvantages as well.

◆ The efficiency and throughput of the network decreases substantially with NAT because every packet sent by the internal network host needs to be modified by the NAT system.

◆ Many applications that directly use physical IP addresses to communicate fail to work through an NAT system because the system hides the actual IP address of the internal host. However, modifying the applications to use domain names instead of physical addresses can circumvent this problem.

◆ Most network monitoring tools give false results because they have no way of knowing about the internal hosts behind the NAT system.

◆ Since the NAT system modifies the original IP packet sent by the internal host, some of the authentication schemes across the networks fail.

♦ If an NAT system is not integrated with the network's auditing and logging system, the correct logging of network traffic becomes very difficult because the NAT system modifies the source IP address within the data packet.

Q. What does overloading an IP address mean?

A. Overloading an IP address implies multiplexing many internal or private IP addresses on a single valid global IP address. Global IP addressing is the most commonly used multiplexing schema. When a global IP address is overloaded using an NAT host, NAT uses the port numbers of the internal network hosts to uniquely identify a host.

Q. What is the difference between static and dynamic address translation?

A. When the network administrator manually configures a network address table for use by a NAT host, it is called *static address translation*. In *dynamic address translation*, the NAT host resolves the mapping using some specified schema, such as the global IP addressing schema.

Q. What is IPSec?

A. *IPSec* is a tunneling protocol for the IP layer that addresses the issue of host-to-host authentication and encryption. IPSec addresses the issue of integrity and privacy of the data between two networks.

Q. What is tunneling?

A. The process of encapsulating data and transmitting it over a network, and then decapsulating the data at the destination network is called *tunneling*. In this process, encapsulated data of one network is sent over another network. L2TP, PPTP, and IPSec are a few examples of tunneling protocols.

Appendix C

In the Wings

In the past few years, firewall technology has become increasingly prevalent. Sales have continuously increased worldwide, mainly because of the increase in Internet usage by various companies. Being connected 24 hours a day, seven days a week increases network vulnerability. Loopholes are discovered on a regular basis, and patches are released as soon as possible.

As the firewall market grows, the concern is on achieving more security with minimal performance compromise. There are some problems with firewalls. For example:

◆ They lack a reliable security mechanism for TCP/IP, which restricts the usage of many services over the network.

◆ They impart restrictions to many useful services when requested through a remote connection. Firewalls normally block such services because they are risky from a security point of view.

◆ Not all traffic is allowed to pass through the firewall because it can lead to a major performance downfall. It can also lead to problems such as bandwidth obstruction.

◆ Existing firewall technology does not provide continuous reauthorization, which can lead to problems such as session stealing.

These problems should be addressed, and a new generation of firewall should be implemented to overcome these problems. IETF (*Internet Engineering Task Force*) developed a set of standards to deal with these problems and increase security by implementing encryption in firewall and Internet communication. These standards are known as IPSec standards, and they introduced IPng (*next generation IP*) and IPv6. These new protocols include an optional security header.

In the future, firewalls will provide some other useful and advanced features. For example:

◆ Application- and network-level firewalls will become more transparent and efficient, which will lead to faster packet filtering.

◆ Firewalls will include encryption, which will facilitate a secure transfer of data between the firewall and the Internet. Organizations will be able to communicate and transfer data through the Internet without any security problems.

Index

3Com Corp, 140
3Com Firewall Family, 142
32-bit Internet addressing system, 17
802.11 PCMICA cards, 37

A

-A option (IPchains program), 253
-A option (IPtables program), 255
access control
  description of, 33
  service-level firewalls and, 251
  SOCKS protocol and, 97
Access Control Lists (ACLs), 135, 271
Access Point Family, 142
accessing FTP servers, 213–214
ACL (Access Control List), 135, 271
Actions tab (Intrusion Detected Properties
    dialog box), 248
Active Server Pages (ASP), 199
Address Resolution Protocol (ARP), 12
addresses
  Ethernet, 48
  IP
    classes, 17–19
    defined, 17
    FAQs for, 309
    global, overloading, 104–105
    hiding, using NAT, 70
    nodes and, 17
    range of values in, 18

specifying in IAS Server installation,
    238
administrators
  best practices for, 294–297
  tips and tricks for, 297–298
Advanced Research Projects Agency
    (ARPA), 3–4, 8–9
Advanced Research Projects Agency
    Network (ARPANET), 3–4
AH (Authentication Header), 113–114
alert command, 289
alert messages, sending
  on intrusion, 247–249
  using SYSLOG command, 271–272
allocation of bandwidth, 233
Alta Vista Firewall, 142
anonymous FTP access, 213
API (Application Programming Interface),
    11, 174
APOP (Authentication POP), 207
Application layer
  OSI model, 11
  TCP/IP, 13, 95
Application-layer firewalls, 74–76, 303–304
application-level filtering, 230–231
application-level gateways. *See* proxy
    servers
Application MIME type, 208–209
Application Programming Interface (API),
    11, 174
application proxies. *See* proxy servers

architecture, firewall
 dial-up, 120–121
 dual-homed host, 122
 dual router, 121–122
 multiple screened subnet, 124
 screened host, 122–123
 screened subnet, 124
 single router, 121
ARP (Address Resolution Protocol), 12
ARPA (Advanced Research Projects
  Agency), 3–4, 8–9
ARPANET (Advanced Research Projects
  Agency Network), 3–4
array member, installing ISA Server as, 235
Ascend SecureConnect, 142
ASP (Active Server Pages), 199
asymmetric encryption, 33
asymmetric key ciphers, 33–34
attachments, e-mail
 overview, 207–210
 viruses in, 41
attacks. *See also* threats
 backdoor entries, 47
 Denial of Service, 47, 50–51
 dictionary-based, 46
 DNS cache poisoning, 52
 FAQs for, 303
 IP half scan, 245
 land attacks, 245
 network attacks, 48–51
 out-of-band, 245
 parameter manipulation, 47–48
 password, 46
 ping of death, 245
 reporting to authority, 222–223
 resource starvation, 52
 responding to, 220–222

routing attacks, 52
 session hijacking, 50–51
 sniffing, 48–49
 spoofing, 49–50, 55
 stack-based buffer overflow, 42–46
 stack smashing, 45
 tips and tricks for, 297
 UDP bomb, 245
 vandalism, 35
 Web application, 46–48, 203
Audio MIME type, 210
audit-trail command, 289
audit trails, 271–272, 287
audits, performing, 30, 33
authenticated FTP access, 213
authentication
 description of, 33
 Kerberos, 98–100
 for users, performing, 67–68
Authentication Header (AH), 113–114
Authentication POP (APOP), 207
authorization
 description of, 33
 third-party, 40
availability, bastion hosts, 162
Avaya VPN Gateways, 142

B

backdoor entries, 47, 53
backups, 222
bandwidth
 allocation of, 233
 consumption, 52
 history of, 4
 improvements to, 5–6

bastion hosts
  availability, 162
  description of, 125–127, 160
  design of, 191–193
  external bastion hosts, 161
  FAQs for, 306–307
  hardening
    documentation, 169–170
    factors for, 160
    hardware setup, 170
    operating system setup, 170–171
    performance tests, 173
    security events, logging, 161
    security measures, 172–173
    service configuration, 171–172
  internal bastion hosts, 161
  public services of, 160
  robustness, 162
  scalability, 162
  system requirements
    hardware specifications, 163–165
    location requirements, 167–168
    operating system, 165–166
    services, 166–167
  UNIX-based, configuring
    overview, 180–181
    service installation, 182–189
    services to disable, 190–191
    services to enable, 189–190
  user interface factor, 163
  victim hosts, 161
  Windows-based, configuring
    overview, 173–174
    SCM (Service Control Manager), 179
    service accounts, 178–179
    service applications, 176–178
    service installation, 174–175
    services to disable, 180–181
    services to enable, 179–180
Bay Networks, 140
best practices for administrators, 294–297
biometric devices, security and, 28
BIOS software, 170–171
bits, 17
bootd service, 190
bootpd service, 190
BorderGuard, 142
BorderWare Firewall Server, 142
bridge, 15
browsers, 20
buffer overflow attacks, 42–46
bytes, 17

C

caching
  distributed, 232
  DNS cache poisoning, 52
  forward caching, 231
  hierarchical caching, 232
  reverse caching, 232
caching proxies. *See* proxy servers
Caldera, 182
callee, 45
caller, 44–45
CBAC (Context-Based Access Control)
  advantages of, 272–273
  Application-layer protocols supported by, 274
  configuring
    access lists, setting up, 279
    Application-layer protocol inspection, 285–286
    generic TCP and UDP inspection, 286

global timeout and threshold parameters, 281–283
inbound access lists, setting, 281
inspection rules, 285–286
interfaces, selecting, 277–279
IP fragmentation inspection, 286
logging and audit trails, 287
outbound access list, setting up, 279–281
required services, determining, 277
router support, checking, 276–277
testing and verifying, 287–290
functions
adding rules to access control lists, 271
alerts and audit trails, 271–272
application-level traffic filtering, 270
intrusion detection, 272
list of, 269–270
stateful inspection of traffic, 270–271
inbound traffic allowed by, 275
limitations of, 273
outbound traffic allowed by, 275
overview, 267–268, 273–274
traffic inspected by, 276
CERN (European Organization for Nuclear Research), 4, 198
CFML (ColdFusion Markup Language), 199
chains
forward chains, 252
input chains, 252
IPchains, 252–254
output chains, 252
Challenge-Handshake Authentication Protocol (CHAP), 111
channels, 213

CHAP (Challenge-Handshake Authentication Protocol), 111
chassis, 164–165
Check Point Next Generation firewall, 141
checklists, for security policies, 136–139
chipsets, 169
choke point security strategy, 58
choke router, 124
cipher, 32
cipher text, 31
circuit gateway, 135
circuit-level filtering, 229
circuit proxies. *See* proxy servers
Cisco IOS firewall features, 267–268
Cisco PIX Firewall Family, 141
Cisco Systems, 140
Class A address format, 18
Class B address format, 18–19
Class C address format, 19
Class D address format, 19
Class E address format, 19
clients, securing, 204–205
ColdFusion Markup Language (CFML), 199
COM (Component Object Model), 233
command channels, 213
commands. *See also* functions
alert, 289
audit-trail, 289
fragment, 289
inspection-name, 285, 289
ip inspect global configuration, 288
ipconfig, 250
java-list access list, 289
max number, 289
ping, 250
route, 250

rpc program-number, 289
SYSLOG, 271–272, 287
timeout, 289
timeout seconds, 289
wait-time, 289
Common Vulnerabilities Exposures
    (CVE), 54
communication, protocol communication,
    14
Component Object Model (COM), 233
components, external and internal, 26
compression, 202
Computer Fraud and Abuse Act, 223
configuring
    bastion hosts, UNIX-based
        overview, 180–181
        service installation, 182–189
        services to disable, 190–191
        services to enable, 189–190
    bastion hosts, Windows-based
        overview, 173–174
        SCM (Service Control Manager), 179
        service accounts, 178–179
        service applications, 176–178
        service installation, 174–175
        services to disable, 180–181
        services to enable, 179–180
    CBAC (Context-Based Access Control)
        access lists, setting up, 279
        Application-layer protocol inspection,
            285–286
        generic TCP and UDP inspection, 286
        global timeout and threshold parame-
            ters, 281–283
        inbound access lists, setting, 281
        inspection rules, 285–286
        interfaces, selecting, 277–279

        IP fragmentation inspection, 286
        logging and audit trails, 287
        outbound access listing, setting up,
            279–281
        required services, determining, 277
        router support, checking, 276–277
        testing and verifying, 287–290
    firewalls
        overview, 144
        packet-filtering architecture, 149–154
        split-screen subnet architecture,
            145–149
connections
    process-to-process, 204
    VPN connection, 107
Connectiva, 182
Context-Based Access Control. *See* CBAC
Control Panel, 174
controlled traffic firewall characteristic, 71
cookies
    disabling, 204
    security issues and, 47
corrective controls, vulnerabilities and, 30
CPU, 169
cron value, 190
cryptography, 31–33
CU-SeeMe, 274
CVE (Common Vulnerabilities
    Exposures), 54
cyber attacks. *See* DoS attacks
CyberGuard Firewall, 142

D

-D option (IPchains program), 253
-D option (IPtables program), 255
daemon process, 169

DARPA (Defense Advanced Research
    Projects Agency), 8
data channels, 213
Data Encryption Standard (DES), 32
Data Link layer, 12
data privacy, 28
data transmissions, 111
datagrams, 16
De-Militarized Zones. *See* DMZ
Debian, 182
decryption, 31–32
dedicated and special purpose routers, 261
dedicated WAN link, 108
Defense Advanced Research Projects
    Agency (DARPA), 8
defense in-depth security strategy, 58
demultiplexing, 87
Denial of Service (DoS) attacks
    bandwidth consumption, 52
    network attacks, 51
    operating system attacks, 51
    overview, 47
    resource starvation, 51
DependOnGroup value, 176
DependOnService value, 176
DES (Data Encryption Standard), 32
Description value, 176
detective controls, vulnerabilities and, 30
deterrent controls, vulnerabilities and, 30
dhcpd service, 190
DHTML (Dynamic HTML), 199
dial-up firewall architectures, 120–121
dialog boxes
    Intrusion Detected Properties, 248–249
    IP address ranges, 238
    IP Packet Filters Properties, 246–247

Microsoft Internet Security and
    Acceleration Server Setup, 236–237
dictionary-based attacks, 46
digital certificates, 28
digital signature, 34
disk space, partitioning, 170
DisplayName value, 176
distributed caching, 232
diversity of defense security strategy, 60
DMZ (De-Militarized Zones)
    FAQs for, 307–308
    overview, 83
    sample of, 268
DNS cache poisoning, 52
DNS (Domain Name System), 4
DNS MX (mail exchange), 193
DNS Server service, 180
domain accounts, 178–179
domain configuration
    packet-filtering architecture, 149
    split-screen subnet architecture, 145
Domain Name System (DNS), 4
domain server, 94
DoS (Denial of Service) attacks
    bandwidth consumption, 52
    network attacks, 51
    operating system attacks, 51
    overview, 47
    resource starvation, 51
dotted decimal notation, 17
dotted quad notation, 17
driver registry parameters, 176–178
dual-homed host
    architecture, 122
    execution on, 93–94
dual router architecture, 121–122
dumpster diving, 40

Dynamic HTML (DHTML), 199
dynamic server-side programs, 202

E

Eagle firewall, 142
e-commerce, 5
elevation of privilege threat, 56
e-mail
  attachments
    overview, 207–210
    viruses in, 41
  composing and delivering, 206
  mail system components, list of, 206–207
  MIME types used in, 207–210
  overview, 205–206
  securing, 210–212
Enable Intrusion Detection option (IP
    Packet Filters Properties dialog box),
    246
Encapsulating Security Payload (ESP), 114
encapsulation, 84–86
encryption
  asymmetric encryption, 33
  DES (Data Encryption Standard), 32
  overview, 31
  public key cryptography, 33
  "shift by three," 32
  symmetric key encryption, 32
end points, tunneling between communica-
    tion, 110
Enterprise edition (ISA Server), 234
enumeration, 38–39
ErrorControl value, 176
ESP (Encapsulating Security Payload), 114
/etc/hosts.allow file, 251
/etc/hosts.deny file, 251

/etc/inetd.conf file, 189
/etc/rc/ directory, 183
Ethernet, 4
Ethernet address, 48
eTrust firewall, 141
European Organization of Nuclear
    Research (CERN), 4, 198
EventLog, 179
exim function, 206
Extensible Markup Language (XML), 199
external bastion hosts, 161
external components, 26–27

F

-F option (IPchains program), 253
fail-safe stance security strategy, 59
FAQs (frequently asked questions)
  for Application-layer firewalls, 303–304
  for attacks, 303
  for bastion hosts, 306–307
  for DMZ, 307–308
  for firewalls, 300–301
  for footprinting, 302
  for IP addresses, 309
  for NAT, 308–309
  for network scanning, 302
  for packet filtering, 301–302
  for proxy servers, 304–306
  for spoofing, 303
FAT file system, 174
File Transfer Protocol. *See* FTP
files
  /ect/hosts.allow, 251
  /ect/hosts.deny, 251
  /etc/inetd.conf, 189
  rc, 183

rc.local, 183
rc.sysint, 183
filter chains, 254
Filter Settings screen (New IP Packet
    Filter wizard), 228
filtering
  application-level, 230–231
  application-level traffic, 270
  circuit-level, 229
  FTP access filters, 230
  H.323 protocol filter, 231
  HTTP rules, 205
  IP packet
    advantages of, 229
    disadvantages of, 229
    overview, 228–229
    prevention of IP spoofing using,
        266–267
    routers and, 266
  packet filtering, 69
    advantages of, 91
    description of, 89
    disadvantages of, 92
    FAQs for, 301–302
    protocol-based filtering systems, 91
    simple packet filtering, 90
    state tracking, 90–91
  POP rules, 212
  RPC filters, 231
  service filtering, 68–69
  SMTP filters, 230
  SMTP rules, 212
  SOCKS filters, 231
  streaming media filters, 231
  Web filter, 230
fingerd service, 190
finwait-time parameter setting, 283

firewalls
  Application-layer, 74–76
  architectures
    dial-up, 120–121
    dual-homed host, 122
    dual router, 121–122
    multiple screened subnet, 124
    screened host, 122–123
    screened subnet, 124
    single router, 121
  Cisco IOS firewall features, 267–268
  configuring, 144
    packet-filtering architecture, 149–154
    split-screen subnet architecture,
        145–149
  controlled traffic characteristic, 71
  establishing VPN using, 71–72
  evaluating, 143–144
  FAQs for, 300–301
  functions of
    authenticating users, 67–68
    filtering services and packets, 68–69
    NAT performance, 69–70
    network scanning, 69
  future development of, 77, 312
  history of, 66–67
  Internet security through, 227–231
  limitations of
    alternative route to data access, 76
    reconfiguration for new protocols, 76
    threats from virus-infected data, 77
  in Linux, implementing, 249
    IPchains, 252–254
    IPtables, 254–255
    packet-filtering firewalls, 251–252
    proxy-based firewalls, 251
    service-level firewalls, 251

system checks, 250

logged traffic characteristic, 71

multi-layered, 227–231

Network-layer, 72–73

in network security, roles of, 70–72

problems with, 312

router-based, 140–141, 262–265

rules, 260

security policies

  checklists, designing, 136–139

  finalizing, 139–140

  guidelines for, 136

  need for, 135–136

selection criteria, 144

single point of contact, 70–71, 93

workstation-based, 141–142

footprinting

  FAQs for, 302

  overview, 35–36

forward caching, 231

forward chains, 252

fragment command, 289

fragment packets port scans, 38

fragmentation inspection, configuring, 286

frames, 44

fraud, Computer Fraud and Abuse Act, 223

frequently asked questions. *See* FAQs

Fscan, 38

FTP access filters, 230

FTP bounce port scans, 38

FTP (File Transfer Protocol)

  creation of, 4

  description of, 212

  servers

    accessing, 213–214

    securing, 214

function calls, 43

functions. *See also* commands

  exim, 206

  maildrop, 206

  main(), 43–44

  postfix, 206

  procmail, 206

  qmail, 206

  second(), 44

  sendmail, 206

  SvcCtrlMain, 179

  third(), 43–44

G

gateway, routers acting as, 263

Gauntlet firewall, 141

Generic Routing Encapsulation (GRE), 112

GET request, 46

global IP address, overloading, 104–105

GNAT Box GB-100, 142

Graphical User Interface (GUI), 67

GRE (Generic Routing Encapsulation), 112

Group value, 177

GUI (Graphical User Interface), 67

H

H.323 protocol filters, 231

hacking. *See also* security

  backdoor entries, 47

  computer-based social engineering skills, 41

  cookies, stealing, 47

  Denial of Service attacks, 47, 50–51

DNS cache poisoning, 52
dumpster diving, 40
footprinting, 36–38
impersonation, 40
in-person, 40
port scanning, 38
resource starvation, 52
routing attacks, 52
scanning, 36–38
session hijacking, 50–51
shoulder surfing, 41
sniffing, 32
spoofing, 49–51
stack-based buffer overflow attacks,
    42–46
sweeping, 37
vandalism, 35
war dialing, 37
war driving, 37
Web application attacks, 46–48
half-open sessions, 284
hard disks, 169
hardening, bastion hosts
documentation, 169–170
factors for, 160
hardware setup, 170
operating system setup, 170–171
performance tests, 173
security events, logging, 161
security measures, 172–173
service configuration, 171–172
hardware
bastion hosts requirements, 170
architecture, 163
chassis, 164–165
display, 164
memory specifications, 164

speed, 163–164
for routers, 261
hardware address spoofing, 49
HCL (Hardware Compatibility List), 181
HDTV (High Definition Television), 5
headers, TCP and UDP, illustration of, 86
hidden form fields, 47
hierarchical caching, 232
High Definition Television (HDTV), 5
hot patches, 170
hot-swapping, 164–165
HTTP (Hypertext Transfer Protocol)
filtering rules for, 205
overview, 46
hub, 15
human-based social engineering, 40–41
hybrid proxy, 95
Hypertext Transfer Protocol. *See* HTTP

I

IBM Firewall, 142
ICMP (Internet Control Message
    Protocol), 37, 73, 86
identity elements, security and, 28
idle-time parameter setting, 283
IETF (Internet Engineering Task Force),
    95, 312
iGateway Family, 142
IGMP, field values, 86
IKE (Internet Key Exchange), 113–114
IM Firewall, 142
Image MIME type, 210
ImagePath value, 177
IMAP (Internet Mail Access Protocol),
    207
impersonation, 40

in-person hacks, 40
inbound data packets rules for, 239–240
inbound traffic allowed by CBAC, 275
inetd value, 190
information disclosure threat, 56
init value, 190
input chains, 252
inspection-name command, 285, 289
inspection rules, 285–286
installing
  ISA Server
    as array member, 235–236
    cache size, 237
    considerations for, 233–234
    custom installation, 235
    IIS server, uninstalling, 237
    IP addresses, specifying range of, 238
    Microsoft ISA Server Setup screen,
      234
    server mode, selecting, 236
  services
    for UNIX-based bastion hosts,
      182–189
    for Windows-based bastion hosts,
      174–175
integrity threats, 55
InterJak 200, 142
internal bastion hosts, 161
internal components, 26–27
International Standards Organization. *See*
  ISO
International Telecommunications Union
  (ITU), 34
Internet
  browsers, 20
  current era of, 5–6
  defined, 2–3

functions of, 20–21
history of, 3–5
ISP, PC connected to Internet through,
  21
LAN (Local Area Network), 21
modems, 21
networks and, 6–7
preliminary stages of, 8
Internet Control Message Protocol
  (ICMP), 37, 73, 86
Internet Engineering Task Force (IETF),
  95, 312
Internet Key Exchange (IKE), 113–114
Internet Mail Access Protocol (IMAP),
  207
Internet Network Information Center
  (InterNIC), 5
Internet Protocol Security (IPSec), 82,
  113–114
Internet Security and Acceleration (ISA),
  74–75
Internet Security Systems Web site, 244
Internet Server API (ISAPI), 202–203
Internet Service Providers. *See* ISPs
Internetwork Operating System (IOS), 262
InterNIC (Internet Network Information
  Center), 5
Intrusion Detected Properties dialog box,
  248–249
intrusion detection
  alert messages, 247–249
  CBAC and, 272
  overview, 244–247
IOS (Internetwork Operating System), 262
IP address
  classes, 17–19
  defined, 17

FAQs for, 309
global, overloading, 104–105
hiding, using NAT, 70
nodes and, 17
range of
specifying in IAS Server installation,
238
values in, 18
IP address ranges dialog box, 238
IP datagram, 85
IP half scan attack, 245
IP header, components of, 85
ip inspect global configuration command,
288
IP packet, 85
IP packet filtering
advantages of, 229
disadvantages of, 229
overview, 228–229
prevention of IP spoofing using,
266–267
routers and, 266
IP Packet Filters Properties dialog box,
246–247
IP protocol, 17
IP routing, 87–89
IP spoofing, 50
IP tracing, 106
IPchains
program, options available in, 253–254
types of, 252–253
ipconfig command, 250
IpEye, 38
IPng (next generation IP), 312
IPSec (Internet Protocol Security), 82,
113–114
IPtables, 254–255

ISA (Internet Security and Acceleration),
74–75
ISA Server
caching in, 231–232
Enterprise edition, 234
features of, 226–227
installing
as array member, 235–236
cache size, 237
considerations, 233–234
custom installation, 235
IIS server, uninstalling, 237
IP addresses, specifying range of, 238
Microsoft ISA Server Setup screen,
234
server mode, selecting, 236
as proxy server, 231
security for, configuring, 238
alert messages, sending on intrusion,
247–249
global rules, 239
inbound data packets, rules for,
239–240
intrusion detection, 244–247
management rules, 240–243
outbound data packets, rules for, 240
protocol rules, 241–242
security policies, 239
Standard edition, 234
ISAPI (Internet Server API), 202–203
ISO (International Standards
Organization)
Data Link layer, 12
overview, 10
Physical layer, 12
ISPs (Internet Service Providers)
history of, 5

PC connected to Internet through, illustration of, 21
ITU (International Telecommunications Union), 34

J

Java blocking, 267
java-list access list command, 289
Java Server Pages (JSP), 199, 202
JavaScript, 199
JSP (Java Server Pages), 199, 202

K

Kerberos
    description of, 98–99
    goals of, 100
    hierarchy of realms in, 99
Kerberos POP (KPOP), 207
kernel-level process, 174
keyserv service, 190
killing processes, 183
KPOP (Kerberos POP), 207

L

-I option (IPchains program), 253
-I option (IPtables program), 255
-L option (IPchains program), 253
-L option (IPtables program), 255
L2F (Layer 2 Forwarding), 112
L2TP (Layer 2 Tunneling Protocol), 109, 112
LAN (Local Area Network), 21
land attacks, 245

Last In First Out (LIFO), 42
Layer 2 Forwarding (L2F), 112
Layer 2 Tunneling Protocol (L2TP), 109, 112
layers
    Application
        OSI model, 11
        TCP/IP, 13, 95
    Data Link (OSI model), 12
    Link (TCP/IP), 14
    Network
        OSI model, 12
        TCP/IP, 14
    Physical (OSI model), 12
    Presentation (OSI model), 11
    Session (OSI model), 11
    Transport
        OSI model, 11
        TCP/IP, 14, 95
LCP (Link Control Protocol), 111
least privilege security strategy, 57–58
Lee, Tim Berners, 198
licenses, 170
LIFO (Last In First Out), 42
Link Control Protocol (LCP), 111
Link layer (TCP/IP), 14
links, dedicated WAN link, 108
Linux, implementing firewalls in
    IPchains, 252–254
    IPtables, 254–255
    overview, 249
    packet-filtering firewalls, 251–252
    proxy-based firewalls, 251
    service-level firewalls, 251
    system checks, 250
list restrictions, 251
Livingston Enterprises, 140

local accounts, 178–179
Local Area Network (LAN), 21
location requirements for bastion hosts, 167–168
locd service, 190
log files, 75
logged traffic firewall characteristic, 71
logging requests, 251
lpd service, 190

M

Mail Delivery Agent (MDA), 206
Mail Transport Agent (MTA), 206
Mail User Agent (MUA), 206
maildrop function, 206
main() function, 43–44
management tasks, Windows 2000 integration for, 232–233
Mandrake, 182
mangle chain, 254
max number command, 289
MDA (Mail Delivery Agent), 206
memory requirements, for bastion hosts, 164
Message MIME type, 207
methods. *See* commands; functions
Microsecure Firewall, 142
Microsoft Internet Security and Acceleration Server Setup dialog box, 236–237
Microsoft ISA Server Setup screen, 234
Microsoft Management Console (MMC), 240
MIME (Multimedia Internet Mail Extension) types
in e-mail, 207–210

list of, 200–202
mitigation techniques, threat modeling, 57
Mitre Corporation, 54
MMC (Microsoft Management Console), 240
Model MIME type, 210
modems, 21
modes
normal mode, 214
PASV, 214
selecting for ISA Server installation, 236–237
modules, 204
motherboards, 169
mountd service, 190
MTA (Mail Transport Agent), 206
MUA (Mail User Agent), 206
multi-layered firewalls, 227–231
Multimedia Internet Mail Extension. *See* MIME types
Multipart MIME type, 207
multiple screened subnet architecture, 124

N

-N option (IPchains program), 253
nat chain, 254
NAT (Network Address Translation), 67
advantages of, 106
description of, 100–101
disadvantages of, 106–107
FAQs for, 308–309
hiding IP addresses using, 70
overloading global IP addressing schema, 104–105
process illustration of, 102
system illustration of, 102

traffic types supported by, 103
NCP (Network Control Protocol), 10
Net Logon, 179
NetBIOS interface, 180
Netcat, 38
Netscan, 38
Netscape Proxy Server, 74
Netscape Server API (NSAPI), 202
NetScreen Family, 142
Network Address Translation. *See* NAT
network attacks, 48–51
Network Control Protocol (NCP), 10
Network File System (NFS), 11
Network layer
    OSI model, 12
    TCP/IP, 14
Network-layer firewalls, 72–73
Network News Transfer Protocol (NNTP),
    68
network scanning
    FAQs for, 302
    preventing, 69
Network Systems Corporation, 140
networks
    connected through routers, illustration
        of, 15
    with different computing devices, illus-
        tration of, 6
    Internet illustration of, 7
    with multiple components, illustration of,
        27
    perimeter, 83
    security model, implementation, 30
    with sub-networks, illustration of, 7
    trusted, 263
    untrusted, 263
    vulnerability scanning, 36

New IP Packet Filter wizard, 228
New Protocol Rule wizard, 241
New Technology File System (NTFS), 237
next generation IP (IPng), 312
NFS (Network File System), 11
nfsd service, 190
Nmap, 38
NNTP (Network News Transfer Protocol),
    68
nodes
    defined, 10
    IP addresses and, 17
    TCP/IP-enabled, communication
        between, 14
normal mode, 214
notation, 17
NSAPI (Netscape Server API), 202
NT LM Security Support Provider, 179
NTFS file systems, 174
NTFS (New Technology File System), 237
nukes. *See* DoS attacks

O

ObjectName value, 177
obscurity security strategy, 61
octet, 17
one-way hash functions, 33–34
Open Systems Interconnection. *See* OSI
    model
OpenPGP, 211
operating system requirements, for bastion
    hosts, 165–166, 170–171
OSI (Open Systems Interconnection)
    model
    Application layer, 11
    layers, list of, 10

Network layer, 12
Presentation layer, 11
Session layer, 11
Transport layer, 11–12
out-of-band attacks, 245
outbound data packets, rules for, 240
outbound traffic, allowed by CBAC, 275
OUTPUT chain, 254
output chains, 252, 254
overloading global IP addressing schema,
  104–105

P

-P option (IPchains program), 253
packet accounting, 252
packet filtering, 69
  advantages of, 91
  architecture, configuring
    domain configuration, 149
    firewall details, 150
    internal network details, 150
    packet-filtering rules, 152–154
    service configuration, 151
  description of, 89
  disadvantages of, 92
  FAQs for, 301
  firewalls and, 251–252
  protocol-based filtering systems, 91
  simple packet filtering, 90
  state tracking, 90–91
packet redirection, 252
packets
  best practices for, 294
  defined, 8
  inbound, rules for, 239–240
  IP packet, 85

outbound, rules for, 240
PAP (Password Authentication Protocol),
  111
parameter manipulation, 47–48
partitioning disk space, 170
password attacks, 46
Password Authentication Protocol (PAP),
  111
PASV mode, 214
PCI (Peripheral Component Interconnect),
  163
perimeter networks, 83
perimeter security, 28
Peripheral Component Interconnect (PCI),
  163
peripherals, 169
Perl/CGI, 199
PhoneSweep, 37
Physical layer (OSI model), 12
pid (process id), 183
ping command, 250
ping of death attacks, 245
ping service, 151
ping sweeping, 37
PKI (Public Key Infrastructure), 33–34
Plug-and-Play, 180
Point-to-Point Protocol (PPP), 111
Point-to-Point Tunneling Protocol
  (PPTP), 109, 112
policies, security. *See* security
policy management, security and, 29
POP (Post Office Protocol), 206–207, 212
port 80, 46
port scanning, 38
ports
  defined, 261
  that routes should block, 264–265

Portus, 142

Post Office Protocol (POP), 206–207, 212

POST request, 46

postfix function, 206

POSTROUTING chain, 254

power failures, 162

PPP (Point-to-Point Protocol), 111

PPTP (Point-to-Point Tunneling
    Protocol), 109, 112

PREROUTING chain, 254

Presentation layer (OSI model), 11

preventive controls, vulnerabilities and, 30

preventive measures
    legal measures, 222–223
    remedial measures, 220–222

privacy. *See* security

privileges, elevation of, 56

process-to-process connections, 204

processes, killing, 183

procmail function, 206

protected storage service, 180

protocol-based filtering systems, 91

protocol communication, 14

protocol rules for ISA Server, creating,
    241–243

protocols
    HTTP (Hypertext Transfer Protocol), 46
    IMAP (Internet Mail Access Protocol),
        207
    IP protocol, 17
    L2TP (Layer 2 Tunneling Protocol), 109
    PAP (Password Authentication
        Protocol), 111
    POP (Post Office Protocol), 206–207
    PPTP (Point-to-Point Tunneling
        Protocol), 109
    rejected, 265

SMTP (Simple Mail Transfer Protocol),
    69

TCP, 16

UDP (User Datagram Protocol), 16

proxy-based firewalls, 251

proxy client, 94

proxy servers
    advantages of, 97
    defined, 74, 92
    disadvantages of, 97–98
    FAQs for, 304–306
    features of, 93–94
    hybrid proxy, 95
    ISA (Internet Security and Acceleration),
        74–75
    ISA server as, 231
    log file generated by, illustration of, 75
    Netscape Proxy Server, 74
    requirements of, 94–95

public key cryptography, 33

Public Key Infrastructure (PKI), 33–34

Python, 199

Q

qmail function, 206

qualitative risk analysis, 29–30

quantitative risk analysis, 29

R

-R option (IPchains program), 253, 255

RAID (Redundant Array of Inexpensive
    Disks), 163

RAM, 169

Raptor Firewall Family, 142

RARP (Reverse Address Resolution
Protocol), 12
rc files, 183
rc.local file, 183
rc.sysint file, 183
RealAudio, 274
RealSecure, 141
Red Hat, 182
Red Hat Linux sample files, 183–188
Redundant Array of Inexpensive Disks
(RAID), 163
rejected protocols, 265
remote access, 109
Remote Access Service, 180
Remote Procedure Call (RPC), 11, 180
reporting attacks, 222–223
repudiation threat, 56
Request for Comments (RFCs), 4
resource starvation, 51
Reverse Address Resolution Protocol
(RARP), 12
reverse caching, 232
rexd service, 190
RFCs (Request for Comments), 4
risk analysis
    qualitative, 29–30
    quantitative, 29
    tips and tricks for, 297
rlogind service, 190
robustness, bastion hosts, 162
routable protocols, 261
route command, 250
routed service, 190
router-based firewalls, 140–141
routers
    blocked ports, 264–265
    bootstrap software, 261
    choke router, 124
    dedicated and special purpose, 261
    defined, 15
    as firewalls, 262–265
    hardware for, 261
    networks connected through, illustration
        of, 15
    overview, 260–261
    rejected protocols, 265
    screening routers, 89
    software for, 262
routing attacks, 52
routing protocols, 261
RPC filters, 231
rpc program-number command, 289
RPC (Remote Procedure Call), 11, 180

S

S/MIMEv3 (Secure MIME Version 3),
    210–211
scalability, bastion hosts, 162
scanning
    network scanning, preventing, 69
    network vulnerability scanning, 36
SCM (Service Control Manager), 174, 179
screened host architecture, 122–123
screened subnet architecture
    network layout diagram for, 192
    overview, 124
    variations to
        bastion host acting as exterior router,
            127
        interior and exterior routers, 126
        multiple bastion hosts, 125–126

multiple exterior routers, 128

multiple perimeter networks, 129

screening routers, 89

scripting languages, 199

SDK (Software Development Kit), 233

second() function, 44

Secure MIME Version 3 (S/MIMEv3),
210–211

SecureIT, 142

security

attacks

backdoor entries, 47

Denial of Service, 47, 50–51

dictionary-based, 46

DNS cache poisoning, 52

FAQs for, 303

IP half scan, 245

land attacks, 245

network attacks, 48–51

out-of-band, 245

parameter manipulation, 47–48

password, 46

ping of death attacks, 245

reporting to authority, 222–223

resource starvation, 52

responding to, 220–222

routing attacks, 52

session hijacking, 50–51

sniffing, 48–49

spoofing, 49–50, 55

stack-based buffer overflow, 42–46

stack smashing, 45

tips and tricks for, 297

UDP bomb, 245

vandalism, 35

Web application, 46–48, 203

audits, performing, 30, 33

authentication, 33

backdoors, 53

for bastion hosts, 172–173

cookies, stealing, 47

cryptography, 31–33

data privacy, 28

decryption, 31–32

digital certificates, 34–35

digital signature, 34–35

e-mail, 210–212

encryption, 31

asymmetric encryption, 33

DES (Data Encryption Standard), 32

public key cryptography, 33

"shift by three," 32

symmetric key encryption, 32

ensuring success of, 30

FTP servers, 214

identity elements, 28

IPSec (Internet Protocol Security), 82

for ISA Server, configuring, 238

alert messages, sending on intrusion,
247–249

global rules, 239

inbound data packets, rules for,
239–240

intrusion detection, 244–247

management rules, 240–243

outbound data packets, rules for, 240

protocol rules, 241–243

security policies, 239

models for, drafting, 26–27

monitoring process, 28–29

network security, implementing, 30

one-way hash functions, 33–34

perimeter, 28

PKI (Public Key Infrastructure), 33–34

policies, establishing, 30, 297–298
  checklists, designing, 136–139
  finalizing, 139–140
  guidelines for, 136
  need for, 135–136
policy management, 29
risk analysis, 29–30
sniffing, 32
strategies for
  choke point, 58
  defense in-depth, 58
  diversity of defense, 60
  fail-safe stance, 59
  least privilege, 57–58
  obscurity, 61
  simplicity, 60–61
  universal participation, 60
  weakest link, 59
threats
  analyzing, 55–56
  computer-based social engineering
    skills, 41
  description of, 29
  dumpster diving, 40
  elevation of privilege, 56
  enumeration, 38–39
  footprinting, 35–36
  human-based social engineering,
    40–41
  impersonation, 40
  in-person hacks, 40
  information disclosure, 56
  integrity threats, 55
  port scanning, 38
  repudiation, 56
  scanning, 36–38
  shoulder surfing, 41
  social engineering, 39–40

STRIDE model, 55–56
sweeping, 37
tampering, 55
third-party authorization, 40
threat modeling, 54, 56–57
war dialing, 37
war driving, 37
trojan horse, 53
viruses, 52–53
vulnerabilities
  assessment categories, 54–55
  CVE (Common Vulnerabilities
    Exposures), 54
  description of, 29, 53–54
  reasons for, 54
Web clients, 204–205
Web server extensions, 202–203
worms, 53
SecurwayGate 1000, 142
Send E-Mail option (Intrusion Detected
    Properties dialog box), 249
sendmail function, 206
Serial Line IP (SLIP), 111
servers
  FTP, accessing, 213–214
  ISA
    caching in, 231–232
    Enterprise edition, 234
    features of, 226–227
    installing, 234–238
    as proxy server, 231
    security for, configuring, 238–249
    Standard edition, 234
  Web servers
    extensions, securing, 202–203
    extra functionality for, 203
    function of, 199–200
    MIME type supported by, 200–202

modules, 204
xinetd, 189
Service Control Manager (SCM), 174, 179
service filtering, 68–69
service-level firewalls, 251
services
of bastion hosts, 166–167
configuring for bastion hosts, 171–172
EventLog, 179
installing
for UNIX-based bastion hosts,
182–189
for Windows-based bastion hosts,
174–175
Net Logon, 179
NT LM Security Support Provider, 179
Plug-and-Play, 180
spooling, 180
Win32, 175
session hijacking, 50–51
Session layer (OSI model), 11
sessions
defined, 11
half-open, 284
shoulder surfing, 41
Simple Mail Transfer Protocol (SMTP),
69, 212
Simple Network Management Protocol
(SNMP), 39
simple packet filtering, 90
simplicity security strategy, 60–61
single point of contact firewall characteristic, 70–71, 93
single router architecture, 121
Slackware, 182
SLIP (Serial Line IP), 111
smart cards, 28

SMTP filters, 230
SMTP (Simple Mail Transfer Protocol),
69, 212
sniffing, 32, 48–49
SNMP (Simple Network Management
Protocol), 39
social engineering
human-based, 40–41
overview, 39–41
Socket Security. *See* SOCKS
SOCKS filters, 231
SOCKS (Socket Security)
advantages of, 96–97
components of, 95
description of, 95
versions of, 96
software
routers, 262
updating, 298
Software Development Kit (SDK), 233
SonicWALL Family, 142
speed requirements, for bastion hosts,
163–164
split-screen subnet architecture, configuring
domain configuration, 145
firewall configuration, 147
subnet configuration, 146–147
spoofing, 55
description of, 49
FAQs for, 303
hardware address spoofing, 49
IP spoofing, 50
preventing, using IP packet filtering,
266–267
spooling, 180
Springtide IP Service Switch, 142
Sputnik, 3

SQL*Net, 274

stack-based buffer overflow attacks, 42–46

stack smashing attacks, 45

stacks

as data structure, illustration of, 42

defined, 42

frame regions in, 44

main() function within, 43

with multiple frames, illustration of, 44

Standard edition (ISA Server), 234

Start value, 177

StartService value, 176

startup scripts, 183

state tracking, filtering process, 90–91

StoneGate, 142

storage, protect storage services, 180

streaming media filters, 231

StreamWorks, 274

STRIDE model, for threat analysis, 55–56

strobe port scans, 38

su root privilege, 183

subnet configuration, split-screen subnet
architecture, 146–147

Sun Screen firewall, 141

SuSE, 182

SvcCtrlMain function, 179

swap value, 190

sweep port scans, 38

sweeping, 37

symmetric key ciphers, 33–34

symmetric key encryption, 32

synwait-time parameter setting, 283

syslodg value, 190

SYSLOG command, 271–272, 287

system accounts, 178–179

system requirements, bastion hosts
hardware specifications, 163–165

location requirements, 167–168

operating system, 165–166

services, 166–167

T

T1 line, 52

T3 line, 52

tampering, security threats, 55

TCP idle-time parameter setting, 283

TCP/IP (Transmission Control
Protocol/Internet Protocol)

Application layer, 13, 95

demultiplexing, 87

encapsulation, 84–86

field values, 86

headers, illustration of, 86

IP routing, 87–89

layers, list of, 13

Link layer, 14

Network layer, 14

packet filtering, 89–92

printing service, 180

protocols, types of, 16–17

requirements for, 13

Transport layer, 14, 95

TCP protocol, 16

TCP segment, 85

TeleSweep, 37

Telnet, 151

testing

CBAC configuration, 287–290

system performance, 173

Text MIME type, 207

tftpd service, 190

third() function, 43–44

threats. *See also* attacks
  analyzing, 55–56
  computer-based social engineering skills,
    41
  description of, 29
  dumpster diving, 40
  elevation of privilege, 56
  enumeration, 38–39
  footprinting, 35–36
  human-based social engineering, 40–41
  impersonation, 40
  in-person, 40
  information disclosure, 56
  integrity threats, 55
  port scanning, 38
  repudiation, 56
  scanning, 36–38
  shoulder surfing, 41
  social engineering, 39–40
  STRIDE model, 55–56
  sweeping, 37
  tampering, 55
  third-party authorization, 40
  threat modeling, 54, 56–57
  war dialing, 37
  war driving, 37
threshold and timeout values, 282–283
tickets, 99
timeout and threshold values, 282–283
timeout command, 289
timeout seconds command, 289
tips and tricks for administrators, 297–298
ToneLoc, 37
traffic
  application-level filtering, 270
  best practices for, 294
  controlled traffic, 71
  inbound, allowed by CBAC, 275

  inspected by CBAC, 276
  logged traffic, 71
  outbound, allowed by CBAC, 275
  stateful inspection of, 270–271
  types, supported by NAT, 103
Transmission Control Protocol/Internet
    Protocol. *See* TCP/IP
transmissions, 111
Transport layer
  OSI model, 11–12
  TCP/IP, 14, 95
tricks and tips for administrators, 297–298
trojan horse, 53
trusted networks, 263
tunneling, 110–111
TurboLinux, 182

U

UDP idle-time parameter setting, 283
UDP (User Datagram Protocol)
  bomb attacks, 245
  description of, 16
  field values for, 86
  headers, illustration of, 86
  overview, 12
  port scans, 38
Uniform Resource Locator (URL), 20
Uninterrupted Power Supply (UPS), 144,
    162
UniRo-Secure, 142
universal participation security strategy, 60
UNIX-based bastion hosts, configuring
  overview, 180–181
  service installation, 182–189
  services to disable, 190–191
  services to enable, 189–190

untrusted networks, 263
UPS (Uninterrupted Power Supply), 144, 162
URL (Uniform Resource Locator), 20
U.S. Department of Justice Web site, 223
User Datagram Protocol. *See* UDP
user interface factors, 163
users, authentication, performing, 67–68
uucpd service, 190

V

vandalism, 35
vanilla port scans, 38
VBScript, 199
VDOLive, 274
victim hosts, 161
Video MIME type, 210
video streaming, 5
Virtual Private Network. *See* VPN
Virtual Reality Markup Language (VRML), 199
viruses, 41, 52–53
VPN connection, 107
VPN (Virtual Private Network)
    advantages of, 114
    description of, 107
    disadvantages of, 114–115
    firewalls and, 71–72
    remote access using, 109
    requirements, 109–110
    tunneling, 110–111
VRML (Virtual Reality Markup Language), 199
vulnerabilities
    assessment categories, 54–55
    corrective controls, 30

CVE (Common Vulnerabilities Exposures), 54
    description of, 29, 53–54
    detective controls, 30
    deterrent controls, 30
    preventative controls, 30
    reasons for, 54
vulnerability assessment, 220

W

wait-time command, 289
walld service, 190
WAN (Wide Area Network), 71, 108
war dialing, 37
war driving, 37
WatchGuard SOHO, 142
weakest link security strategy, 59
Web application attacks, 46–48, 203
Web clients, securing, 204–205
Web filters, 230
Web servers
    extensions, securing, 202–203
    extra functionality for, 203
    function of, 199–200
    MIME types supported by, 200–202
    modules, 204
Web sites
    Internet Security Systems, 244
    U.S. Department of Justice, 223
WEP (Wired Equivalent Protocol), 37
Wide Area Network (WAN), 71, 108
Win32 services, 175
Windows 2000, for unified management, 232–233
Windows-based bastion hosts, configuring overview, 173–174

SCM (Service Control Manager), 179
service accounts, 178–179
service applications, 176–178
service installation, 174–175
services to disable, 180–181
services to enable, 179–180
Winscan, 38
Wired Equivalent Protocol (WEP), 37
wizards
  New IP Packet Filter, 228
  New Protocol Rule, 241
WolfPac Firewall, 142
workstation-based firewalls, 141–142
worms, 53
WWW (World Wide Web), 198

X

-X option (IPchains program), 253
xinetd server, 189
XML (Extensible Markup Language), 199

Z

-Z option (IPchains program), 253

fast&easy® web development

Adobe LiveMotion
fast&easy web development

Less Time. Less Effort. More Development.

Don't spend your time leafing through lengthy manuals looking for the information you need. Spend it doing what you do best—Web development. Premier Press's *fast & easy® web development* series leads the way with step-by-step instructions and real screen shots to help you grasp concepts and master skills quickly and easily.

GAME DEVELOPMENT.
IT'S SERIOUS BUSINESS.

"Game programming is without a doubt the most intellectually challenging field of Computer Science in the world. However, we would be fooling ourselves if we said that we are 'serious' people! Writing (and reading) a game programming book should be an exciting adventure for both the author and the reader."

—André LaMothe,
Series Editor

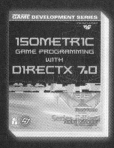

The Premier Press *fast&easy* series

Fast Facts, Easy Access

Offering extraordinary value at a bargain price, the *fast & easy* series is dedicated to one idea: To help readers accomplish tasks as quickly and easily as possible. The unique visual teaching method combines concise tutorials and hundreds of screen shots to dramatically increase learning speed and retention of the material. With the Premier Press *fast & easy* series, you simply look and learn.

The Official Family Tree Maker®
Version 9 Fast & Easy®
1-931841-02-0
U.S. $18.99 ▪ Can. $28.95 ▪ U.K. £13.99

Microsoft® Windows®
Millennium Edition Fast & Easy®
0-7615-2739-7
U.S. $18.99 ▪ Can. $28.95 ▪ U.K. £13.99

Paint Shop Pro™ 7
Fast & Easy®
0-7615-3241-2
U.S. $18.99 ▪ Can. $28.95 ▪ U.K. £13.99

Quicken® 2001
Fast & Easy®
0-7615-2908-X
U.S. $18.99 ▪ Can. $28.95 ▪ U.K. £13.99

Microsoft® Works Suite 2001
Fast & Easy®
0-7615-3371-0
U.S. $24.99 ▪ Can. $37.95 ▪ U.K. £18.99

Microsoft® Access 2002
Fast & Easy®
0-7615-3395-8
U.S. $18.99 ▪ Can. $28.95 ▪ U.K. £13.99

Microsoft® Excel 2002
Fast & Easy®
0-7615-3398-2
U.S. $18.99 ▪ Can. $28.95 ▪ U.K. £13.99

Microsoft® FrontPage® 2002
Fast & Easy®
0-7615-3390-7
U.S. $18.99 ▪ Can. $28.95 ▪ U.K. £13.99

Microsoft® Office XP
Fast & Easy®
0-7615-3388-5
U.S. $18.99 ▪ Can. $28.95 ▪ U.K. £13.99

Microsoft® Outlook 2002
Fast & Easy®
0-7615-3422-9
U.S. $18.99 ▪ Can. $28.95 ▪ U.K. £13.99

Microsoft® PowerPoint® 2002
Fast & Easy®
0-7615-3396-6
U.S. $18.99 ▪ Can. $28.95 ▪ U.K. £13.99

Microsoft® Word 2002
Fast & Easy®
0-7615-3393-1
U.S. $18.99 ▪ Can. $28.95 ▪ U.K. £13.99

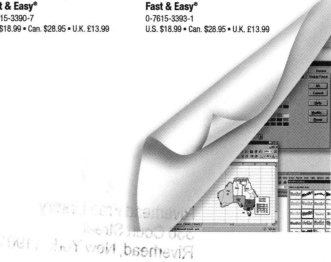

Premier Press
www.premierpressbooks.com

Call now to order
(800)428-7267

Fast & Easy is a registered trademark of Premier Press. All other product and
company names are trademarks of their respective companies.